Good Girl
Messages

Good Girl Messages

How Young Women Were Misled
by Their Favorite Books

Deborah O'Keefe

CONTINUUM

NEW YORK   LONDON

2000

The Continuum International Publishing Group Inc
370 Lexington Avenue, New York, NY 10017

The Continuum International Publishing Group Ltd
Wellington House, 125 Strand, London WC2R 0BB

Printed in the United States of America

Library of Congress Cataloging in Publication Data

O'Keefe, Deborah.
   Good girl messages: how young women were misled by
their favorite books / Deborah O'Keefe.
      p.   cm.
   Includes index.
   ISBN 0-8264-1236-X (alk. paper)
   1. Children's stories, American—History and criticism.
2. Girls in literature.   3. Children's stories, English—
History and criticism.   4. Young women—Books and
reading.   5. Conduct of life in literature.   6. Girls—Books
and reading.   7. Sex role in literature.   I. Title.

PS374.G55 O44 2000
810.9'352054—dc21   99-088181

For my husband Dan, who always believed in this book,
and
my three amazing sons

and
For all the other mid-century girls who loved reading
more than anything else in the world

Contents

Acknowledgments

I am very grateful to all the relatives, friends, and acquaintances who told me about their experiences with childhood reading—sharing strong opinions and important memories. This book would have been impossible without the collection of my own children's books that my mother preserved through decades of household confusion, and without the secondhand bookstores of Vermont, New York, Massachusetts, and California. In many of these stores I found booksellers who are virtually omniscient. The staff of the Chappaqua, NY, Library gave knowledgeable help. The late Terrence Des Pres encouraged me greatly, reading chapters of my manuscript at the Bread Loaf Writers' Conference. Special thanks should go to smart and helpful friends Penny Stillinger, Marion Perret, and Sherry Chappelle; and to perceptive editors Justus George Lawler and Evander Lomke.

Note

One technical matter should be explained. This book contains many prose passages from children's books. I present those quotations in small-capital letters, to make them easily distinguishable from the rest of my text, and to provide a slight sense of the texture—the flavor—of that bigger-print childhood reading. When I quote from other kinds of works, books *about* children's literature or books on other subjects, I revert to conventional punctuation.

· 1 ·

Horizontal Heroines

THERE WAS A HIGH WAINSCOTING OF WOOD ABOUT THE ROOM, AND ON TOP OF THIS, IN A NARROW GILT FRAMEWORK, RAN A ROW OF ILLUMINATED PICTURES ILLUSTRATING FAIRY TALES, ALL IN DULL BLUE AND GOLD AND SCARLET AND SILVER. ON ONE SIDE OF THE ROOM WAS A BOOKCASE FILLED WITH HUNDREDS—YES, I MEAN IT—WITH HUNDREDS AND HUNDREDS OF BOOKS. THE CARPET WAS OF SOFT GRAY, WITH CLUSTERS OF GREEN BAY AND HOLLY LEAVES. THE FURNITURE WAS OF WHITE WOOD, ON WHICH AN ARTIST HAD PAINTED SNOW SCENES AND GROUPS OF MERRY CHILDREN RINGING BELLS AND SINGING CAROLS.

I got hold of this book somehow in 1946 when I was seven, though it had been published in 1886. Of all the descriptions I loved in my own books—Dorothy's emerald chamber with the green fountain, Peter Pan's cave, Heidi's loft—this bedroom was perhaps the most alluring. I used to wish I lived there; I admired, even envied the owner of the room—an invalid who died on her eleventh birthday.

THE LITTLE CHILD LAY MONTH AFTER MONTH A PATIENT, HELPLESS INVALID, IN THE ROOM WHERE SHE WAS BORN. THE SHUTTERS COULD ALL BE OPENED AND CAROL COULD TAKE A REAL SUN-BATH IN THIS LOVELY GLASS HOUSE, OR THEY COULD ALL BE CLOSED WHEN THE DEAR HEAD ACHED OR THE DEAR EYES WERE TIRED. LOVE-BIRDS AND CANARIES HUNG IN THEIR GOLDEN HOUSES IN THE WINDOWS, AND THEY, POOR CAGED THINGS, COULD HOP AS FAR FROM THEIR WOODEN PERCHES AS CAROL COULD VENTURE FROM HER LITTLE WHITE BED.

To suffer, to withdraw, to give; these were girls' verbs. My brain has an indelible memory of one illustration in *The Birds' Christmas Carol*. A naked baby, golden as an angel, stands on her mother's lap. One hand clings to the mother's neck, while the other offers a cookie to a startled brother. The caption reads, "Her tiny hands forever outstretched in giving."

SUCH A GENEROUS LITTLE CREATURE YOU NEVER SAW! A SPOONFUL OF BREAD AND MILK HAD ALWAYS TO BE TAKEN BY MAMMA OR NURSE BEFORE CAROL COULD ENJOY HER SUPPER; WHATEVER SWEETMEAT FOUND ITS WAY INTO HER PRETTY FINGERS WAS STRAIGHTWAY BROKEN IN HALF TO BE SHARED WITH DONALD, PAUL, OR HUGH; AND WHEN THEY MADE BELIEVE NIBBLE THE MORSEL WITH AFFECTED ENJOYMENT, SHE WOULD CLAP HER HANDS AND CROW WITH DELIGHT. "WHY DOES SHE DO IT?" ASKED DONALD THOUGHTFULLY. "NONE OF US BOYS EVER DID."

Virtuous as she was as a baby, Carol became more saintly as her illness set in. From her bed she arranged to send books from her own collection every week to the Children's Hospital, with a little note in each. As her eleventh birthday (Christmas Day, of course) approached, she asked her family to withhold their usual presents and donate the money instead to a celebration for the poor Irish family in the back alley. "I SHALL GIVE THE NINE RUG-GLESES A GRAND CHRISTMAS DINNER HERE IN THIS VERY ROOM. AND AFTERWARDS A BEAUTIFUL CHRISTMAS TREE, FAIRLY BLOOMING WITH PRESENTS. AFTER WE'VE HAD A MERRY TIME WITH THE TREE WE CAN OPEN MY WINDOW AND ALL LISTEN TOGETHER TO THE MUSIC AT THE EVENING CHURCH-SERVICE." That Christmas night, after the nine overjoyed Ruggleses went home, Carol's "loving heart quietly ceased to beat."

This makes me sob even now, middle-aged and ironic. I used to read and reread Kate Douglas Wiggin's story about Carol. I loved the luxury—how easy and graceful it was to be generous—and especially the gorgeous immobility of the heroine. In my childhood stories the best girls were passive, still. It was understood that not every girl came naturally to this exalted state but the rebellious ones were urged to emulate the saintly ones, and they usually gave in by the end of the book or at least the end of the series.

For several years I have been re-reading my childhood books from a fiftyish perspective—re-reading them with delight and with horror. I also talked to friends and relations about their favorite childhood books. They had much to say and their responses tended to echo my own conclusions about the books I read as a mid-century girl. So did the books and articles I read about children and children's literature. In these chapters I will be looking at the books themselves and the messages they sent their young readers.

Women of my age remember a passionate devotion to their girlhood reading. They claim, as I do, to have been profoundly influenced by it; the question is, what kind of influence? Some say they were inspired by heroines who were "plucky" and independent—I know a woman who claims that she got her detective's license because of Nancy Drew. Even if this is true, I am convinced that many girls were damaged by characters, plots, and themes in the books they read and loved. *Good Girl Messages: How Young Women Were Misled by Their Favorite Books* will present some opinions that are not particularly controversial: most of us would agree that invalidism and early death are not the ideal goals for a young girl. Other issues are more complex.

First, some readers and researchers maintain that if girls do not encounter strong female models in their reading, they can and will identify with the male models. I am skeptical about this. Surely many girl readers learned from their reading that females are the bystanders and the comforters and the sufferers, not the adventurers. A second question concerns the "cop-out" plot pattern: In the many books where a young girl starts out lively and active but ends up ladylike and docile, were girl readers more strengthened by her early independence or weakened by her ultimate passivity?

Another issue involves the relation of females to authority and aggression, of girls to their elders. I found a popular plot pattern in which a girl is faced with a harsh, grim, powerful adult but manages to disarm him or her through the strength of her own passive, girlish virtue. Does this plot demonstrate the power of the unaggressive, loving maiden—or does it encourage a tendency to deny hostility and avoid confrontation at all costs?

The fourth question is about the mixed messages sent by groups of characters in which only one of the females has characteristics which are not traditionally feminine—must she be the exception and they the normal context, the default? The final question asks what qualities are desirable in a girl or woman. The favorite girls' books of my generation proclaimed that certain qualities were valuable. Some, like sensitivity and helpfulness, we still consider positive, but others which we consider negative today, like submissiveness and self-denial, are portrayed in these books as inevitably interwoven with the positive qualities.

My next chapters will talk about these issues, and will illustrate in various ways my belief that girls' fiction told its readers to be permanently girlish. Chapter 2 will set girls' reading in the context of books read by boys or by children of both genders. Chapters 3, 4, 5, and 6 will tell in lurid detail what my mid-century books said about how girls should behave and how they should relate to elders and to contemporaries. A final chapter will examine some of the books read by girls *since* 1950, showing that amazing, heartening changes are taking place in girls' fiction.

Lying in Bed—Invalids or Dolls

Carol Bird's life-and-death in her little white bed among the maidenhead ferns was especially uplifting, but my childhood was populated by hundreds of other fictional girls who were also sweet and sacrificing, who were often presented in images of stillness, paralysis. In Carol withdrawal from life revealed sanctity. Other girls in fiction revealed that withdrawal could bring comfort and protection. Heidi's little hay-bed under the roof was a terrific retreat, for instance—like a warm, soft coffin with a good view of the Alps. Even Jane Moffat, not a weak girl normally, spent a whole day sitting still in a bread bin outside a store, because she thought the police wanted her for making faces at the superintendent-of-schools.

My enjoyment of Carol Bird's death was echoed by Ann Douglas in *The Feminization of American Culture* (1977): "As a child I read with formative intensity in a collection of Victorian sentimental fiction, a legacy from my grandmother's girlhood. . . . I followed the timid exploits of innumerable pale and pious heroines. But what I remember best, what was for me as for so many others the archetypically satisfying scene in this domestic genre, was the death of little Eva in *Uncle Tom's Cabin*. A pure and beautiful child in a wealthy Southern family, little Eva dies a lingering and sainted death of consumption. Her adoring papa and a group of equally adoring slaves cluster in unspeakable grief around her bedside while she dispenses Christian wisdom and her own golden locks with profuse generosity."

An even more morbid book is one I discovered recently and did not know as a child (fortunately for my mental health). *In the Closed Room* (1904) by Frances Hodgson Burnett (author also of the less psychotic *Secret Garden*) boasts not just one dead girl but three, in just 130 very small pages—a record, I believe. Seven-year-old Judith was fascinated by tales of her Aunt Hester, who had the same white skin and big eyes Judith had and who died suddenly at fifteen. When Judith's parents became caretakers in an empty mansion, another dead girl appeared to her: the beautiful child who recently died in the locked room on the fourth floor. That little girl with burnished hair welcomed her into the bedroom of death, saying "YOU HAVE COME TO PLAY WITH ME." Judith was delighted—she had always had A VAGUE BELIEF THAT SHE HERSELF WAS NOT QUITE REAL. The two children played with their dolls for some days, then walked happily over the roof terrace onto a BROAD, GREEN PATHWAY COVERED WITH TREMBLING BELL-LIKE FLOWERS, where Aunt Hester was waiting to greet them.

If you are confined or paralyzed, in a bed or a box, the chances are that your behavior will be blameless, your decisions simple, your emotions placid. If you are unreal to boot, inanimate, you are even safer. As a tot, my favorite Beatrix Potter book was not *Peter Rabbit* or *Benjamin Bunny*, with their virile raids on the vegetable garden, but *The Tale of Two Bad Mice* (1904). The heroines were mistress and servant in a doll's house. IT BELONGED TO TWO DOLLS CALLED LUCINDA AND JANE; AT LEAST IT BELONGED TO LUCINDA, BUT SHE NEVER ORDERED MEALS. JANE WAS THE COOK; BUT SHE NEVER DID ANY COOKING, BECAUSE THE DINNER HAD BEEN BOUGHT

READY-MADE, IN A BOX FULL OF SHAVINGS. THERE WERE TWO RED LOB-
STERS, AND A HAM, A FISH, A PUDDING, AND SOME PEARS AND OR-
ANGES. THEY WOULD NOT COME OFF THE PLATES, BUT THEY WERE
EXTREMELY BEAUTIFUL.

A gross animal principle intruded one day into this delightfully
static, nonthreatening world. Two warm, hairy, sensual mice van-
dalized the doll's house and stole its contents. They smashed the
shiny, artificial paint-and-plaster food. WHAT A SIGHT MET THE EYES
OF JANE AND LUCINDA, when they came back in their perambulator.
LUCINDA SAT UPON THE UPSET KITCHEN STOVE AND STARED, AND JANE
LEANED AGAINST THE KITCHEN DRESSER AND SMILED; BUT NEITHER OF
THEM MADE ANY REMARK. Later, the mice left them a shilling for
damages and swept up the mess. The dolls seemed untouched by
the incident. The last illustration shows them lying rigid, in a little
bed piled high with comforters, a sight most comforting to timorous girl readers.

In *What Katy Did* (1872), Susan Coolidge created both a horizontal heroine and a cop-out pattern. Katy was a tomboy until an
accident immobilized her for several years. Inspired by her permanently crippled and therefore saintly aunt, Katy lay in bed a
long time, became virtuous, and was finally cured. She was no
longer independent and sassy. Another girl dramatically though
temporarily immobilized was Wendy in *Peter Pan* (1904). Jealous
Tinker Bell incited the Lost Boys to shoot at Wendy as she flew
near their island, pretending that Peter wanted them to. The hap-
less Tootles hit her with an arrow. A juicy scene ensued in which
all the boys stood around aghast at what they had done in killing
the beautiful girl brought to them as a friend and mother. She
recovered, but only after the boys and the readers had experienced
the usual frisson of painful delight at the sight of an innocent,
pretty maiden, dead.

One type of static image especially intrigued me. Girls at one
time apparently enjoyed putting on shows that involved not actions but scenes without movement, tableaux vivants. These heroines, already cozily confined in their feminine clothes and
customs, reached an apotheosis when they stood frozen before
admiring audiences as sacrificial Pocahontases or, best of all, lay

dead on a barge like the Little Colonel playing the Lily Maid of Astolat.

The stiffest, most passive heroine of all was not acting, or dead or sick or under a spell; she was wooden. *Hitty, Her First Hundred Years* (1929) tells of a doll who was carved in the early 19th century in Maine. We hear, in Hitty's own voice, a story which peculiarly combines total paralysis with dangerous adventure. The doll traveled on a whaling ship to the South Seas, in the care of the captain's little daughter; she was shipwrecked, worshipped by natives, exhibited in a snake charmer's act, and so on. Whatever happened, her prim little face retained the same ladylike smile; her posture remained rigid. She was conscious but unable to speak or act.

I SAY I WAS UNABLE TO LIFT A FINGER. I MUST CONFESS THAT THE OLD PEDDLER HAD SEEN FIT TO GIVE ME ONLY ONE ON EITHER HAND, AND THAT A THUMB, WITH ALL THE REST LEFT IN ONE SOLID PIECE LIKE A MITTEN. Compare Hitty with another wooden character—Pinocchio, a boy. When Pinocchio was made he started leaping about, causing trouble, making mistakes—always moving, learning, doing. His career was a dynamic movement toward a moral self; Hitty's was static. She was fingerless, pure, and unchanging, incapable of error, incapable also of moral growth.

Hitty, the ultimate victim, realized that there were drawbacks to her sort of life but she was grateful for its advantages: PHOEBE HAD A SMALL BASKET, IN WHICH I WAS ALLOWED TO RIDE. SHE HAD LINED IT NEATLY WITH LEAVES THAT FELT PLEASANTLY COOL AND SMOOTH. IT WAS A HOT AFTERNOON IN LATE JULY, AND I WAS THANKFUL TO BE OUT OF THE DUST AND GLARE OF THE ROAD. IT SEEMED TO ME THAT THIS WAS ONE OF THE MANY TIMES WHEN IT WAS NICE TO BE A DOLL.

As a child I enjoyed reading about Hitty and learning how nice it was to be a doll but she made me uneasy. I sensed that her paralysis was less comfortable and less sentimental than, say, Carol Bird's. The illustrations in *Hitty* are, in fact, most unnerving. Her author, Rachel Field, consciously or unconsciously had found a perfect image for passivity menaced by more vital forces. The doll is pictured floating stiffly under the water while sea plants and creatures coil about her; she is shown standing at attention in her proper New England garb while a cobra points its phallic self at her midriff. She could not help herself out of a predicament, but she could endure and maintain her composure. She realized it was peculiar when the natives worshipped her as an idol, WHEN THEY MADE THEIR QUEER GRUNTINGS BEFORE MY TEMPLE. BUT THEY NEVER KNEW IF I FELT BORED OR FRIGHTENED. I CONTINUED TO SMILE DOWN UPON THEM AS SERENELY AS IF I HAD BEEN BACK ON A STATE OF MAINE MANTELPIECE. I HAD BEEN MADE WITH A PLEASANT EXPRESSION, SO IT WAS REALLY NO CREDIT TO ME. The passive heroine in my children's books managed to stay calm and still, even when faced with lascivious men and their queer sexual gruntings. It is possible that such models helped teach girls how to respond to abuse or harassment: with a Hitty-like, glazed passivity.

The Doll's House by Rumer Godden showed some insight into the plight of a doll and, metaphorically, of a girl: IT IS AN ANXIOUS, SOMETIMES A DANGEROUS THING TO BE A DOLL. DOLLS CANNOT CHOOSE; THEY CAN ONLY BE CHOSEN; THEY CAN'T "DO"; THEY CAN ONLY BE DONE BY; CHILDREN WHO DO NOT UNDERSTAND THIS OFTEN DO WRONG THINGS, AND THEN THE DOLLS ARE HURT AND ABUSED AND LOST; AND WHEN THIS HAPPENS DOLLS CANNOT SPEAK, NOR DO ANYTHING EXCEPT BE HURT AND ABUSED AND LOST. In addition, dolls NEVER HAVE TO ALTER, THEY NEVER HAVE TO GROW. When the doll family was threatened, all they could do was wish very hard; sometimes their wishing seemed to affect the behavior of people around them, but only slightly, in a mild, indirect way. The other important fact about these doll people was that they yearned to be played with. That is what made them alive; that is what they were for. I find it interesting that this book appeared in 1947, at the end of the period I am examining. When Godden describes so explicitly the dolls' state of powerlessness and pain, maybe she is heralding an era of increasing awareness.

The Doll's House contains a familiar female plot pattern as well as a set of familiarly victimized characters. The dolls could not be heard by humans and they could do practically nothing to affect their fates, but by a superhuman—or rather superdoll—effort one of them sacrificed her life to save her little boy. Birdie the wife, mother, and housekeeper is a touching character; like many other

women she WAS NOT QUITE RIGHT IN THE HEAD. THERE WAS SOME-
THING IN HER HEAD THAT RATTLED. SHE WAS ALTOGETHER GAY AND
LIGHT, BEING MADE OF CHEAP CELLULOID, BUT ALL THE SAME, NICELY
MOLDED AND JOINED AND PAINTED. This pretty, shallow doll-
woman, timid and confused, saw her child about to be burned
and managed to fall onto the candle, knocking him away. The
little girl owner exclaimed, "WASN'T BIRDIE BEAUTIFUL WHEN SHE
WENT UP IN THAT FLAME? LIKE A FAIRY, LIKE A BEAUTIFUL KIND OF
SILVER FIREWORK." The only significant action a doll-woman is ca-
pable of is self-immolation.

Folk tales gave us the Sleeping Beauty (she made herself vulnerable by pricking her finger), and Snow White in her glass coffin
(she erred in accepting the poisoned apple). It is clear in such cases
that a hostile person hurt the heroine, yet somehow the heroine
was guilty too, had "brought it on herself," and needed to atone
in a purgatorial paralysis. Adult books also show situations like
this, where the woman at once innocent and guilty is disposed of
by being immobilized. Eighteenth-century Clarissa, after being violated while drugged, could only waste away and die. When her
death was imminent she cheerfully ordered an exquisitely etched
coffin and kept it in her bedroom. "She writes and reads upon it,
as others would upon a desk."

The image persists, in many versions, of a woman whose action
consists of decreasing action, increasing stillness. In Hemingway's
"An Alpine Idyll," a peasant's wife dies in their mountain hut in
December. He couldn't bring her out to be buried until May, and
when he did so the priest made him explain the battered appearance of the corpse's face. " 'When she died I made the report and
I put her in the shed across the big wood. When I started to use
the big wood she was stiff and I put her up against the wall. Her
mouth was open and when I came into the shed at night to cut
up the big wood, I would hang the lantern from it.' 'It was very
wrong,' said the priest. 'Did you love your wife?' 'Ja, I loved her,'
Olz said. 'I loved her fine.' "

From my present perspective, I appreciate this version of the
frozen princess legend—the horror of what was done to her, what
she turned into, what her husband failed to feel. I can see that

female helplessness is destructive and offers no defense against aggression. But mature perspective is easily shoved aside; my buried conviction about frozen princesses is that those Rapunzels, locked in their snazzy towers waiting to be rescued, were not to be pitied. The version found in children's books is hard to erase, the notion that inanition is beautiful and virtuous. Poe had the same idea, with his theory that no topic is more poetic than the death of a beautiful young woman.

How Girl Readers Responded

In recent years I have found myself brooding about this childhood reading. No one is unaware now of the problems, blatant and insidious, caused by the traditional view of women as passive and powerless. The influence of childhood reading outside of school, however, has not been discussed in much detail. I want to show how most stories read by girls in my generation presented female characters as more or less obedient, fearful, and helpless. I hope especially to illustrate: to dramatize for a new generation traditional female images they may have encountered more theoretically than forcefully; to confront my own generation with some images that may still be lurking behind their confident façades producing conflict and distress; to remind us all how pervasive and powerful were these models which, we believe, have faded into a stale joke.

I will not claim that girls' fiction had certain clear effects on their readers, good, bad, or mixed. It is possible that the girls' books available in my era contributed to a pattern of dependency and subservience, but they were certainly not the only or primary factor in such behavior, and surely some girls were helped to a wider, freer perspective by children's books. The traditional "feminine" qualities in our books influenced me and others like me, but we read them partly because we were already in sympathy with those qualities. Such immersion in reading can be an *instance* of passive, escapist, "feminine" behavior as much as it is a spur to such behavior. But I also believe that our girlhood reading did more than reflect our particular personalities—that they both helped us and harmed us in complicated ways. In this book I will be acknowledging the help while emphasizing the harm. If hundreds of stories told girls that aggression must be denied or endured or placated, never challenged, if countless heroines were praised for subjugating their own needs in order to serve others, it is hard to believe that these messages had no effect.

As Bob Dixon reasonably points out in *Catching Them Young: Sex, Race and Class in Children's Fiction* (1977), "Anyone interested in how ideas—political ideas in the broadest and most important sense—are fostered and grow up in a society cannot afford to neglect what children read. . . . There are people who, apparently, feel a desperate need to believe that nothing children read has any effect on them at all. It seems to me much more reasonable to believe that everything that happens to us, including literature, has some kind of effect which will vary with the individual." One male friend recalled the influence of Howard Pease, "who wrote adventure stories about ships that always seemed to be in pea-soup fogs and who probably caused me to join the Navy."

I have heard in various forms a "doctor" anecdote about the way children learn from the culture around them rather than from direct experience. Maccoby and Jacklin report one version in *The Psychology of Sex Differences* (1974): they describe "the case of a 4-year-old girl who insisted that girls could become nurses but only boys could become doctors. She held to this belief tenaciously even though her own mother was a doctor. A child gradually develops concepts of 'masculinity' and 'femininity' and when he has understood what his own sex is, he attempts to match his behavior to his conception. The generalizations he constructs do not represent acts of imitation, but are organizations of information distilled from a wide variety of sources."

And one of these sources, of course, is "his"—or her—reading. I find myself wondering about the childhood reading of a woman mentioned in the *New York Times* in 1982. Her behavior reveals traditional "feminine" qualities many women fear they still have—the inability to think straight and the inability to act decisively.

Ozark, Mo., April 4 (UPI): Betty Tennis has resigned as city clerk after the town council discovered she had bought 87 gross, or 12,528, ballpoint pens for $7000. City Attorney Jim Eiffert said Mrs. Tennis had explained that a salesman had offered her "a good deal on some ballpoint pens," and she ordered *six* gross. When more pens arrived, she kept paying, he said. The clerk thought she had no choice but to accept the additional pens. "She thought she ordered them all," Mr. Eiffert said.

It's not clear what caused the confusion of Betty Tennis, but her ineptitude feels familiar and so does her method of solving a problem by doing nothing. Her behavior seems like the sort of thing one might expect from a woman raised on tales of Carol Bird and Elsie Dinsmore and Hitty.

The books I want to discuss, all published before 1950 and some long before that time, cover a broad spectrum. Some portrayed female life in ways that seem grossly, even pathologically limited to us today. Others sent a more complicated message, often through the "cop-out pattern," where heroines ultimately gave up their independent vision and subsided into traditional behavior. I am certainly not arguing that girls should have been pointed toward the pole opposite to submissiveness, traditionally male qualities which are just as harmful—selfishness, rigidity, aggression, and the need to dominate. Some of my childhood books showed the positive side of "female" qualities—sympathy, cooperation, flexibility—along with the negative, and I would not claim that their influence was entirely baleful. But most of this mid-century reading did assume that being submissive was part of being cooperative, that being sympathetic required denigrating yourself. The good girl always let the boy win the prize and if a girl was not naturally inclined to do so, by the end of the book she had learned to be more submissive.

Alison Lurie, in her 1990 book *Don't Tell the Grown-ups*, strikes an encouraging note about traditional children's stories. While admitting that many children's books do push a conventional viewpoint, Lurie describes classic children's books as wonderfully anarchic, freeing young readers through their "subversive" viewpoints even though adults think the children are being conservatively socialized. I would not deny that some of the classic stories are indeed subversive—but many are not. Lurie's analysis does not consider the conservative thrust of so many fictional messages that told girls to follow traditional patterns and reinforced their desire to do so.

In addition, many of the "greatest" children's books are not necessarily the favorite reading of children; often they prefer the less complex, less great works, stories which make them feel comfortable and reinforce rather than subvert the status quo. Since many well-loved books did offer cop-out plots and only token strong females, if any, I cannot agree that—before the late twentieth century—*most* children's fiction tended to subvert a repressive status quo.

Whether children's books merely represented feminine values and stereotypes or whether they also successfully inculcated them, these books were an enormous presence in the lives of many girls in the pre-television and early-television era. Anyone who has been or has known a child devoted to reading understands that certain books get re-read so often they are almost memorized. Other books that do not strike an important chord at the moment get forgotten, but the crucial ones are mauled and battered, stained with Hershey bars, and remembered forever, viscerally. A child can tell you the details of her favorite story, even the position on the page of certain passages. A woman friend said: "My sisters to this day complain about how they were dragged to the library whenever I had to babysit for them. One of them swears she remembers crying in her stroller while waiting for me at the library."

Pre-1950 children's fiction did not, of course, constitute a uniform mass of propaganda. Only a few books ignored gender stereotypes (in *The Peterkin Papers* all family members, male and female, exhibited equal, sublime foolishness) or contradicted them (in *The Secret Garden*, Mary was neither weak nor dependent nor sweet). Many books exhibited simple-minded sexism in a form easy to resist, making "female" behavior seem unappealing and ridiculous even to a mid-century good-girl type. In *Peter Rabbit*, the female bunnies smugly ate bread and milk and blackberries in their claustrophobic cave while brother Peter slept off his masculine adventures; they got the blackberries, but he got all the fun.

The really extreme Victorian books, like *Elsie Dinsmore* with its murky masochism, repelled my generation and couldn't be taken seriously:

"DEAR PAPA, I LOVE YOU SO MUCH," ELSIE REPLIED, TWINING HER ARMS AROUND HIS NECK, "I LOVE YOU ALL THE BETTER FOR NEVER LETTING ME HAVE MY OWN WAY, BUT ALWAYS MAKING ME OBEY AND KEEP TO RULES."

But another large group of books presented the constructive qualities of the traditional image of women (cooperation, sympathy, flexibility) as bound together with the destructive (helplessness, subservience), so that the whole package was hard to separate or reject. In *The Five Little Peppers*, for instance, Polly's struggles to feed and cheer her brothers and sisters in spite of poverty made her touching as well as saccharine. It may have been salutory to read about the love and sociability of the March sisters in *Little Women* but unhealthy to realize that the achievement of Beth, in wasting away and dying, was more purely, radiantly female than that of Jo, in merely living and growing and writing.

The more interesting girls' books were not gross and single-minded; they did not present bizarre little saints like Elsie Dinsmore. But they were not what we, today, would call liberating. They were full of haunting images of girls with tear-stained faces gazing worshipfully at the boys who saved them from disaster; images of girls swooning pitifully on beds of pain; images of cheerful girls rolling pastry into tiny tarts, of earnest girls plumping pillows for their invalid uncles; images of girls on a quiet river, smiling but demure, holding parasols, drifting, sitting still—while being rowed downstream by muscular young men who were in charge of all the significant action.

When I try to imagine an ideal life for a little girl, I think, against my better judgment, of *The Beautiful Story of Doris and Julie*. This was a book from my mother's childhood that enchanted me when I was about five, filling my incipient soul with ribbons and ringlets, with fluffy girls in small boats on small, safe ponds. All I can remember of the plot is a benevolent aunt, tears, hugs, picnics and treats, possibly a furry dog; but it was the ringlets and the dolls' tea-set that really got to me. If I could find a copy of

Doris and Julie today, I would be disgusted but enthralled. In *Good Boys and Dead Girls* (1991), Mary Gordon points out that, "The image of the moving boy has been central in American writing. Men have freedom, autonomy, movement. Women prevent movement." Discussing male novelists, she remarks on "a habit of association that connects females with stasis and death; males with movement and life."

Recently, a sizable number of writers and researchers have analyzed certain types of stories read by young girls, notably fairy tales, school readers, and picture books. The free-time reading of school-aged girls has been discussed in less detail, though some attention has been paid to girls' series fiction. The books to be considered here are the books that surrounded me between 1943 when I was four and started to read, and 1953 when I turned fourteen, graduated from ninth grade and left the only school I had so far attended. Most of the stories were American but many were English. Almost all presented characters who were white, middle-class, and Anglo-Saxon, because that was the kind of book being published. This distressing limitation did not bother me as a child, as I myself was white, middle-class, and Anglo-Saxon. Children who were not, however, may have been upset to find that, according to the best authority of fiction, they did not exist. These were heinous omissions, but they are not my subject here, which is middle-class girls at mid-century reading whatever fiction was available about girls.

Notice the overlapping of the generations. I did read books that appeared in the 1940s, but many of my favorites were from the 1920s, the turn of the century, or earlier—not just transcendent classics, but also delightful junk books that celebrated the stereotypes of their times. When I now consider the strong heroines in recent children's fiction I am encouraged; but when I remember my own obsession with the Little Colonel, a winsome girl who flowered in Kentucky in the 1890s but still hung around in Connecticut in the 1940s, I am not so confident that our children will avoid contact with destructive models we think we have destroyed. I learned from the current *Books in Print* that *The Birds' Christmas Carol* has recently been reprinted in three editions—a book I had thought safely buried in the archives of morbid sexism.

Girls as a group were always more involved than boys were in reading, an activity that is girlish in that it earns approval from one's elders and requires sitting still for long periods of time. Reading habits were so firmly split by gender that men in their fifties apologized to me, with embarrassment still intense, for once having read a girls' book. One told me, "I read one Nancy Drew mystery and enjoyed it but never read another because it was for girls." But girls who liked boys' books, instead of or in addition to books considered proper for themselves, always read them with no apology. Boys' stories were higher in the hierarchy of seriousness and girls could read them without shame.

In my day, books most popular with boys included *Tom Sawyer* and *Huckleberry Finn*, *Treasure Island*, Kipling's *Jungle Books*, and maybe the Hardy Boys. Favorite books of girls included Alcott's *Little Women*, the Nancy Drew books, *Heidi*, and *The Secret Garden*. Realistic, family-and-friends-and-school stories were read primarily by girls. A majority of the books I will discuss in later chapters—books beloved by girls at least up to the mid-twentieth century—are stories of children in a real world. It may be a contemporary, familiar world; or the fiction may be set in a time or place that is different but nonetheless realistic, possible. From the Moffats to the Saturdays, in the books of Alcott and of Wilder and hundreds of others, stories of family and community life appealed to girls. The adventure stories preferred by boys involve journeys, quests, battles, struggles to survive and win.

When you compare the *Little Women* type of book with the *Robinson Crusoe* type you can see the essential difference: To say that boys liked action stories is to say that they were interested in whether the hero achieved his personal goals. To say that girls liked character stories is to say that they cared most about social interaction, about achieving a relationship or a reconciliation. I think boys liked adventure stories because the focus was individual, the values heroic, while girls liked family-and-friends stories because the focus was social; the qualities they most admired were sensitivity, cooperation and sacrifice.

I must state this clearly: I believe these differences in boy and girl perspective and behavior were caused by culture rather than biology. With time, we may eradicate or at least reduce them. But girls in this period loved books that encouraged them to be girlish and boys relished books that told them how to be boyish; these messages still resonate decades later. Surely I am not the only middle-aged person surrounded by juvenile, fictional ghosts.

I will be looking at some extreme cases—storybook girls who spent their lives beautifully lying down—along with girls who were not bedridden but whose main activities were obeying and fearing, housekeeping and comforting, enduring and above all sacrificing. Most of these female actions could be done sitting down, without much physical exertion. Even housekeeping was partly sedentary, involving as it does shelling peas and mending. Many years later, my friends and I seem to have grown beyond the wilting, sedentary female ideal of our childhood. My generation has changed greatly since our youth, that blessed time when princesses sat on top of glass hills, withholding the favor of their golden apples. We have moved beyond the domestic realm and have won some battles. But some of our external actions and internal conflicts suggest that we are not rid of the passive princess, of the old attitudes so eloquently described by Susan Brownmiller in her 1983 book *Femininity*.

Fear, evasion, self-pity, self-contempt—these are not always visible. Some women who seem to function well may be undermined by the secret belief that they must remain permanently subordinate and that they can meet aggression only with politeness and a glazed, doll-like smile. Confidence can be weakened by too many old messages: "Gentlemen first." "Always be tactful." "Don't fidget; sit still." It's hard to replace them with newer messages: "Don't be apologetic." "Win a point even if another person has to lose." "Let someone else clean up the vomit." Gloria Steinem begins *Revolution From Within* (1992) with the following passage: "The idea for this book began a decade ago when even I, who had spent the previous dozen years working on external barriers to women's equality, had to admit there were internal ones, too. Wherever I traveled, I saw women who were smart, courageous, and valuable, who didn't *think* they were smart, courageous, or valuable. . . . It was as if the female spirit were a garden that had grown beneath the shadows of barriers for so long that it kept growing in the same pattern, even after some of the barriers were gone."

A woman I know said that childhood reading "left me with vastly overblown romantic notions, and ill-prepared for the realities I was to encounter." Decades after the Girl Scout campfires and the girls' storybooks, many female hearts are still made of S'mores, those repellent and irresistible objects that Girl Scouts made by squashing blobs of melted chocolate and marshmallow between damp graham crackers. Soft as a S'more, we may still rely on acquiescence to solve problems, rather than initiative.

So to me, and perhaps other girls of my time, a woman sitting still or permanently horizontal was not pitiful but comfortable or saintly. Staying home sick was a treat for me, especially since I was not sick often or seriously. The long, still day in bed gave life a most desirable drifting quality. When I was sick-in-bed my mother would bring out the ceremonial objects the occasion called for. One was a wooden tray with legs, pale blue and decorated appropriately with a white narcissus. The other was a large squashy backrest. Its triangular bulk leaned at such a comfortable angle that you could never get tired of resting; its fat arms stuck out just far enough to envelop and nurture. Bed may have been the place where I had nightmares or shuddered at shadows outside, but it was also the sanctuary where I could listen to the radio soap opera "Hilltop House" in between chapters of *An Old-Fashioned Girl* and drink cocoa from the narcissus tray.

My earliest memory is of a woman lying in bed. We had a live-in sitter for a while, and Sally slept in my bedroom. The image is vivid: I woke and saw this young woman with a thin face and dark hair lying in a bed across the room, reading and eating grapes. She looked safe, and beautiful, and right, and I went back to sleep.

Here is a genuine school report on a good, meek little girl, preserved by my mother. "Beginners class, January 1944: Early in the year, Debby was very shy and almost painfully self-conscious with adults." My weaknesses were in the tradition of maidenly timidity so no one minded. And, I'm gratified to note, they recognized my potential for heroine status: as they said on the report card, *"She is completely relaxed at rest period."* I knew already that a girl is most herself in a reclining position, though I didn't understand some implications of that notion.

The plane has just taken off from Kennedy and won't come down again till San Francisco, in the dark. Am I exhilarated because I am on vacation and have no large or small responsibilities for two weeks? Because I will be meeting interesting people? I am exhilarated, to speak honestly, because I will be confined leaning back in a small seat for five hours with a blanket on my knees, and I will read two simple-minded mystery books, and a lady will bring me small, bland things to eat in tidy little dishes. While my husband makes assertive gestures waving his hands to help the pilot fly properly, I sit quite still, content. It's disgusting but true: I am like Hitty, relishing my wooden passivity; glad to be moving, but through no motion of my own.

· 2 ·

Fluttery Girls, Bloody-Minded Boys: Where Girls Fit In

A man I know said that he grew up on "good, old-fashioned blood-and-guts cowboys, Indians, soldiers and baseball heroes." Another told me wistfully, "I devoured junky wonderful boys' fiction about how our hero persevered to win The Big Game and Get the Girl." "The message of these books was always clear," another former boy pointed out: "the celebration of fair play, honesty, sportsmanship, bravery and modesty. In retrospect those virtues counted for little in a world rushing towards war and mass destruction." Those books sent unrealistic messages to boys, just as Elsie and Hitty and Carol Bird gave lessons in submissiveness to girls. Boys may have faced expectations that were impossibly high and heroic but at least they learned from their reading that life was an adventure and all roads were open to them.

Just as "woman" has traditionally been subsumed under the broader heading of "man," girls' books have constituted a limited sub-category of children's fiction. Boys' books were the norm, not just a separate genre. A man I happen to be married to confesses to something that he now considers dreadful but not surprising. As a boy he conceived a plan of reading alphabetically all the books in the children's room of the library, but the plan broke down. Along about "C" he was enjoying a book on Eskimos, but suddenly noticed the author's name: it was a woman.

Of course he had to stop reading the book. It couldn't possibly be any good.

In *Jill Came Tumbling After* (1974), Elaine Showalter claims that the reading of girls tells them that "the masculine viewpoint is considered normative and the feminine viewpoint divergent. Women are expected to identify as readers with a masculine experience and perspective, which is presented as the human one." The question is whether girls can identify with Jim Hawkins or Huck Finn, strengthening their young selves without paying some terrible price. Carolyn Heilbrun, in *Reinventing Womanhood* (1979), is more optimistic than Showalter: "If women can take as their own the creative possibilities, the human aspirations once the property of men only, can they not also adopt male role models in their struggle for achievement? I believe that women must learn to appropriate for their own use the examples of human autonomy and self-fulfillment displayed to us by the male world." Heilbrun believes that females must "choose male literary models and reinterpret them to address women. Ultimately, there are no male models, there are only models of selfhood from which woman chooses to learn.

"From fairy tales onward, women's fantasies have been of themselves as the sleeping figure a man will awaken. Yet in stories, as in life, even women can learn to identify with the protagonist, to be the quester, not 'she who is sought.' In stories, as in life, it is the male figure whom society has hitherto allowed to be the protagonist, who must, therefore, for a time, be the model."

The British writer Susan Cooper agrees with Heilbrun. In the *New York Times* in 1975, she questioned the usefulness of deliberately presenting adventurous heroines instead of heroes, so that "Little Jane can identify with them; little John can admire. It's a false premise: an adult neurosis foisted upon children. I don't believe little Jane gives a damn that Jack the Giant Killer is a boy. Lost in the story, she identifies with him as a *character*, just as little John shares Red Riding Hood's terror of the wolf without reflecting that, of course, she's only a girl. Response to fairy tale, as to all myth, is subconscious, unrelated to such superficial elements. We are all mixtures of male and female; reading stories isn't going to change that."

This position cannot be dismissed. Some girls enjoyed writers like Rudyard Kipling, Jack London, Robert Louis Stevenson, and Daniel Defoe. Identifying with the male protagonists, they may have undergone the liberating experience Heilbrun describes. On the other hand, they may have noted that in these adventures females were absent or insignificant or passive, and they may have learned to value themselves accordingly—such an outcome is equally plausible. And even if some benefited from reading a "boys' " author, other girls turned away. I know how I felt about those authors: They had nothing to offer; their choices and concerns were not mine, on either a realistic or a fantasy level. Those who did identify with male protagonists must surely have been aware to some extent that, being girls, they were not the real thing; they must always have known that they were the Other sex—making the best of it, only pretending to be the essential, human One, the male. Those girls who enjoyed boys' books in the period when I was young were probably the ones who already tended to be active and independent. The ones who could have profited most from identifying with a strong male model would have been the milder ones like myself, who wouldn't have dared make that leap.

Even today girls continue to play a lesser role in children's popular culture. In the *New York Times* of April 7, 1991, Katha Pollitt offered a complaint as a mother of young daughters. "Somehow or other, only boys get to go On Beyond Zebra or see marvels on Mulberry Street. Frog and Toad, Lowly Worm, Lyle the Crocodile, all *could* have been female. But they're not. Do kids pick up on the sexism in children's culture? You bet. Preschoolers are like medieval philosophers: the text—a book, a movie, a TV show—is more authoritative than the evidence of their own eyes. The sexism in preschool culture deforms both boys and girls. Little girls learn to split their consciousness, filtering dreams and ambitions through boy characters while admiring the clothes of the princess. The privileged and daring can dream of becoming exceptional women in a man's world—token Smurfettes. The others are taught to accept the more usual fate, which is to be a [female] passenger car drawn through life by a masculine train engine." In discussing boy characters as models for girl readers, I fear that

Pollitt describes the situation more realistically than Heilbrun and Cooper. The situation is definitely changing, as parents try to lessen the damage to daughters and media people start to see market potential in girls. But at best the change is slow, uneven.

Who Read What

THEY ALL WENT OFF TO DISCOVER THE POLE,
OWL AND PIGLET AND RABBIT AND ALL;
IT'S A THING YOU DISCOVER, AS I'VE BEEN TOLE
BY OWL AND PIGLET AND RABBIT AND ALL.
EEYORE, CHRISTOPHER ROBIN AND POOH
AND RABBIT'S RELATIONS ALL WENT TOO—
AND WHERE THE POLE WAS NONE OF THEM KNEW. . . .
SING HEY! FOR OWL AND RABBIT AND ALL!

For A. A. Milne's characters, the exciting outside world was less appealing than their own comfortable world, the inner circle of friends and friendly places. You might lose your tail or get lost on an expedition or fall in a pit, but you were always surrounded by The People who helped you in practical ways and gave you good things to eat and made sure you didn't get your feelings hurt. Winnie the Pooh's forest society had a neat hierarchy, with Rabbit's Friends and Relations at the bottom and Christopher Robin at the top, pointing upward to the even wiser storyteller. While this society was hierarchical, it was also supportive and harmonious, delightfully cozy. A child reader was on the inside, *with* The People though pleasantly wiser than they; the rest of the world was excluded.

The trip to the North Pole was a typical communal adventure in Pooh land. Pooh's rhyme immortalized the occasion with its epic list of participants. Children reading the story probably did not notice that, according to Pooh's list, The People of the forest were all male. Kanga, the only female character in the stories, was not mentioned in the poem's list, even though she did go on the expedition. Kanga's entire role was to be Mother, dispensing medicine and urging caution to her baby and to others. She was essential but never important. She was not what Milne would call One of Us (rather, she was what Simone de Beauvoir would call the Other) and apparently she did not deserve listing in Pooh's catalogue. The list condescended to mention Rabbit's relations at the bottom but nobody would SING HEY! for Kanga.

The Pooh books were among my early favorites and I don't think I wondered why all the characters except one were "he." Depending on my mood, I would identify with Piglet, meek and snivelling but sweet, or with Eeyore, who was grouchy and gloomy but interesting, so I was in fact identifying with male characters. At an older stage my friends and I would give each other nicknames out of Winnie the Pooh. One fall day in my sophomore year in college, three friends and I bicycled into a woodsy glade and sat around reading (self-consciously) from Winnie the Pooh. These animals were less conspicuously male than boy characters in realistic fiction, but they were still males.

I cannot perceive the female-free world of Winnie the Pooh as being in itself a major trauma for girls, but it is a typical pattern and the effect of such books is perhaps cumulative. A fantasy world offers children life in its essence, a complex image that is enormously forceful and evocative. Other stories repeat Milne's almost-all-male pattern; some fantasy stories include *both* male and female. Are there any popular fantasy worlds before 1950 that are almost entirely *female*? I can't think of any. The Alice and Oz books have female protagonists and other strong female characters, but even they do not offer a community that is all or mostly female, which would be a counterpart to the male Milne world. In a revealing book called *Communities of Women* (1978), Nina Auerbach documents a long tradition of attitudes toward female groups: They were considered ludicrous or else dangerous and corrupting, because women together were felt to "ignite each other's grossness."

Another male idyll like the one in *Winnie the Pooh* (1926) was created in Kenneth Grahame's *The Wind in the Willows* (1908). When Toad, the one character who didn't appreciate the animals' perfect world, went out into the imperfect human world, a few females played small roles in the story. But the central society of the animals contained no female members—only a father, Otter, and no mothers. Perhaps that's why all the animals seemed so free. Women belonged with the alien humans, not with the warm, comfortable animals.

Like Winnie the Pooh's world, the society of Rat and Mole had limits, specific ones: when Mole first came to the river bank, Rat pointed out the dangerous Wild Wood and beyond it the Wide World that no respectable animal had anything to do with. As long as the little band of male animals stuck together, they could keep out the outside world. So, when Rat and Mole escaped from the snowstorm into Badger's home and Otter followed them there, the gang rejoiced in their safe haven, their male solidarity.

IN THE EMBRACING LIGHT AND WARMTH, WARM AND DRY AT LAST, WITH WEARY LEGS PROPPED UP IN FRONT OF THEM, AND A SUGGESTIVE CLINK OF PLATES BEING ARRANGED ON THE TABLE BEHIND, IT SEEMED TO THE STORM-DRIVEN ANIMALS THAT THE COLD AND TRACKLESS WILD WOOD JUST LEFT OUTSIDE WAS MILES AND MILES AWAY. WHEN SUPPER WAS FINISHED AT LAST, AND EACH ANIMAL FELT THAT HIS SKIN WAS NOW AS TIGHT AS WAS DECENTLY SAFE, AND THAT BY THIS TIME HE DIDN'T CARE A HANG FOR ANYBODY OR ANYTHING, THEY GATHERED ROUND THE GLOWING EMBERS OF THE GREAT WOOD FIRE, AND THOUGHT HOW JOLLY IT WAS TO BE SITTING UP *SO* LATE, AND *SO* IN-DEPENDENT, AND *SO* FULL.

This society, of course, was still hierarchical: Badger the gruff country gentleman was at the top, with his unpretentious but wealthy estate; the bottom here contained the young (Mole's field-mouse Christmas carolers and Badger's hedgehog visitors) and the miscellaneous residents of the river bank. Each was comfortable in his home and happy in his role. Again, Badger's den was vividly drawn:

IT SEEMED A PLACE WHERE HEROES COULD FITLY FEAST AFTER VIC-TORY, WHERE WEARY HARVESTERS COULD LINE UP ALONG THE TABLE AND KEEP THEIR HARVEST HOME WITH MIRTH AND SONG, OR WHERE TWO OR THREE FRIENDS OF SIMPLE TASTES COULD SIT ABOUT AS THEY PLEASED AND EAT AND SMOKE AND TALK IN COMFORT AND CONTENT-MENT. I adored *Wind in the Willows*, not noticing consciously the men's club or sweaty locker room aspect. This world was astonishingly real; did girls therefore feel *less* real, diminished?

Winnie the Pooh and *The Wind in the Willows* were usually read in the early years of childhood. Their male emphasis set a pattern that was followed throughout the fiction read by older boys and some girls—through stories of adventure, history, animals, mystery, and fantasy. More boys than girls liked adventure books and sports stories; more girls liked fantasies and mysteries and especially realistic fiction—stories about family and friends and community.

Some boys liked fantasies and animal stories and mysteries too—but only when they offered high energy plot and action. Boys' science fiction resembled heroic adventure (Jules Verne, the Tom Swift series); they were less taken with broad fantasy societies like those of Oz or Pinocchio. Boys' animal stories were the kind closest to adventure tales (*Call of the Wild, Silver Chief*), while girls read the domestic horse books of Mary O'Hara (*My Friend Flicka*), and Marguerite Henry (*Misty*), stressing character more than plot. Boys admired the animal as individual *hero* being tested in the wild (with triumphant or tragic results), while girls loved the animal as *victim* of society or as socialized *friend*.

As for mysteries, boys read the Hardy Boys and Sherlock Holmes series, while girls were devoted to Nancy Drew and, to a lesser extent, Cherry Ames and Sue Barton (two other girls' mystery series). A mystery is an adventure of a social kind, an adventure with a solution rather than just an outcome. A crime has torn the social fabric, which must be restored. I suspect that girls appreciated the moral, social element in mysteries more than boys did. Girls' mysteries like Cherry Ames, even when thin and superficial, present a texture of social relations. Sherlock Holmes is practically an adventure hero: the crimes he solves are challenges to his own problem-solving brilliance and his ability to vanquish opponents, more than they are immoral attacks on a society. And Holmes's relation to Watson is on the simplest level, that of warrior to worthy subordinate, Crusoe to Friday. Even in mysteries, boys preferred to see a hero testing himself, reaching for a goal—not a person working out problems with other people. Is it fanciful to conclude that boys admired the triumph of ego, and girls the comforting reassertion of superego?

Boys' Reading

Before turning to female favorites, I want to look at some books that probably haunt the memories of middle-aged and elderly *men*, the books that were read by boys—or by many boys and some girls. Some were not *written for* but were *read by* children. It is worth considering the themes and values boys encountered in their favorite adventure stories. Males typically showed themselves to be brave (facing danger and hardship, taking risks), dominant and ambitious (fighting to win and beat others and achieve a goal), resourceful (solving problems, making plans), and independent (escaping restrictions, acting without help or with only the help of subordinates). These were qualities most characteristic of the male characters, most alien to the female.

Robinson Crusoe (1719) was the master of these virile qualities. His was the most extreme male adventure story: one man testing himself against human and non-human enemies, aided only by a sidekick who's clearly presented as an inferior. He arrived on his desert island in a heroic manner, unlike the passive way a heroine would be floated ashore. Enormous waves threatened to drown him or dash him on the rocks. Five times, as a wave swept wildly over him, he held his breath and struggled toward shore; he would not stop fighting. Crusoe's ingenuity is legendary: I HAD NEVER HANDLED A TOOL IN MY LIFE, AND YET IN TIME BY LABOR, APPLICATION, AND CONTRIVANCE, I MADE AN ABUNDANCE OF THINGS, EVEN WITHOUT PROPER TOOLS, AND SOME WITH NO MORE TOOLS THAN AN ADZ AND A HATCHET.

Crusoe was stalwart in carrying out his plans and defending his turf, but mostly he spared us the bloody-minded competitiveness so popular in other boys' stories. That quality is especially prized in *The Three Musketeers* (1844). Dumas described a time of political intrigue when the French Queen's partisans were violently at odds with supporters of the King and Cardinal. The book's energy lies in the witless, boastful aggressiveness of the Musketeers: LOOSE IN THEIR WAYS, BATTLE-SCARRED, THE MUSKETEERS ROAMED THE CITY, LOUNGING IN THE TAVERNS OR STROLLING IN THE PUBLIC WALKS, SHOUTING, TWIRLING THEIR MUSTACHES AND RATTLING THEIR SWORDS. THEY TOOK IMMENSE PLEASURE IN JOSTLING

THE GUARDS OF MONSEIGNEUR CARDINAL WHEN THEY MET. THEN THEY WOULD DRAW THEIR SWORDS IN THE OPEN STREET, AMID A THOUSAND JESTS, AS THOUGH IT WERE ALL THE GREATEST SPORT IN THE WORLD. SOMETIMES THEY WERE KILLED, OFTEN THEY DID THE KILLING. I have always been baffled as to why anybody finds these antics interesting. Simplistic male images are just as stupid as simplistic female images, and a lot more violent.

Probably the bloodiest of heroes was Tarzan (1912). TO KILL WAS THE LAW OF THE WILD WORLD HE KNEW. FEW WERE HIS PRIMITIVE PLEASURES, BUT THE GREATEST OF THESE WAS TO HUNT AND KILL. After battling an enormous boar, the young Tarzan feasted: THE APE-MAN HAD NO KNIFE, BUT NATURE HAD EQUIPPED HIM WITH THE MEANS OF TEARING HIS FOOD FROM THE QUIVERING FLANK OF HIS PREY, AND GLEAMING TEETH SANK INTO THE SUCCULENT FLESH. AH, BUT IT HAD BEEN DELICIOUS! NEVER HAD HE QUITE ACCUSTOMED HIMSELF TO THE RUINED FLESH THAT CIVILIZED MEN HAD SERVED HIM, AND IN THE BOTTOM OF HIS SAVAGE HEART THERE HAD CONSTANTLY BEEN THE CRAVING FOR THE WARM MEAT OF THE FRESH KILL, AND THE RICH, RED BLOOD. (At least he ate only those slain enemies who were not human.) "I AM TARZAN," HE CRIED. "I AM A GREAT KILLER. THERE BE NONE AMONG YOU AS MIGHTY AS TARZAN. LET HIS ENEMIES BEWARE." THE YOUNG LORD GREYSTOKE BEAT UPON HIS MIGHTY BREAST AND SCREAMED OUT ONCE MORE HIS SHRILL CRY OF DEFIANCE.

Tarzan had the strength and speed of a wild beast, but was also ludicrously rational and noble. He saved the weak and injured, protected women and peaceable natives, adapted to the mores of Paris, and sacrificed his inheritance as Lord Greystoke for the sake of the woman he loved. Burroughs called him godlike, and enjoyed describing his sinuous, rippling muscles along with his less tangible virtues. His creator saw Tarzan as the finest type of unspoiled gentleman; American boys agreed. His habit of chewing the necks of wild beasts and sucking their blood apparently was considered a lovable male foible.

Favorite boy books certainly included *Treasure Island* and *Huckleberry Finn*. Some of Jim Hawkins's adventures happened by chance, like his overhearing the pirates' plans while submerged in an apple barrel, but Jim was still a major actor in the battles and schemes of *Treasure Island* (1883). Though a mere lad, he recaptured the ship by shooting the grisly pirate left on board as a guard. "WELL," SAID I, "I'VE COME ABOARD TO TAKE POS-SESSION OF THIS SHIP, MR. HANDS; AND YOU'LL PLEASE REGARD ME AS YOUR CAPTAIN UNTIL FURTHER NOTICE." Captured by the pirates again, he swaggered in the heroic manner: "HERE YOU ARE, IN A BAD WAY: SHIP LOST, TREASURE LOST, MEN LOST; AND IF YOU WANT TO KNOW WHO DID IT—IT WAS I! I WAS IN THE APPLE BARREL THE NIGHT WE SIGHTED LAND, AND I HEARD YOU. AND AS FOR THE SCHOONER, IT WAS I WHO CUT HER CABLE, AND IT WAS I THAT KILLED THE MEN YOU HAD ABOARD OF HER. THE LAUGH'S ON MY SIDE; I'VE HAD THE TOP OF THIS BUSINESS FROM THE FIRST; I NO MORE FEAR YOU THAN I FEAR A FLY. KILL ME, IF YOU PLEASE, OR SPARE ME." For a hero, modesty is not required.

Young David Balfour in Stevenson's *Kidnapped* (1886) carried on much like Jim: I HAD NEVER FIRED WITH A PISTOL IN MY LIFE. BUT IT WAS NOW OR NEVER; I CRIED OUT, "TAKE THAT!" AND SHOT INTO THEIR MIDST. I MUST HAVE HIT ONE OF THEM. THE WHOLE PLACE WAS FULL OF THE SMOKE OF MY OWN FIRING. THERE WAS ALAN, STANDING AS BEFORE ONLY NOW HIS SWORD WAS RUNNING BLOOD TO THE HILT, AND HIMSELF SO SWELLED WITH TRIUMPH AND FALLEN INTO SO FINE AN ATTITUDE, THAT HE LOOKED TO BE INVINCIBLE. RIGHT BEFORE HIM ON THE FLOOR WAS MR. SHUAN, ON HIS HANDS AND KNEES; THE BLOOD WAS POURING FROM HIS MOUTH.

The scene seems endless, with the shouting and leaping and slashing: THE ROUND-HOUSE WAS LIKE A SHAMBLES; THREE WERE DEAD INSIDE, ANOTHER LAY IN HIS DEATH AGONY ACROSS THE THRESHOLD; AND THERE WERE ALAN AND I VICTORIOUS AND UNHURT. HE TURNED TO THE FOUR ENEMIES, PASSED HIS SWORD CLEAN THROUGH EACH OF THEM, AND TUMBLED THEM OUT OF DOORS ONE AFTER THE OTHER. AS HE DID SO HE KEPT HUMMING AND SINGING AND WHISTLING TO HIMSELF. HIS EYES WERE AS BRIGHT AS A FIVE-YEAR OLD CHILD'S WITH A NEW TOY. There may be irony in Stevenson's voice as he presents these proud, bloody scenes, but the child reader is not interested in such subtleties. Imagine the multitude of boys who have brandished shiny pistols and swords over the last century, each of them becoming David Balfour as he cries out "Take that!" to the villains.

* * *

These observations about the boldness and cleverness of the male hero are unoriginal—only too familiar—but as I will offer many instances of the girlish messages of girls' books, it seems fitting to include also specific examples of behavior that was considered admirably boyish in boys' fiction. *Kidnapped* and *Treasure Island* stressed the warlike side of the male image, then, and *Robinson Crusoe* the resourcefulness; the most important quality in *Tom Sawyer* (1876) and *Huckleberry Finn* (1884) was independence.

Tom struggled to escape one constricting force after another—punishments, schooling, chores, bedtime, clothes, all the expectations of his benign world. HE LOOKED EXCEEDINGLY IMPROVED AND UNCOMFORTABLE. THERE WAS A RESTRAINT ABOUT WHOLE CLOTHES AND CLEANLINESS THAT GALLED HIM. He escaped this civilizing physically in outrageous escapades and mentally in outrageous tales and fantasies. If a girl character of that era had climbed out the window at night or run away to an island leaving everyone to think she was dead, she would have incurred something worse than the head-shaking "Land sakes!" that Tom earned. At the end of *Tom Sawyer* Tom urged wild Huck to stay in town and live with the Widow Douglas, but not in the cop-out spirit of a girls' story; he simply wanted his friend nearby, to join in new adventures. Tom did not end up with his spirit broken like Rebecca of Sunnybrook Farm and Anne of Green Gables.

Huck Finn, of course, is the ultimate emblem of male independence. HUCKLEBERRY CAME AND WENT, AT HIS OWN FREE WILL. HE SLEPT ON DOORSTEPS IN FINE WEATHER AND IN EMPTY HOGSHEADS IN WET; HE DID NOT HAVE TO GO TO SCHOOL OR TO CHURCH, OR OBEY ANYBODY; HE COULD GO FISHING OR SWIMMING WHEN AND WHERE HE CHOSE; NOBODY FORBADE HIM TO FIGHT; HE COULD SIT UP AS LATE AS HE PLEASED; HE NEVER HAD TO WASH, NOR PUT ON CLEAN CLOTHES; HE COULD SWEAR WONDERFULLY. IN A WORD, EVERYTHING THAT GOES TO MAKE LIFE PRECIOUS THAT BOY HAD. From this first appearance, through adventures on the island and raft, to his final vow to avoid being "sivilized" by lighting out for the territory ahead of the rest, Huck Finn never compromised his freedom.

Besides courage, ambition, resourcefulness, and independence, two other male characteristics were traditionally important: Loyalty to something beyond yourself and insight into other people's true nature appear in both male and female characters, but in significantly different forms. From their books, boys learned to be loyal to a team, an ideal, as members of the team or sometimes as leaders. A male protagonist could be intensely loyal to an abstract code or to a superior—king or captain—but his subordinate position, usually, was freely chosen, dignified, and important to the superior. In *Ivanhoe*, Richard the Lion-Hearted was involved in the plot as the hero's revered king and mentor, but the king kept his identity hidden and behaved more like a comrade to Ivanhoe than a sovereign. A character might be a junior member of his team, like Ivanhoe or Jim Hawkins, but his distance below the senior members is not great, and his behavior is never subservient.

The role of apprentice is appropriate to a boy, as he is younger and less experienced than the elders. He knows that this junior position is temporary; he will become leader himself one day. Girls show their loyalty from a position permanently secondary; they are locked into a hierarchy where women are leaders to the children and the weak—but followers to their husbands and other men in authority. The nurse will always be below the doctor and the little sister below her brother. In girls' books you see cheerful obedience more often than proud loyalty; the female character stands at a greater distance from the object of her loyalty than does a male character.

Themes of male loyalty were important in a number of the boys' best adventure stories. Some solitary heroes, like Tarzan and Cooper's Natty Bumppo, were loyal to a code of behavior, a moral or religious conviction, rather than a specific person or group. Natty Bumppo, called Deerslayer and Hawkeye, was strong and clever like Tarzan, and brave enough to endure Indian torture without flinching. His most notable quality, though, was the forthright honesty that caused him frequently to halt the action and pontificate about his moral code. In *The Deerslayer* (1841) he announced: "I HOLD IT TO BE ONLAWFUL TO TAKE THE LIFE OF MAN, EXCEPT IN OPEN AND GENEROUS WARFARE" and "A WHITE MAN'S GIFTS ARE CHRISTIANIZED, WHILE A REDSKIN'S ARE MORE FOR THE WILDERNESS. THUS, IT WOULD BE A GREAT OFFENSE FOR A WHITE MAN TO SCALP THE DEAD; WHEREAS IT'S A SIGNAL VARTUE IN AN INDIAN. THEN AG'IN, A

WHITE MAN CANNOT AMBOOSH WOMEN AND CHILDREN IN WAR, WHILE A REDSKIN MAY." The Deerslayer kept his word loyally, but he followed no master—only his conscience.

Kipling's stories are always about allegiance to a virile code. He showed a boy-hero training for life under the ruthless Law of the Jungle in *The Jungle Books* (1894), another learning to follow the rules of the great espionage Game in *Kim* (1901). Clearly, each boy was destined to become a leader when his training was complete. Mowgli learned to obey the laws of justice and cruel revenge: "WHAT IS THE LAW OF THE JUNGLE? STRIKE FIRST AND THEN GIVE TONGUE." Kipling and the animals taught Mowgli a xenophobic devotion to his own team—the Master Words were "WE BE OF ONE BLOOD, THOU AND I," AND A FAVORITE SAYING WAS "NORTH ARE THE VERMIN; SOUTH ARE THE LICE. *WE* ARE THE JUNGLE." Even as a little boy, Mowgli loved "killing right and left," proving his boldness and power over enemies. THERE WAS NOTHING MOWGLI LIKED BETTER THAN TO PULL THE WHISKERS OF DEATH AND MAKE THE JUNGLE FEEL THAT HE WAS THEIR OVERLORD. His affection toward his teammates had an exalted and erotic tone; leaning upon his friend the snake after a battle, HE FELT KAA GROW BIGGER AND BROADER BELOW HIM AS THE HUGE PYTHON PUFFED HIMSELF OUT, HISSING WITH THE NOISE OF A SWORD DRAWN FROM A STEEL SCABBARD. Loyalty to the Law and those within the Law was the basis for all civilization, and those who lacked the Law were, like the Monkey People, detestable and wretched. American boys apparently loved this murderous colonial, racist stuff.

Kim, a more sophisticated tale, also concerns the development of a boy who must combine the primitive strengths of a lower society (Indians in *Kim* equalling jungle animals in *The Jungle Books*) with the godlike virtues of the colonial male. The book's excitement lay in the spy adventure, the deadly Game that tested young Kim's loyalties. One adviser taught him: "IS NOT THE LITTLE GUN A DELIGHT? IT IS BORNE IN THE BOSOM NEXT THE SKIN, WHICH, AS IT WERE, KEEPS IT OILED. NEVER PUT IT ELSEWHERE, AND PLEASE GOD, THOU SHALT SOME DAY KILL A MAN WITH IT." This is an odd way of pleasing God, but inspiring to male youth in Kipling's era and mine.

Insight into people's character is the other quality besides loyalty that takes a different form in girls' and boys' books. Girls' stories stress empathy and sympathy and include few characters who are really bad. Some are difficult or unhappy but can be cajoled by an understanding female person; others *seem* bad but turn out to be good inside or reformable through the power of feminine goodness. Boys' stories, on the other hand, delight in grossly wicked characters and morally ambiguous characters. Boy protagonists defeat or escape bad people who challenge them; and they figure out the truth about the ambiguous characters.

What interests me particularly is that a male hero does not expect people to change. He tries to understand them so he can define them as friend or enemy, superior or inferior, and deal with them successfully; but he does not hope to reform the bad or improve the flawed. While the heroine's world cannot tolerate the existence of real, implacable villains, the hero's world needs them. Boys must win, so they need somebody to beat; girls must create harmony, so they need somebody to help. Each has an insight into character that is appropriate to his or her purpose, the males wanting to get on with the achieving of their personal goals and the females wanting to understand and advance the goals of people around them.

So in *Treasure Island* Long John Silver could be Jim's treacherous enemy and his fascinating mentor, without the inconsistency being resolved. *Kidnapped* was a murky mixture of right and wrong action and allegiance. In the Tarzan books John Clayton was an appealing young man even though reprehensible when he claimed the title, knowing that Tarzan was the real Lord Greystoke. Mark Twain had mixed characters like Muff Potter, who was a no-account low-life but did not deserve to be convicted of a crime he didn't commit. It is safe to generalize that boys' stories told boys to be realistic, keen in *judging* others, fair but skeptical; girls' stories told girls to be idealistic, keen in *understanding* others, generally trusting and making allowances. While trust and empathy are fine things (I prefer books that teach children how to understand an outcast rather than how to unmask and torture a traitor), it would probably improve these girls' lives if they could learn to identify the traitors too, and not always deny that hostility exists.

These traditional male characteristics found in earlier fiction did not disappear in twentieth-century children's books. For example, the sea stories of Howard Pease written in the 1940s follow the old patterns. Pease's teenage protagonists usually acted alone. One rescued a comrade who was tied up at a voodoo ceremony in a Caribbean jungle; one lived broke in New York by sleeping in Central Park and working as a furnace-tender; one escaped bandits in Mexico by zooming down a dangerous mountain road in a defective car. A typical hero, Tod Moran in his Mexican adventure had an annoying habit of exhorting himself to do better in a crisis: HOW FAR, TOD WONDERED, WOULD A CAR FALL BEFORE IT HIT THE RIVER? HUNDREDS OF FEET, PROBABLY THOUSANDS. DRIVE STEADY, TOD MORAN— DRIVE STEADY! Another time, THERE WAS NO HELP AT HAND, NOT EVEN AN AX OR A SHOVEL. BUT THERE WERE NUMBERLESS DEAD PALM FRONDS IN THAT TROPICAL GROWTH AND PLENTY OF GRAVEL. FURTHERMORE, HE HAD TWO HANDS. TIME TO GET TO WORK, TOD MORAN!

The most absurd twentieth-century examples of brave, clever, independent boy heroes appeared in a 1928 book I found recently in a secondhand store, *Mystery and Adventure Stories for Boys, Four Complete Books*. It interested me because its cover resembled the cover of a book I liked as a child, and it was obviously a companion volume. The girls in *Mystery Stories for Girls, Four Complete Books* (just called *mysteries* in the female book, not *adventures*) were fairly well characterized and their escapades were fairly plausible. The boys' stories were different; they had wooden characters with no motivation, and impossible events with no connecting plot, presented in a dreary, stale style. Transitions were effected with this degree of sophistication: "WE ARE ADRIFT ON THE ICE!" CRIED ANDY. "WE ONLY ESCAPED FROM ONE DANGER TO FALL INTO ANOTHER!"

What these boys' stories *did* have was all the stereotypes of boy heroes. One lad lived on a Naval Air Station. THE CALL OF THE OPEN SPACES SEEMED INBORN IN THE SMITH FAMILY. ANY BOY WHO HAS RED BLOOD IN HIM, AND BILLY WAS NO ALICE-SIT-BY-THE-FIRE, IS BOUND TO BECOME INFECTED BY SUCH ENVIRONMENT. Later in the young career of "Billy Smith—Exploring Ace," he was being attacked in a jungle: WHILE TWO OF THE LITTLE MEN ATTACKED HIM IN FRONT, THE OTHER SPRANG UPON HIS BACK. QUICK AS THOUGHT, BILL CAUGHT AT THE ARM ENCIRCLING HIS THROAT AND CATAPULTED THE SAVAGE OVER HIS HEAD. IN THE INSTANT'S RESPITE THE LAD MANAGED TO DRAW HIS REVOLVER AND, AS THE THIRD NATIVE RAISED HIS STONE-TIPPED CLUB TO STRIKE, BILL PISTOLED HIM. The "Boy Ranchers" had just as much fun: WITH DISTINCT FEELINGS OF JOY, AND NO ALARM WHATEVER, NORT AND DICK WATCHED THE HANDS OF SLIM AND BABE SLIDE TOWARD THEIR HOLSTERS, WHERE NESTLED THEIR .45 GUNS. . . . BUD AND HIS COUSINS SAW A SIGHT WHICH THRILLED THEM THROUGH AND THROUGH. IN THE MIDST OF AN ENCAMPMENT OF TENTS, SEVERAL MEN WERE KNEELING, USING PACKS AND BAGGAGE AS A BARRICADE. THEY WERE FIRING OVER THIS LINE OF DEFENSE AT OBJECTS UNSEEN, BUT WHICH WERE EASILY GUESSED TO BE HUMANS, WITH MORE OR LESS SINISTER MOTIVES.

The plucky orphan boys in "Through the Air to the North Pole" showed their ingenuity in handling a peculiar airship that was electric and involved both a propeller and an immense phallic gas bag SHAPED LIKE A CIGAR, BIG IN THE MIDDLE AND TAPERING AT BOTH ENDS. When the airship was disabled, the boys showed its inventor how to repair it. "HAVE YOU ANYTHING TO MEND THE SILK BAG WITH?" WENT ON THE BOY—"IF YOU'LL LET ME I'LL CLIMB UP AND MEND THE HOLE THE EAGLE MADE." "DARE YOU DO IT?" CRIED THE OLD PROFESSOR, HOPE SHINING IN HIS FACE. THE ANSWER, NATURALLY, WAS, "TRY ME AND SEE!" The boys in these "Four Complete Books" were invariably bold and smart, and they shared the sensuous joys of being loyal members of the team, "one of us": THOUGH THE BOYS PROTESTED AT BEING MADE TO REMAIN IN BED, THE OLD MAN INSISTED. HE MADE THEM TAKE OFF MOST OF THEIR CLOTHES, AND THEN BROUGHT OUT SOME LINIMENT. UNDER HIS DIRECTION JACK AND MARK RUBBED THEMSELVES WELL, AND EXPERIENCED ALMOST IMMEDIATE RELIEF. This may be a traditional kind of male experience, but I personally would not be pleased if I learned my own sons had taken off their clothes and experienced almost immediate relief supervised by this old man and his wonderful rubbing technique.

Girls in Boys' Books

In looking at the messages boys received from their own reading, I don't want to neglect the female characters. They were mostly absent or insignificant; when present they were weak, suffering, and saintly. Girl and women characters in boys' stories fall into four types. Some are unreliable, frivolous, vain. Some are sweet, appealing, and weak. Some are nurturing. A very few are strong and resourceful—to some degree. These few women who try to take action in a crisis almost always fail; their little efforts fizzle and they are rescued by men.

Robinson Crusoe ignored women. *Treasure Island* noticed Jim's mother briefly but showed her to be incompetent: early in the book, her muddled behavior almost got herself and Jim caught by the pirates. Kipling mentioned only a few women characters perfunctorily, usually of the maternal type. The one woman in Kipling's *Captains Courageous* was Harvey's rich mother, who had spoiled him so abominably that the entire book was devoted to turning him into a brave young man instead of a mama's boy. No girl characters in Kipling's books shared in the boys' adventures, even in a subordinate position.

Lorna Doone (1869) presents a lush array of female stereotypes. John Ridd, the shrewd and forthright hero, had a mother who was stupid and fluttery; one sister who was clever and sharp-tongued and physically deformed (since intelligence in females traditionally appeared along with some abnormality); and another sister who was sweet and feminine. Sister ANNIE WAS OF A PLEASING FACE AND VERY GENTLE MANNER, WITHOUT ANY AIRS, ONLY TRYING TO GIVE SATISFACTION. IF SHE FAILED, SHE WOULD GO AND WEEP, BELIEVING THE FAULT TO BE ALL HER OWN, WHEN MOSTLY IT WAS OF OTHERS. BUT IF SHE SUCCEEDED IN PLEASING YOU, IT WAS BEAUTIFUL TO SEE HER SMILE, TAKING NOTE HOW TO DO THE RIGHT THING AGAIN FOR YOU.

Alas, submissiveness in "little" Annie was not accompanied by good judgment. She was so easily swayed that she fell for an obvious trick and turned over to an enemy a priceless diamond necklace. The family chastised her but were not suprised at her witlessness and soon became reconciled to the loss. Other conventional females were the crude but loyal "little" maidservant Gwenny and John's long-suffering "little" cousin Ruth, who hid her unrequited love for John and dedicated herself to saving the life of his wounded bride Lorna after the doctor declared her officially dead. Ruth proved herself almost of heroine quality not just by sacrificial actions but by fainting several times.

The champion fainter and head heroine was Lorna Doone herself. Lorna was not presented as an unusually timid girl. She occasionally spoke up for herself, gently. Once she actually helped her lover by waking him when he fell asleep while standing guard against an expected attack. Nonetheless, her most notable qualities were confusion and a tendency to faint.

At one point, Lorna was living on the Ridds' farm, having been rescued by John from her relatives the Doones, a cruel robber band. She sensed that she could be doing something useful around the farm but, in the words of her beloved John, IT WAS QUITE IN VAIN TO TELL HER THAT SHE WAS EXPECTED TO DO NOTHING, AND FAR WORSE THAN VAIN (FOR IT MADE HER CRY SADLY) IF ANYONE ASSURED HER THAT SHE COULD DO NO GOOD AT ALL. SHE EVEN BEGAN UPON MOTHER'S GARDEN, BEFORE THE SNOW WAS CLEAN GONE FROM IT, AND SOWED A BEAUTIFUL ROW OF PEAS, EVERY ONE OF WHICH THE MICE ATE. This Dora syndrome (which I name after David Copperfield's feeble child-bride) presents the most lovable maiden as the one who is physically weak and mentally vacant.

As for physical weakness, Lorna Doone was perfectly healthy but had a sensitivity that manifested itself through swooning, an activity that her suitor John found titillating. At their first childhood meeting, in John's words, SHE SHRANK TO ME, AND LOOKED UP AT ME, WITH SUCH A POWER OF WEAKNESS, THAT I AT ONCE MADE UP MY MIND TO SAVE HER, OR TO DIE WITH HER. A TINGLE WENT THROUGH ALL MY BONES, AND I ONLY LONGED FOR MY CARBINE. Years later, when John sneaked into the robbers' den to rescue her, she was weak and ill because her cousin Carver was trying to starve her into submission: SHE HAD FAINTED AWAY, AND LAY BACK ON A CHAIR, AS WHITE AS THE SNOW AROUND US. Then, THE TENDER HUE FLOWED BACK AGAIN INTO HER FAMISHED CHEEKS AND LIPS. SHE GAVE

ME ONE LITTLE SHRUNKEN HAND. LATER, LORNA WAS SO FAR OP-
PRESSED WITH ALL THE TROUBLES OF THE EVENING THAT SHE LAY
QUITE MOTIONLESS, LIKE FAIREST WAX IN THE MOONLIGHT.

When Lorna and John spoke up to the evil uncle and defied his
power over her, she naturally fainted once more: SHE FELL INTO
MY ARMS; AND THERE SHE LAY WITH NO OTHER SOUND, EXCEPT A GUR-
GLING IN HER THROAT. And on another occasion, after learning
good news about her uncertain parentage, Lorna LAY BACK ON THE
GARDEN BENCH, WHILE HER COLOUR WENT AND CAME; AND ONLY BY
THAT, AND HER QUIVERING BREAST, COULD ANYONE SAY THAT SHE
LIVED AND THOUGHT. Most frightening, lustful cousin Carver
Doone came after her once with "his long gun" when she was
alone outside. THE MAIDEN, ALTHOUGH SO USED TO TERROR, LOST ALL
PRESENCE OF MIND, AND COULD NEITHER SHRIEK NOR FLY, BUT ONLY
GAZE, AS IF BEWITCHED. FRIGHT HAD STRICKEN HER STIFF AS STONE. To
torment her, Carver fired right at her feet, WITH NO SIGN OF PITY
IN HIS FACE, BUT A WELL-PLEASED GRIN AT ALL THE CHARMING PALSY
OF HIS VICTIM.

I am multiplying examples of Lorna's wilting tendency to show
that it is no minor, incidental element in the story. The very core
of *Lorna Doone* was John's love for Lorna, and the core of that love
was his noble strength and her miserable weakness, which the
author himself worshipped and described in endless detail. Black-
more and his hero found nothing unattractive about Lorna's "little
shrunken hand," "gurgling throat," "quivering breast," and
"charming palsy." They found it natural that the heroine's most
common posture was "stiff as stone," "like fairest wax."

After all this, the wedding scene was inevitable: AFTER THE PAR-
SON HAD BLESSED US, LORNA TURNED TO LOOK AT ME, WITH A SUB-
DUED GLANCE. HER EYES TOLD ME SUCH A DEPTH OF COMFORT THAT I
WAS ALMOST AMAZED. DARLING EYES, MOST LOVING EYES—THE SOUND
OF A SHOT RANG THROUGH THE CHURCH, AND THOSE EYES WERE
FILLED WITH DEATH. LORNA FELL ACROSS MY KNEES, A FLOOD OF
BLOOD CAME OUT UPON THE WOOD OF THE ALTAR STEPS; AND AT MY
FEET LAY LORNA, TRYING TO TELL ME SOME LAST MESSAGE OUT OF HER
FAITHFUL EYES. Cousin Carver had struck again. I try not to mar
this touching scene by noticing that Lorna's eyes were described
in terms suitable to a cocker spaniel. Lorna survived to live hap-

pily with John and their brood. A strong, honorable man wins his prize, and the best prize in an adventure is the golden treasure or, more likely, the golden lady who out-languishes all the others. Or often both.

Women in the Tarzan books were like Lorna Doone: they were basically feeble, in spite of slight differences in courage and competence. A servant accompanied the white travelers shipwrecked on the African shore (in order to amuse the author by being fat and a "Negress"). This Esmerelda was even more confused and terrified than her mistress Jane. Once when the two women were besieged by a lion while waiting in their hut, Jane tried to protect herself and Esmerelda, her inferior (as the superior men would try to protect Jane). Predictably the effort came to naught. Jane shot at the lion, only grazing it though she shot at close range, and then fainted. She was saved by the arrival of Tarzan, who could do with his bare hands what Jane could not do with a loaded rifle. In another story Jane escaped from her captors in a jungle camp, stole a gun, and made her way back to the river and the ship of her friends. The reader starts to hope that this time she may accomplish something useful, but foolish mistakes caused her downfall. AFTER ALL HER PAINS, HER HEROIC STRUGGLE FOR FREEDOM HAD FAILED. WITH A STIFLED SOB SHE GAVE UP THE UNEQUAL BATTLE.

Jane appeared more often and more appropriately in a horizontal position, as when we see her floating unconscious in a small boat: While Tarzan DANCED AMONG HIS NAKED FELLOW SAVAGES, THE FIRELIGHT GLEAMING AGAINST HIS GREAT, ROLLING MUSCLES, THE PERSONIFICATION OF PHYSICAL PERFECTION AND STRENGTH, THE WOMAN WHO LOVED HIM LAY THIN AND EMACIATED IN THE LAST COMA THAT PRECEDES DEATH BY THIRST AND STARVATION. Later Jane was tied up on the stone altar of savages preparing for sacrifice. SHE TREMBLED IN AN AGONY OF FRIGHT. DURING THE GROTESQUE DANCE OF THE VOTARIES, SHE LAY FROZEN IN HORROR, NOR DID SHE REQUIRE THE SIGHT OF THE THIN BLADE AS IT ROSE SLOWLY ABOVE HER TO ENLIGHTEN HER AS TO HER DOOM. AS THE HAND BEGAN ITS DESCENT, JANE PORTER CLOSED HER EYES AND SENT UP A SILENT PRAYER—THEN SHE SUCCUMBED TO THE STRAIN UPON HER TIRED NERVES, AND SWOONED.

A woman who faces too great a trial will simply give up and absent herself, like Jane and like Tarzan's mother, Alice, in the first book. When Alice and her husband were shipwrecked alone at the jungle's edge, Greystoke declared that "WORK MUST BE OUR SALVATION. WE MUST FACE WHATEVER COMES, BRAVELY" and he got right to work. The lady bemoaned her fate for a while and then quietly went mad. Until she died, Lady Greystoke thought she was back in England with her servants and her furniture.

In truth, while these women did not exactly enjoy their torments and captivities, in the eyes of their male author they did long to be abducted by the *right kind* of strong, overpowering savage. When Tarzan first carried off Jane he had not yet learned human speech and she had no idea what this apelike creature was up to; nonetheless, after a token struggle, SHE GAVE UP THE FUTILE EFFORT AND LAY QUIETLY. A FEELING OF DREAMY PEACEFULNESS STOLE OVER JANE AS SHE SANK DOWN UPON THE GRASS WHERE TARZAN HAD PLACED HER, AND AS SHE LOOKED UP AT HIS GREAT FIGURE TOWERING ABOVE HER, THERE WAS ADDED A STRANGE SENSE OF PERFECT SECURITY. Despite his savage training Tarzan knew by instinct that a human lady is to be protected and so the perfect match came about, the godlike primitive man and the passive lady. And young readers were told once again that the traditional advice to maidens being raped is reasonable: "Give up the futile effort and lie quietly," in a state of "dreamy peacefulness."

The best-known novelists of historical adventure, Walter Scott and James Fenimore Cooper, created rousing but stereotypical heroines. They both liked to provide a strong woman as contrast to a weak heroine. The strong woman was often a sympathetic character, but she never won out in the end. Cora, the strong sister in *The Last of the Mohicans* (1826), died nobly trying to save her honor and her sister Alice. And even she was often lumped with Alice in the category of feeble females: THE TREMBLING SISTERS WERE COWERING IN THE FAR CORNER OF THE BUILDING. When the allies took a large cache of weapons, everybody got one except the sisters. Similarly, Scott's strong and intelligent women could be admired but must be punished. Rebecca, the beautiful and virtuous "Jewess" in *Ivanhoe* (1820), was exiled while blonde Rowena, dim and dreary, wed the hero.

In *Tom Sawyer* and *Huckleberry Finn*, Mark Twain gave us an ambiguous view of feminine stereotypes. He both supported the conventional picture of woman and undercut it with his satire. Tom eloquently explained to his friends the nature of women: First you kidnap them and then "YOU SHUT UP THE WOMEN, BUT YOU DON'T KILL THEM. THEY'RE ALWAYS BEAUTIFUL AND RICH, AND AWFULLY SCARED. YOU TAKE THEIR WATCHES AND THINGS, BUT YOU ALWAYS TAKE YOUR HAT OFF AND TALK POLITE. WELL, THE WOMEN GET TO LOVING YOU, AND AFTER THEY'VE BEEN IN THE CAVE A WEEK OR TWO WEEKS THEY STOP CRYING AND AFTER THAT YOU COULDN'T GET THEM TO LEAVE. IF YOU DROVE THEM OUT THEY'D TURN RIGHT AROUND AND COME BACK. IT'S SO IN ALL THE BOOKS." And Huck learned that women enjoy dying as well as being kidnapped. Staying at the Grangerford family's house, he wondered at the gloomy drawings on a bedroom wall depicting young ladies weeping over a dead bird, leaping off a bridge in the moonlight, and "leaning pensive on a tombstone." The late Emmeline Grangerford had produced these drawings along with mournful poetic tributes to anyone who died, until she herself pined away and died at the age of 14.

The reader realized that these morbid females were ludicrous and unrealistic, satirically described images from romantic fiction. But Tom Sawyer's own real adventures—as distinguished from his play-acting fantasies—involved a real maiden who was equally pitiful and swooning. When Tom and Becky got lost in the cave they behaved very much like traditional strong hero and weak heroine. They both became terrified and desperate but Tom took on two virile tasks—to find an escape route and to protect Becky. Hers was a totally female role: AT LAST BECKY'S FRAIL LIMBS REFUSED TO CARRY HER FURTHER. FATIGUE BORE SO HEAVILY UPON BECKY THAT SHE DROWSED OFF TO SLEEP.... BECKY GAVE LOOSE TO TEARS AND WAILINGS. HE PROPOSED TO EXPLORE ANOTHER PASSAGE. BUT BECKY WAS VERY WEAK. SHE HAD SUNK INTO A DREARY APATHY AND WOULD NOT BE ROUSED. SHE SAID SHE WOULD WAIT, NOW, WHERE SHE WAS, AND DIE—IT WOULD NOT BE LONG. Tom's dogged exploring saved the two of them. Afterwards they needed a few days to recover: TOM GOT ABOUT, A LITTLE, ON THURSDAY, AND WAS NEARLY AS WHOLE AS EVER SATURDAY; BUT BECKY DID NOT LEAVE HER ROOM

UNTIL SUNDAY, AND THEN SHE LOOKED AS IF SHE HAD PASSED THROUGH A WASTING ILLNESS. For all the Mark Twain humor, Tom and Becky are no different from Tarzan and Jane or John Ridd and Lorna Doone. They do not shatter the gender stereotypes or even make them quiver.

I myself knew nothing that would challenge gender stereotypes— I didn't even *know* any boys or men, to talk to and listen to. My father was loving but elderly and a bit remote. I had no brothers or male playmates. At school I never thought of boys as real people who might consider me a real person. The split between boy and girl worlds was absolute, and the boy world was clearly the more serious, taking up more physical and mental space.

I went to movies a lot (we had no TV)—cowboy and World War II movies as well as musicals where Doris Day sang in a sleigh or kissed West Point cadets. These cheerful musicals starred boy-next-door actors like Mickey Rooney and Van Johnson. They were likable, but not fascinating like the virile Western-and-War actors: William Holden, Gregory Peck, John Wayne, Henry Fonda, Robert Taylor. Real men were inscrutable and strong, almost omnipotent; not funny, or fun. I greatly admired my own much older, handsome half-brother, a submarine officer. Fred looked a bit like William Holden, and since I saw him seldom, my brain got the two of them jumbled together on the same plane of reality.

A neighbor family had a girl my sister's age and a boy one year older than I. The two older girls were great friends. When they graduated from ninth grade, Paul and I were left to wait at the schoolbus stop together for two more years. He was a quiet, pleasant lad, I believe. In that time we didn't exchange a single word, except once when the bus didn't show up. I was terrified he might talk, and glad that he didn't. We never looked each other in the eye.

Animal Stories

In my youth all children, girls and boys, were encouraged to enjoy stories about real (as distinguished from fantasy) animals. Teachers and parents liked the conservative values taught in these books; children liked the adventures and the noble beasts. School reading lists offered *Lassie* and *Black Beauty* and *Call of the Wild* as enthusiastically as *David Copperfield* and *Huckleberry Finn*. Animal stories may not seem aimed at one sex more than the other, but male and female reactions to animal books differed. Boys of my generation liked books of the animal-as-hero type (such as *Call of the Wild*), while girls liked animal-as-partner-and-friend-to-a-young-human books (like *Misty*). Again, girls chose stories about relationships; boys chose stories about an individual—a hero's struggle to prove himself, to succeed triumphantly or fail tragically.

Examining various animal books, those read by girls and those read by boys, you see the patterns found in other genres—males dominate and thrive, take risks and find adventures; only a few females are present and they are weak, incompetent, or insignificant. In addition to the animal *hero* present in all these books, the animal-as-partner authors also provided a young human *protagonist*, who owned or tamed the animal hero. How many of these young people were girls? Only one—Velvet Brown, who had to dress as a boy so she could race the horse herself and who was much weaker and more vulnerable than the boy protagonists in other animal stories.

In animal books children learned about a hierarchical, usually harsh world, much like that of *Kidnapped* or *Kim*, and they learned the right way to live in it—with strength, courage, cleverness, and loyalty. In the boys' animal-as-hero books, ruthlessness, even brutality, were also essential. Life in the wild was a violent struggle against the cruel natural world: Wolves' MENACING GROWLS, SAVAGE YELPS, AND BRITTLE CRUNCHING AND RIPPING TELL THE STORY OF THE FEAST, in the opening scene of *Silver Chief* (by Jack O'Brien, 1933) and in countless grim descriptions by Jack London, Albert Payson Terhune, and Ernest Seton Thompson. The hero of Jack London's *White Fang* (1906) KNEW THE LAW WELL—TO OPPRESS THE WEAK AND OBEY THE STRONG. HE ALSO KNEW THAT THE LAW WAS: EAT, OR BE EATEN. This is meant literally; the book described a famine in which dogs ate dogs and men ate dogs.

Our memories of one wild animal book, Felix Salten's *Bambi* (1929), are softened by images from the Disney movie, but in fact the book contained no singing skunks or flitting butterflies—instead, a brutal sequence of killings, battles, and natural disasters. BAMBI HURLED HIMSELF ON RONNO WITH REDOUBLED FURY. A PRONG BROKE FROM RONNO'S ANTLERS WITH A LOUD SNAP. RONNO THOUGHT HIS FOREHEAD WAS SHATTERED. THE NEXT MOMENT A TERRIFIC BLOW TORE OPEN HIS SHOULDER. This was the right behavior to win the heart of a doe: After Ronno slunk away bleeding, Faline came out of the thicket. "THAT WAS WONDERFUL," SHE SAID LAUGHINGLY to Bambi. "I LOVE YOU."

These struggling animal heroes were *male* and stupendously heroic, even when they were destroyed by nature or society. "HE'S NO ORDINARY HORSE. . . . HE'S BEAUTIFUL, SAVAGE, AND NOBLE," was said of Satan, son of the Black Stallion (1947). HE WAS MONSTROUS, AND HIS BLACK BODY GLISTENED IN THE SUN. IT WAS A BEAUTIFUL BUT UNEARTHLY SIGHT AND HENRY WAS AFRAID. Heroic Buck, at the end of *Call of the Wild*, was running with the wolves, LEAPING GIGANTIC ABOVE HIS FELLOWS.

These beasts were all noble and wonderful, and except for Lassie and Misty and Flicka every one I know of was male. Their power lay in their maleness, so that Ken in *Thunderhead* (1943) was terrified that his beautiful stallion, if gelded, would lose his strength and spirit. Now, with his hormones intact, the horse's LEGS WERE LONG AND POWERFULLY MUSCLED, HIS NECK MASSIVE AND ARCHED. STRENGTH, POWER AND WILFULNESS WERE STILL HIS OUTSTANDING CHARACTERISTICS. KEN HAD SEEN THE COLTS BEFORE GELDING, THE POWER THAT FLOWED THROUGH THEM LIKE HOT LAVA, MAKING THEM REAR AND PLAY AND FIGHT AND WRESTLE; MAKING THEIR TAILS AND MANES LIFT LIKE FLYING BANNERS. AND HE HAD SEEN THEM AFTER. SEEN THE CHANGE IN THE CARRIAGE OF THE HEAD, THE LOOK OF THE EYE, THE GENERAL BEHAVIOR. It's that power flowing like hot lava that impressed a pre-adolescent human reader.

Reading the animal-as-hero books, you might feel pity and terror, but not outrage: you couldn't argue with the natural order of things. The girls' animal-as-victim books, on the other hand, called for indignation because it was human society that hurt and destroyed the animals. *Black Beauty* (1877) was especially loved by girls. In this classic story, the horses encountered a series of bad or good owners. They worshipped and obeyed the good masters; with the bad ones they could suffer bravely or just give up, but like girl characters in other kinds of childhood stories these victim-animals must be passive. Horse characters in *Black Beauty* were brave or snivelling; human characters were kind and empathetic or else cruel. Silver Chief and Buck and White Fang bored me silly, but I reread many times *Black Beauty* and also more comfortable books where animal characters have devoted young human owners.

In animal-as-partner books liked by many girls, the youthful hero tamed or trained an animal (horses, dogs, a fawn) and developed an intense relationship with it. Cooperation and empathy were valued but nature and the social order were still stern and youthful characters had to be tough and mature. Often they made terrible sacrifices because of some kind of loyalty: Joe in Eric Knight's *Lassie Come-Home* (1940) saw his dog sold because the family was poor. At least he got Lassie back in the end, while Jody in *The Yearling* (1939) and Travis in *Old Yeller* (1956) had to shoot their beloved pets themselves, to save the family. (Jody's fawn could not be stopped from eating all the crops, and Travis's hound had been bitten by a rabid wolf while defending the farm.)

These are stories of growth and initiation in a menacing world. Fourteen-year-old Travis took charge of his family's remote and primitive farm for months while Papa was away. Paul in *Misty* was allowed to join the men in a dangerous rescue mission after a flood ravaged an island full of wild ponies. You got fearsome bloody scenes here (bear attacks, pig castrations and calf deliveries that went wrong), as violent as the scenes in the animal-as-hero books. You also got a lot of warmth and affection between human and animal and among humans as well, and girl readers seemed to like this.

In all these animal tales (except for *National Velvet* where the heroine and her mother are central but both are in some way freakish) the female presence is minimal, marginal, and dull. The boy may have had a younger sister or admiring girl neighbor, but his relations with her were stereotyped. *Misty* (1947) was typical: THE BOY WAS TALLER THAN THE GIRL AND LED THE WAY. "QUIT ACT-

ING LIKE A GIRL, MAUREEN!" and so on, little touches repeated insidiously often.

National Velvet (1935) was the most interesting girl character but also the saddest, because she was depicted as not really up to the challenge she set herself. I remember as a child being bothered that Velvet kept vomiting under the slightest stress and that she fainted at the end of her triumphant race. She was both bold and timorous, determined and feeble. The odd combination seems to reflect undigested ambivalence rather than the psychological complexity Enid Bagnold probably intended. Velvet and her trainer Mi were both committed to her secret plan that she should ride The Piebald in the Grand National race disguised as a boy, but Velvet's role in the planning was passive. She had never seen the racecourse, and the night before the race Mi tried to coach her on the details of various jumps. SHE SAID AT ONCE, "DON'T TELL ME A THING MORE. I WANT JUST TO SLIDE ALONG TILL IT'S TIME, THINKING OF NOTHING AT ALL." Velvet's boy-counterparts in other horse books knew exactly what they were doing; Alec and Ken and the others insisted on being masters of their fate. They wouldn't dream of "just sliding along."

Mothers were visible in the animal-as-partner books, helpful or strict. Either way, they were out of touch with the young hero's problems. The mother in *Lassie* meant well but just didn't understand. ("OH, MY HEAVENS! SHALL I *NEVER* HAVE ANY PEACE AND QUIET IN MY HOME?") Jody, the boy in *The Yearling*, concluded that, WOMEN WERE ALL RIGHT WHEN THEY COOKED GOOD THINGS TO EAT. THE REST OF THE TIME THEY DID NOTHING BUT MAKE TROUBLE. His view was not presented ironically. For one thing, Jody's attitude was shared by his father: HE WINKED AT JODY AND JODY WINKED BACK. THERE WAS NO USE IN TRYING TO EXPLAIN TO HER. SHE WAS OUTSIDE THE GOOD MALE UNDERSTANDING. And Jody was going to be initiated into this proper role: HE LIKED TO LIE FLAT ON HIS BELLY ON THE EARTH BEFORE THE CAMP-FIRE, WHILE MEN TALKED. THEY HAD SEEN MARVELS. HE FELT HIMSELF MOVING INTO A MYSTIC COMPANY. THE HUNTING TALK OF MEN WAS THE FINEST TALK IN THE WORLD. It is disconcerting to find this "good male understanding," which sounds like bad Hemingway, in a 1939 novel that is in other ways sensitive and intelligent.

In victim books like *Black Beauty*, women characters were more remote and even more thinly developed. They appeared in predictable nurturing roles, as angels trying to help the suffering animals. Females were even less visible in the animal-hero books. Albert Payson Terhune's stories about collies featured The Mistress, who was lovable and not stupid: she showed a certain low cunning and spunk in getting what she wanted for her dogs. Even she was weak and sickly, though, and needed to be protected by her devoted dogs from an array of dangers and mishaps. Female dogs in Terhune were less noble than males—fickle or unreliable or incompetent, causing trouble for patient, protective, male dogs.

Other animal-hero books had virtually no female characters. One appeared in *Call of the Wild* (1903). She and her husband and brother bought Buck's dog team to travel through the Yukon, with no skill or experience. Meeting serious difficulties, they reacted to hardship in different ways. MERCEDES NURSED A SPECIAL GRIEVANCE—THE GRIEVANCE OF SEX. SHE WAS PRETTY AND SOFT, AND HAD BEEN CHIVALROUSLY TREATED ALL HER DAYS. BUT THE PRESENT TREATMENT BY HER HUSBAND AND BROTHER WAS EVERYTHING SAVE CHIVALROUS. IT WAS HER CUSTOM TO BE HELPLESS. THEY COMPLAINED. SHE MADE THEIR LIVES UNENDURABLE. SHE NO LONGER CONSIDERED THE DOGS AND SHE PERSISTED IN RIDING ON THE SLED. SHE WAS PRETTY AND SOFT, BUT SHE WEIGHED ONE HUNDRED AND TWENTY POUNDS— A LUSTY LAST STRAW TO THE LOAD DRAGGED BY THE WEAK AND STARVING ANIMALS. The men begged her to get up and walk, and at one point forcibly removed her from the sled. THEY NEVER DID IT AGAIN. SHE LET HER LEGS GO LIMP LIKE A SPOILED CHILD, AND SAT DOWN ON THE TRAIL until they gave in and slung her back on the sled.

In these heroic stories animals were very noble and men were almost as noble, like stalwart John Thornton, the good master of *Call of the Wild*, and Jim Thorne, the equally brave Mountie of *Silver Chief*. But women did not share in the general nobility; they were represented by pretty, soft Mercedes, whining and sulking in the snow.

* * *

Whether characters were human or just beasts, whether settings were savage or civilized, the common denominator in animal books was that the universe is hierarchical. The perspective was less democratic and more elitist than in many other children's genres. It's true that the power structure in families and peer groups was important in most children's fiction; but animal tales seemed to allow their authors to talk freely about the strong vs. the weak, the best vs. the lowest, in terms that supposedly class-free Americans traditionally find disturbing. A thirst for power is more palatable when seen as an inevitable part of the natural order and embodied in animals rather than in people.

Characters in these books were firmly positioned in one or more systems of power—a town, a society, or some sort of team or band. Boys like *Black Stallion*'s Alec and *Flicka*'s Ken and *Old Yeller*'s Travis had problems with parents and teachers who had power over them; the parents in turn had problems with money and powerful employers and officials. The creatures in the wild animal books respected whatever inexorable pecking order surrounded them, even while they fought to rise higher within it. These books were rife with rules and codes to follow or break, horseraces and dogshows and savage battles to win or lose, with superiors and inferiors. They had a rousing martial spirit. Some of the authority figures were in fact military, as in several of Terhune's books and in O'Hara's Flicka books, where Ken's father was an austere West Point-trained officer. The author of *Silver Chief* gloried in this mystique: THE CODE OF THE MOUNTED IS STERN. THE MEN WHO WEAR THE UNIFORM ARE CAREFULLY CHOSEN, AND ONCE IN THE SERVICE THEY REALIZE THAT THE WORD "FAILURE" IS UNKNOWN. THEY ARE GIVEN ASSIGNMENTS, OFTEN DESPERATE AND FILLED WITH DANGERS AND HARDSHIPS, BUT GENERALLY THEY ARE LEFT TO THEIR OWN RESOURCES AS HOW BEST TO CARRY THROUGH THESE TASKS. EXCUSES ARE NOT ACCEPTED.

In girls' stories goals and rewards were usually less measurable—a picnic with a new friend, not a Best of Breed ribbon; a reconciliation with a grim old uncle, not a promotion to the front of the dog-team; a solution to some household problem, not the slaughter of one's rival. Male-oriented animal stories acknowledged strict natural and social hierarchies, and they offered two routes to the top.

Some people and animals were hopeless, of course, and could never move upward. Casual racism and xenophobia were commonplace in these books: Terhune used expressions like "He went at it like a white man," and so did Will James in *Smoky*. Terhune also presented stereotyped Italians and Germans and Mexicans, and in *Lad: A Dog* (1919) there was a revolting scene in which the collie defended his house from a burglar: BEFORE THE WINDOW HAD RISEN AN INCH, LAD KNEW THE TRESPASSER WAS A NEGRO. ALSO THAT IT WAS NO ONE WITH WHOSE SCENT HE WAS FAMILIAR. A SET OF HOT-BREATHING JAWS FLASHED FOR HIS JUGULAR, AND THE GRAZE LEFT A RED-HOT SEARING PAIN ALONG THE NEGRO'S THROAT. The author seemed delighted with his vision of the burglar slashed viciously, sprawled senseless, and trussed up by the police. He never referred to the man as anything but "the Negro." Almost all these stories included some such figures who were considered human or animal garbage, below the lowest end of the power hierarchy.

Those who were not beyond hope might succeed through personal excellence or through something these authors like to call "blood." Storybook animals were described as good soldiers and loyal knights. (Terhune's Buff was "LIKE THOSE KNIGHT-ERRANT FOLKS WHO USED TO GO THROUGH THE COUNTRY RESCUING FOLKS IN DISTRESS.") They defeated rivals and rescued loved ones with courage, stamina, and intelligence, like any fictional human hero. And their bloodlines were pure. Many fights in these books were between a thoroughbred horse or dog and a surly, misshapen enemy of ignoble birth. Writers in the first half of this century could still get away with glorifying the value of undiluted genes.

LASSIE HAD SOMETHING THAT THE OTHERS HAD NOT. SHE HAD BLOOD. SHE WAS A PURE-BRED DOG, AND BEHIND HER WERE LONG GENERATIONS OF THE PROUDEST AND BEST OF HER KIND. THIS THEORY OF BLOOD LINES IN ANIMALS IS NOT AN EMPTY ONE. WHERE THE MONGREL DOG WILL WHINE AND SLINK AWAY, THE PURE-BRED WILL STILL STAND WITH UNCOMPLAINING FEARLESSNESS. In *The Island Stallion* (1948), Steve would do anything to prevent a hideous disaster coming to the island where he was camping: If he didn't help the beautiful red stallion get over his wounds, a grotesque mutant rival stallion would take over the herd of mares and corrupt the bloodlines forever. But in these books, the mongrel races always lost; Steve went home happy in the knowledge that his beloved Flame was busy impregnating all the wild mares. A hierarchy must be constantly defended against low enemies, but genes and gallantry will win out.

It is rather touching to think of the children who read these books and followed the struggles of the growing stag or stallion or pup fighting against his peers and preparing to challenge the old leader of the pack: this boys' reading was part of the boys' own preparation. If you are going to tell your young men that winning is the most important goal, the animal world—red in tooth and claw—is a good place to illustrate that goal. Some young women also may have read these stories about brutal competition in a harsh hierarchy, but they learned to recognize their own role in the competition: as adjuncts to the principal competing males—they could be nurse to the warriors, or perhaps the prize being fought over. They could appreciate the adventures of Buck and Buff and Bambi, and Ken and Alec and the others, but only as cheerleaders.

Girls were bystanders at the eroticized encounters of man and his male subordinate, the slightly inferior but always loyal beast. SILVER CHIEF GLIDED TOWARD THAT HAND. AS IT CLOSED OVER HIS MUZZLE, THE REALIZATION CAME OVER HIM THAT HE HAD FOUND HIS MASTER AGAIN, AND FOR THE FIRST TIME IN HIS LIFE HIS BIG TAIL STIRRED SWIFTLY. THE DELIGHT OF THE REUNION SEEMED TO SURGE MORE AND MORE DEEPLY UPON THE DOG, AND HIS HAPPINESS MOUNTED. HE BECAME FRANTIC WITH JOY. HE PLUNGED UPWARD, PRESSING CLOSE TO HIS BELOVED MASTER'S SIDE, AND AS THORNE CAUGHT HIM AROUND HIS SHOULDERS IN THE OLD LOVE HUG, HE BROKE INTO WILD BARKS OF DELIGHT. There are some places where girls don't fit in at all, in the old love hug.

It's not surprising that boys in my day didn't read girls' books. It is also not surprising that *some* girls *did* read boys' books in addition to their own: what they learned about the male world and its hierarchies did not challenge their traditional female world. Girls' and boys' systems of values and power did not conflict; they were interdependent. The lives of all the Carol Birds—frail saintly heroines—implicitly gave meaning to the strenuous exploits of their male relatives, friends, and pets. But even though heroes did accept responsibility for protecting their women, these animal books revealed that the highest, most intense, most satisfying interaction was that of the hero and the other males on his team (animal or human), those who followed the same code and shared the "good male understanding."

$\cdot\ 3\ \cdot$

What Girls Could Do, without Losing Their Girlishness

Outdoor Stuff

Rod's voice came from the barn door. "Go up easy, and you'll be able to catch him." Terry moved slowly forward. Her heart beat faster, and her knees felt suddenly queer. She wasn't used to horses just loose in a field. Specially not farm horses with ugly, clumsy feet. If she took just one step nearer, she would reach its halter. But it might kick out at her, it might bite. Terry stepped forward and reached the halter. She had the colt! It moved back suddenly, eyes rolling, ears forward. Terry let go as though she had been bitten. "Sissy!" Johnny called. Terry felt the thick, frightened beating of her heart. She wasn't used to colts. They had no right to expect her to catch it.

Hobby Horse Hill, by Lavinia Davis, was published in 1939, as I was being born. Some eight years later I was delighted to read about Terry. I understood this heroine, quivering with physical and social fears. By the end of the story she had developed enough confidence to head off a runaway at a horse show. Her new courage was admirable because it did not exceed proper feminine limits. Her adventure was dangerous but not very. She still knew her place in this horsey world: When her father bought her the magnificent hunter that was adored by her cousin Rod, Terry traded the hunter to Rod for his comfortable, dumpy pony. Everybody was pleased. SHE THOUGHT OF THE LONG, HAPPY DAYS NEXT SUMMER WITH ROD ON CASSANDRA; AND FROSTY—NICE, FUNNY-LOOKING LITTLE FROSTY, WHO WAS MORE FUN THAN ANY HUNTER THAT HAD EVER LIVED—ALL HER OWN. It was all right to be heroic in a minor way, as long as you didn't do it too far from civilized support services; as long as you stayed humble and chose the funny-looking insignificant horse for your own.

Physical activity used to worry a lot of girls. I admire friends who play tennis and work out, but I've always felt about sports the way Terry did when she couldn't catch the colt: envious, ashamed, resentful; inferior and somehow morally superior—an unattractive mixture of emotions. Here is where girls' books fit in. Plenty of boys in my childhood days were just as fearful or incompetent as girls, and plenty of girls were active and resourceful. But by and large, children's books then reinforced in girls any tendency to be whiny and wimpy; in boys they sternly discouraged fears or failures, any sense of limitations. This perhaps was harder on sensitive or uncoordinated boy readers; they must have hated the scorn heaped on fictional boys who didn't make the grade.

I recently read a remark by Mary Pipher that makes good sense, in her foreword to a book about raising boys (William Pollack's *Real Boys*, 1998). Noting that some people argue about whether, these days, girls or boys face more difficulties in their development, Pipher says, "I don't like 'suffering contests.' " Both girls and boys need to deal with stereotyped gender expectations, and they all deserve help from adults. It's not a competition.

What girls read in my day was perhaps less immediately threatening than what boys read, but perhaps more insidious: Everybody knows that a girl is naturally scared and muddled. She need only learn to handle unpleasant situations without panic. She is not expected to *act*, in any serious and independent way, but she should know how to react properly—with minimal common sense and judgment. In housekeeping and child-rearing she should be efficient; in other activities she will be forgiven for incompetence and praised for modesty, humble ambitions, achievements of a conventional and conservative sort. Understandably, heroines kept aims and expectations low.

Terry's idea of a real nightmare happened at a fancy-dress horse drill. SUDDENLY PIGEON PUT HER HEAD DOWN! THE NEXT MINUTE SHE TROTTED TO THE CENTER OF THE RING. TERRY COULD HEAR LAUGHTER ABOVE THE SOUND OF THE BAND. IT WAS AWFUL. WORSE THAN A NIGHTMARE. SHE COULD DO NOTHING! IN ANOTHER MINUTE SHE WOULD BE THROWN OFF AND IT WOULD BE ALL OVER. TERRY PRAYED THAT THE GROUND MIGHT OPEN UP AND SWALLOW HER. And what does a boy rider consider a nightmare? Being dragged over an empty beach by the wild stallion he was tied to, like Alec in *The Black Stallion;* or riding a crazed colt through a forest fire as he did in a later book. Or putting iodine on another savage stallion who was wounded in a remote valley, like Steve in *The Island Stallion.* In Mary O'Hara's books about Flicka, Ken faced challenges like spending the night in an icy river to cure his fevered horse; cutting down a cow whose stomach and udder were torn and impaled on barbed wire; camping alone in the mountains for six weeks just before blizzard season, in order to hunt for his lost stallion and pack of mares.

Terry's most dangerous moment came when she tumbled off the beautiful hunter on a soft trail in Connecticut—and her real fear was of disapproval, not of failure. Her terrain was not a desert island or mountain ranch, but only "Hobby Horse Hill," an ex-urban estate. A hobby horse is a toy, not real life.

Horse books are especially revealing. They offer a world that is not supernatural but is closer to fantasy than is the world of pedestrian children's books. Most children cannot own horses. Their ordinary lives may include a household pet, a team sport, a little excursion; but a horse represents something extraordinary, impractical but conceivable. Devotion to horse books is not limited to owners or riders of horses. It can appear in any child who likes to imagine controlling a beast lovable but bigger and stronger than himself or herself.

But look at the horsey girl in fiction, as distinguished from the horsey boy. One of my favorite young riders, Connie in the 1939 book *Silver Birch* (by Dorothy Lyons), was the type called spunky. Like Ken in the Flicka books and Alec in the Black Stallion books, she tamed horses that strong men had given up as hopeless. But the background of her adventures was a settled, protective society, with Girl Scout chums and dancing class—no uncouth racetracks or desert islands, only local horse shows in Minnesota like the ones Terry rode in in Connecticut.

Connie tamed Silver Birch until she felt the horse was ready for a trial ride. When she mounted, she had to go through a few minutes of frantic galloping, but nothing like Ken's wild ride in the mountains, when he stuck on the back of Thunderhead while the twisting, biting, racing stallion rounded up his mares. And when Connie in the sequel, *Midnight Moon,* made a desperate bet with a sadistic horseman that she would tame that man's mistreated horse or else give him her own mare, Silver Birch, she really took no risk. Unknown to her, Aunt Lou checked to make sure the bet was not legally binding—Connie would not have lost Silver Birch to him even if she had failed with the other horse. A girl must have a safety net. This is Connie's injury:

ONE AFTERNOON SHE RETURNED LATER THAN USUAL WITH A PAIN-FUL LIMP. "CONNIE, WHAT DID YOU DO TO YOURSELF?" "JUST TURNED MY ANKLE, MOM. DON'T FRET," SHE ANSWERED GAILY, THINKING, "IF MOTHER HAD EVER SEEN THAT SPILL!" "COME RIGHT IN THE KITCHEN THIS MINUTE AND SOAK IT IN HOT AND COLD WATER BEFORE I BAN-DAGE IT."

Now Ken's injury: SUDDENLY THE EAGLE LOOSED HIS HOLD AND ROSE VERTICALLY IN THE AIR. KEN'S SHIRT WAS SOAKED WITH BLOOD ACROSS HIS MIDDLE. BLOOD WAS RUNNING DOWN HIS CHIN FROM HIS CUT LIP. ALL DOWN THE RIGHT SIDE OF HIS HIP HE WAS MINUS PANTS AND THE FLESH WAS RAW. HIS CLOTHES WERE IN RIBBONS AND HIS RIGHT WRIST LAMED. THE HEEL OF THE HAND WAS COVERED WITH TINY CUTS AND ABRASIONS INTO WHICH GRAVEL AND DIRT WAS GROUND. BUT WHAT BOY KNOWS WHEN HE HAS HAD ENOUGH? BEFORE KEN WASHED AND BOUND UP HIS WOUNDS, PLASTERING THEM WITH AD-HESIVE CARRIED IN HIS FIRST-AID KIT, HE DID A LITTLE MORE INVESTI-GATING, DETERMINED TO FIND OUT WHERE THE ENTRANCE TO THE VALLEY WAS. When Connie upset her mother by turning her ankle, she was the same age as Ken of the blood-soaked shirt.

Green Grass of Wyoming (1946), the third book about Ken the riding hero, introduced also a riding heroine. Carey is described as a tough and sensible girl (she did not panic when lost in a blizzard), but her main ordeal was standing up to a domineering grandmother. Ken's life even as a child included doctoring and training valuable, dangerous animals. His father considered him dreamy and impractical but Ken showed himself capable of very practical action: he rescued his mother from a raging bull; he dynamited the exit from a mountain valley to save his stallion from being killed or gelded. Carey, on the other hand, spent most of her childhood changing clothes. Her finest triumph came one summer at Ken's ranch when she defied her grandmother and announced her daring ambition: she was determined to go to Vassar.

I have not mentioned one of the most famous of horse stories, a book I read many times. A good book can deal with stereotyped roles and transcend them; *National Velvet* gave us a weird and loving world where males and females alike teemed with quirks and sensitivities. The characters were unique, not defined by gender stereotypes. A child reading this book learned about dreams and fears and obsessions. (One sister thought only of mating canaries; the groom was terrified of the sea; the little brother kept his spit in a bottle and fiddled with his food till he threw up.)

The child reader was stretched by this, but she learned once again that girls were more vulnerable than boys. Girls could do astonishing things, like Velvet's mother Araminty who swam the English Channel in a storm years before, and like Velvet who won the Grand National on her piebald, disguised as a boy jockey. A woman, it seemed, could rise above her liabilities, but only with a male mentor. (Velvet's friend and trainer was the son of her mother's old swimming coach.) And her unique ability must be marred by some physical cross to bear—punishment, or a sign of her election. Araminty in middle age was awesomely obese. Velvet herself had buckteeth and painful braces; she had a habit of vomiting practically everything she ate; and she fainted after crossing the finish line, in her moment of triumph. A girl may dream and achieve her dream, but only through incredible nerve, because she is not really made for such efforts. After her triumph her spark is forever smothered, as Araminty's was by her mountain of flesh. Is that what Velvet's creator is saying?

Velvet's motive was to put her horse in the history books and above all to make him happy. All the stories I know about girls and horses shared this emphasis on service and society. When Connie tamed Silver Birch and Midnight Moon, she had to undo the harm done earlier by male owners. She gave and ultimately received love and trust. Her goal was to bring the horses gently into her peaceful, small world of Memorial Day parades.

Boys' horses were described in a different spirit. A boy rider did not invite his horse to join in a life of social harmony; he wanted rather to move, himself, out of the everyday world and partake of the horse's savage power. Ken, Steve, and Alec went in for wild, untamed stallions. (Ken loved his mare Flicka protectively, but not with the awe he reserved for the stallion Thunderhead.) They admired their stallions as sexual creatures. The stallion was big and independent and violent; he fought rival stallions, bit and bossed his foolish pack of mares. The boy rider, exhilarated, assumed some of the strength of his galloping stallion. Ken actually rode Thunderhead as he rounded up his mares.

THE HEAD WAS THAT OF THE WILDEST OF ALL WILD CREATURES—A STALLION BORN WILD—AND IT WAS BEAUTIFUL, SAVAGE, SPLENDID, A STALLION WITH A WONDERFUL PHYSICAL PERFECTION THAT MATCHED HIS SAVAGE, RUTHLESS SPIRIT. ONCE AGAIN ALEC FELT HIS BODY GROW WARM WITH EXCITEMENT. . . . HE KNEW FULL WELL THE DANGER THAT WAS HIS WHEN HE LET HIM LOOSE ON THE TRACK. ONCE HE GOT HIS HEAD HE WAS NO MORE THE BLACK THAT ALEC KNEW—BUT ONCE AGAIN A WILD STALLION THAT HAD NEVER BEEN CLEARLY BROKEN, AND NEVER WOULD BE!

A stallion was above ordinary restraints. But Velvet's piebald was only a gelding. Connie and Terry rode mares, and their moments of high delight were moments of social solidarity, of civilization. FROSTY WHINNIED, A GAY, EXCITED WHINNY, AND TWO OTHER HORSES ANSWERED FROM BELOW. SOMEWHERE IN THE DISTANCE SOMEONE WAS BURNING LEAVES. TERRY SNIFFED THE SHARP, DELICIOUS SMELL, AND LOOKED DOWN AT THE HORSES AND HOUNDS.

Riding has always been considered an appropriate sport for girls. When I took riding lessons as a child, I enjoyed trotting down a woodsy path on an old fat horse, but jumping was torture and doing tricks standing on a horse's back was worse. After all,

I had vowed to spend my life sitting down. There, I think, is the secret of riding as a girls' sport. They do it sitting down. In riding as in swimming, the girl is supported by a power not her own. She must show good form and discipline, she must provide direction and control speed—but she does not put forth the type of crude energy needed in running sports. So, for this one girl of the 1940s and perhaps others, riding and swimming were pleasant when not too stressful. At a slow canter, my favorite gait, I could float over the fields. In a quiet lake (the sea was too forceful), I could drift along in a reverie. But playing-fields and courts were detestable.

Since I dreaded active sports so intensely, I thought that losing the use of one's legs, the way Carol Bird did, sounded appealing—as long as it didn't hurt. Hands and eyes were a different matter; you have to be able to eat and read. *The Birds' Christmas Carol* confirmed the idea that physical activity is incompatible with the highest kind of female virtue: IT WAS WITH A PANG OF TERROR HER MOTHER AND FATHER NOTICED, SOON AFTER SHE WAS FIVE YEARS OLD, THAT SHE BEGAN TO LIMP, EVER SO SLIGHTLY; TO COMPLAIN TOO OFTEN OF WEARINESS, AND TO NESTLE CLOSE TO HER MOTHER, SAYING SHE "WOULD RATHER NOT GO OUT TO PLAY, PLEASE." The thing would be to find a disease with genteel symptoms like weakness and weariness, nothing disgusting. Then you wouldn't have to go outside to play.

Summer camp was more benign than school, for me, and I did not hate team sports there quite so much. But they were still a heavy burden. My pleasantest athletic experience happened one summer when I was hit in the head by a baseball bat. That day I was playing catcher. When a batter nicked the side of my temple, blood gushed forth and I was taken to an emergency room— whence I returned with a tiny amount of pain and an enormous gauze turban. For a week I got to rest and eat and read. I milked the awe-struck sympathy and attention of the camp community, until the unimpressed head counselor made me take off the filthy bandage and stop acting pitiful.

This hatred of sports distressed me in two ways: I disliked having to take part in them, and I disliked knowing that some girls liked them. My books helped me here. They showed that it was natural for a girl to enjoy injuries more than effort, with-drawal more than competition. This fictional pattern seemed to authorize avoiding basketball, hockey, and anything else that re-quired running. I was relieved when my 13-girl seventh grade class formed its 11-member field hockey team and I was one of the two left out; scorer and timer were intellectual jobs, I decided.

Years later in college I joined a band of like-minded girls who studied the avoidance of those blue gym suits—straight tunics with very thick, itchy, matching cotton underpants. (You wore the underpants so that a windy bike ride down the hill by Paradise Pond would not expose your maidenly crotch.) We got out of wearing gym suits entirely, by signing up for bowling, hiking, or archery each term. For those pseudo-sports we could stay in our discreet Bermuda shorts and skip the exertion of changing. We could signal our scorn for the sweaty athletes, and our allegiance to Sleeping Beauty and the sedentary ideal. Even Heidi, the great outdoor heroine, really spent her time strolling a short distance up mountain paths to the pasture and then sitting all day, picking wildflowers and watching the goats frisk.

Indoor Stuff

"IT'S FUN TO TAKE CARE OF THESE DARLING ROOMS," ROSIE DECLARED AGAIN AND AGAIN. "THEY'RE SO LITTLE I FEEL WE OUGHT TO BUY A DOLL'S BROOM AND A DOLL'S CARPET-SWEEPER AND A DOLL'S DUST-PAN AND BRUSH. I NEVER SAW SUCH SWEET FURNITURE IN ALL MY LIFE, AND HOW I LOVE THE ROOF SLANTING DOWN LIKE THAT!" "I FEEL THAT WAY TOO—EXACTLY AS THOUGH I WERE PUTTING A DOLL'S HOUSE IN ORDER," LAURA COINCIDED HAPPILY.

Maida's Little House, by Inez Haynes Irwin, was published in 1921. Maida and her friends charmed me; they were learning the housekeeping secrets of adult females but they had little respon-sibility and less work. Maida's father, a very rich Bostonian, scooped up eleven young friends of his daughter's and deposited them at his seaside place for the summer. Mr. Westabrook stayed in the mansion, but the young people were alone in the Little House, a charming old farmhouse on the estate—alone, that is, except for two motherly souls to tend the six smaller children, and Zeke and Floribel to do the cooking and cleaning.

This summer was to be educational for the bigger six. The three boys had to care for the vegetable garden and tennis court, while the three girls did the flowers daily and the cooking on Thursdays. All six had to keep their rooms tidy. This staggering workload almost proved too much for them, but by the end of the summer they were proclaimed excellent and experienced workers. This seemed the right way to look at housework. I loved the idea of keeping a home cozy and colorful, but the reality was too much work. Except for an occasional forced bout of vacuuming, my contribution to housework was drawing faces on our dusty furniture.

IMMEDIATELY AFTER BREAKFAST, ROOMS WERE MADE SPECKLESS. WITH THE GIRLS, THIS CONTINUED TO BE A KIND OF GAME. THEY NOT ONLY PRIDED THEMSELVES ON KEEPING THEIR CHAMBERS CLEAN, BUT THEY ACTUALLY TRIED TO MATCH THE FLOWERS THEY PLACED THERE TO THE CHINTZES AND WALLPAPERS.

It was the stability, the settled pattern, that seemed valuable. Girls learned to do set things at set times; so did boys. The pigeonhole quality was a delight. No square pegs in sight, only the right shape pegs for the right shape holes. Any detail or incident seemed wonderful when it reinforced traditional patterns or definitions of proper behavior: THE HOUNDS BURST INTO A RUN, LEAPED UP AND LICKED HER FACE. MAIDA STAGGERED UNDER THE ONSLAUGHT (of course), BUT ARTHUR EXPERTLY SEIZED THEIR COLLARS, HELD THEM.

One kind of description was especially thrilling: the matching of specific objects or colors to specific people. This was fitting, satisfying, like an art form that encourages small, harmless variations within a tight, formal pattern. THE THREE LITTLE GIRLS TUMBLED PELL-MELL INTO THE FRONT ROOM. IT DID NOT DIFFER MUCH FROM MAIDA'S OR FROM LAURA'S ACROSS THE WAY—EXCEPT WHERE THE KEY-NOTE OF MAIDA'S WALLPAPER AND CHINTZES WERE YELLOW, THAT OF ROSIE'S WAS CRIMSON AND LAURA'S BLUE. IN EACH THERE WAS A DOUBLE CANOPIED BED; A LITTLE OLD-FASHIONED CRICKET; TWO QUAINT LITTLE OLD-FASHIONED CHAIRS. BUT ALL THESE THINGS DIFFERED IN DETAIL AND ALTHOUGH THE ROOMS SHOWED A SIMILARITY, THEY ALSO SHOWED AN INDIVIDUALITY.

It must have been comforting for fictional girls and their readers to feel they were exactly like each other but with some small, picturesque difference to make them special. Maida's author may have read of the Little Colonel's delightful house party, or may simply have used the same convention: Each girl at that house-party stayed in a room of a different color, suiting her personality. The girls received four identical puppies, named them all Bob, and distinguished them only by collar ribbons of blue, green, yellow, and pink. There may be similar books in which *boys* confirm their unique personalities mainly by the colors of their bedspreads, but it doesn't seem likely.

I am not into housework, as they say. My floors need waxing; the dark, beamed dining room benefits from its dim light. My closets contain filthy, unidentifiable objects that could be animal, vegetable, or mineral. I refuse to spend time on obsessive cleaning. But the ghost of Nancy hovers near, filling me with guilt. When *Nancy Keeps House* by Helene Laird came out in 1947, it bore for me the authority of the Bible, and greater readability. The book is written as a narrative but each chapter ends with Nancy's list of instructions for a certain chore. Her mother was preparing twelve-year-old Nancy to keep house, while she was off producing a new baby.

"WHEN I GO TO THE HOSPITAL YOUR FATHER WILL HAVE TO BE TAKEN CARE OF. HE'LL NEED SOMEONE TO GET HIS MEALS AND MAKE THE BEDS AND PUT HIS LAUNDRY AWAY AND—OH—DO THE THINGS I DO FOR HIM NOW." It never seemed odd that a callow kid could be taught all this but not the able-bodied husband. Leaving him aside, it's a reasonable idea to train a girl this age, or a boy, to run things efficiently. The creepy part was the attitude. Housework was not seen here as something useful that can be handled smoothly; it was something cute and jolly, light as meringue.

Here is Nancy considering the lessons that are about to begin: SOME OF THE KIDS HAVE TO DO HOUSEWORK AND DON'T SEEM TO MIND IT, SO IT MUSTN'T BE SO BAD. MOTHER NEVER ACTS LIKE SHE HATES IT. IN FACT, NANCY THOUGHT WITH SURPRISE, SHE ACTS AS THOUGH SHE LIKES IT USUALLY; SHE HUMS AND WHISTLES, SOMETIMES SHE RECITES POETRY; OR SHE LISTENS TO THE NEWS OR A CONCERT ON THE RADIO. MAYBE I'LL LIKE IT TOO.

And this is Nancy's mother on dishwashing: "WHEN I'M ALONE I PROP UP A BOOK OF POETRY ON THE WINDOW SILL AND MEMORIZE A POEM OUT LOUD WHILE I'M WASHING DISHES. IT REALLY IS FUN." Nancy, having learned beds, cobwebs, and toilets, prepared for laundry day: HER MOTHER DOWNSTAIRS IN THE KITCHEN COULD HEAR HER SINGING.

> TODAY'S WASHDAY,
> TODAY'S WASHDAY,
> MONDAY'S WASHDAY, THE SUN IS BRIGHT AND
> SHINING, AND THE WIND IS BLOWING TOO.

MRS. LELAND LAUGHED BECAUSE IT SOUNDED SO FUNNY, BUT SHE WAS GLAD THAT NANCY WAS IN A GOOD HUMOR AND SEEMED TO BE LOOK-ING ON WASHDAY AS A BIG ADVENTURE.

How relieved I was as a child in the 1940s—knowing my future would hold housekeeping and child tending—to read that such work is easy and joyous and that washday is an adventure. "THAT'S ONE OF THE SATISFYING THINGS ABOUT DOING HOUSEWORK, NANCY. YOUR RESULTS ARE SO PLAIN TO BE SEEN. AND WAIT TILL THE BABY COMES; THEN YOU'LL FIND OUT WHAT'S REALLY FUN—TO PICK UP A CRYING, WET, HUNGRY BABY AND BATHE HIM, AND DRESS HIM, AND FEED HIM, AND THEN SEE HIM SMILE OR FALL ASLEEP FROM SHEER COM-FORT." Nancy's mother's babies apparently didn't cry for hours or throw up on her clothes.

Nancy was a thinly conceived character, flimsy enough that a reader with gumption might withstand her influence. But Rebecca Rowena Randall of Sunnybrook Farm (1903, by Kate Douglas Wiggin) was a person to reckon with. A voluble and volatile child, she shocked her maiden aunts with her impetuous antics. Over the years she lived with them, though, they came to appreciate her virtues.

They did take pride in her school honors, but the scene of her graduation is perfunctory compared to a high moment earlier in the book. Rebecca had gone to a church meeting in place of her aunts, who were sick. She had been forced to invite the visiting missionary family back for the night. The aunts despaired at the news; they were unaccustomed to guests, and too weak with their colds to prepare properly. Then Rebecca revealed her truly feminine nature and abilities. REBECCA DASHED UPSTAIRS LIKE A WHIRLWIND. SHE HAD ONLY TO PULL UP THE SHADES, GO OVER THE FLOORS WITH A WHISK BROOM, AND DUST THE FURNITURE. THE AUNTS COULD HEAR HER SCURRYING TO AND FRO, BEATING UP PILLOWS AND FEATHERBEDS, FLAPPING TOWELS, JINGLING CROCKERY. SHE HAD GROWN TO BE A HANDY LITTLE CREATURE. SO THAT WHEN SHE CALLED HER AUNTS AT FIVE O'CLOCK TO PASS JUDGMENT, SHE HAD ACCOMPLISHED WONDERS.

Next morning, when Aunt Miranda crawled downstairs from her sickbed to start breakfast, she was astonished. THE SHADES WERE UP AND THERE WAS A ROARING FIRE IN THE STOVE; THE TEAKETTLE WAS SINGING AND BUBBLING. AND PUSHED OVER ITS CAPACIOUS NOSE WAS A HALF SHEET OF NOTE PAPER WITH "COMPLIMENTS OF REBECCA" SCRAWLED ON IT. THE COFFEEPOT WAS SCALDING, THE COFFEE WAS MEASURED OUT IN A BOWL. THE COLD POTATOES AND CORNED BEEF WERE IN THE WOODEN TRAY, AND "REGARDS OF REBECCA" STUCK ON THE CHOPPING KNIFE. THE BROWN LOAF WAS OUT, THE WHITE LOAF WAS OUT, DOUGHNUTS WERE OUT, THE MILK WAS SKIMMED, THE BUTTER HAD BEEN BROUGHT FROM THE DAIRY.

Never mind that Rebecca wrote good poems and led her class in school, she could also do the important things like getting out the cold potatoes. Her identity was dependent on the bubbling teakettle, as she made clear by affixing her name tag to it. All proper girls in these storybooks could do household work neatly and happily, whether rich like Maida, rambunctious like Rebecca, or destitute like Polly in *The Five Little Peppers*—who made delectable cakes for her siblings even though her stove didn't work right.

The domestic girl child with the most admirers had to be Wendy in J. M. Barrie's *Peter Pan* (1904), mother and housekeeper to a whole island full of Lost Boys. IT WAS ALL ESPECIALLY ENTRANCING TO WENDY, BECAUSE THOSE RAMPAGIOUS BOYS OF HERS GAVE HER SO MUCH TO DO. REALLY THERE WERE WHOLE WEEKS WHEN, EXCEPT PERHAPS WITH A STOCKING IN THE EVENING, SHE WAS NEVER ABOVE GROUND. THE COOKING, I CAN TELL YOU, KEPT HER NOSE TO THE POT. A lot of real housewives could understand that state of never getting above ground, though they might not find it quite so entrancing. In *Little Men* (1871) also, make-believe housewifely activities were described as totally delightful: Meg's small daughter Daisy reached a peak of transcendent happiness when she was given a tiny fake kitchen with a stove and a sink that really worked.

What did I do to emulate these young ladies? Not the housework, since I didn't have the fun with it that my heroines did. Cooking came closer to my ideal of graceful dabbling. One Christmas brought a marvelous cookbook for children, with pink and white squares on the cover, chocolate cornstarch pudding on one lefthand page, and buttery caramel cornflake ring on the facing page. My favorite foods were sweet, soothing, or slimy.

I probably learned to cook a few protein or vegetable items, but what I remember is pie and cake and brownies and cookies and fudge. It sounds sticky and unhealthy now, especially when I remember the exploding pudding can. One recipe simply said to steam an unopened can of sweetened condensed milk for several hours. By magic the contents turned into an oozy caramel pudding of unspeakable, orgasmic sweetness. I made this pudding from time to time until once I let the water around the can boil away. The explosion left caramel spots on the wall and ceiling that could never be removed. I was embarrassed at such public evidence of my sweet tooth, but knew it was expected in a little girl.

A few other activities filled my childhood, beside reading and drinking cocoa from rose china cups by the fire. I do not count the deeds that I was prodded to do, like playing football with my sister and learning to ride a bike (that took two years). Houses fascinated me, in the form of floorplans—an image of a home without the grubby details. I would pore over house plans in the newspaper real-estate section and magazines, then would draw my own, making tiny rearrangements in a common design. You could change some windows and doors and bathrooms and still have your basic familiar House. The smaller the better; a two-bedroom house was most fun, like a doll's house.

It may be that I caught my house-plan craze in Girl Scouts. One of the badges I earned there was for proficiency in "Architecture," and I see from a 1947 *Scout Handbook* that one of the requirements was to make a detailed houseplan. Today I marvel that I spent six or seven years in Girl Scouting, earning badges in all kinds of indoor, outdoor, and community activities. The pleasure, I suspect, was in the rigid structure of the program. I could even enjoy blazing a trail or sewing a button—if told precisely what to do, accompanied by other girls, and supervised by smiling adults.

Girl Scouts learned traditional female values; their "Laws" stressed obedience and helpfulness:

A GIRL SCOUT'S HONOR IS TO BE TRUSTED.
A GIRL SCOUT IS LOYAL.
A GIRL SCOUT'S DUTY IS TO BE USEFUL AND TO HELP OTHERS.
A GIRL SCOUT IS A FRIEND TO ALL AND A SISTER TO EVERY OTHER GIRL SCOUT.
A GIRL SCOUT IS COURTEOUS.
A GIRL SCOUT IS A FRIEND TO ANIMALS.
A GIRL SCOUT OBEYS ORDERS.
A GIRL SCOUT IS CHEERFUL.
A GIRL SCOUT IS THRIFTY.
A GIRL SCOUT IS CLEAN IN THOUGHT, WORD, AND DEED.

You didn't need initiative to get badges, just an ability to follow instructions and check off lists. For each proficiency badge there was a list of requirements and a picture of the badge itself, bearing the symbol for the activity and a caption. These pictures give me now a Proustian shiver of recognition—Home Nurse ("Symbol: Hospital bed"), Cook ("Symbol: Mixing bowl, milk, and cup"), Clerk ("Symbol: Telephone"), One World ("Symbol: Globe"), Hostess ("Symbol: Tea cup and saucer"). These pictures seemed beautiful. In the Scout Handbook, each symbol was surrounded by a thick stripey circle, representing the threaded rim of the cloth badge you received and sewed on your uniform. This tight circle gave a look of completeness to each symbol; all the proper female activities were rounded off so firmly. Child Care Badge, Landscaper Badge, Photography, Basketry, Farm Safety, Musician, Cat and Dog, Reader, Bird . . .

CHECK THE HAZARDS IN YOUR OWN HOUSE . . .
MAKE YOUR PATIENT COMFORTABLE . . .
PRACTICE PACKING A SUITCASE QUICKLY . . .
ONE BOWEL MOVEMENT A DAY IS ESSENTIAL. START THE DAY RIGHT BY
   TAKING CARE OF THIS EARLY. . . .

Here, surely, were Truth and Beauty. The Girl Scout Handbook told me all I knew on earth and all I needed to know.

A nasty little book turned up in a secondhand bookstore recently: *The Sunbonnet Twins, A Story in Verse and Music for Little Tots*, by "Uncle Milton," dated 1907. It consists of seven colorful pictures and a song for each picture. The pictures show a pair of tiny twins engaged in proper housewifely activities for each day of the week:

> ON MONDAY MORN WITH SLEEVES ROLLED HIGH,
> WE WASH AND HANG THE CLOTHES TO DRY;
> WE HELP OUR MAMA ALL THE DAY,
> WE NEVER SHIRK, NOR THINK OF PLAY:
> WE ARE THE SUNBONNET TWINS, YOU SEE,
> AND WE ARE AS GOOD AS WE CAN BE.

The twins are identical. These bonneted miniature women are exactly like each other, and in the entire book of pictures, *they have no faces*.

> ON SUNDAY MORN ALL CLEAN AND SWEET,
> WE GO TO CHURCH JUST DOWN THE STREET;
> WE NEVER WHISPER NOR DO A THING,
> 'CEPT HOLD A BOOK AND TRY TO SING:
> WE ARE THE SUNBONNET TWINS, YOU SEE,
> AND WE ARE AS GOOD AS WE CAN BE.

Adult Stuff

Young girls learned how to behave partly from their reading. They also learned what they would be doing as adults. Serious, paid work outside the home was unheard of. Some ambitions were almost respectable—art, literature, teaching—but generally a talented girl would sacrifice her plans to help someone she loved. When a child heroine showed a genius for teaching, writing, or such, by the end of the book she would be renouncing her Big Chance, as sure as the hero got the princess in a fairy tale.

This cop-out pattern has been much discussed. "A Feminist Look at Children's Books," by Feminists on Children's Media (1974), describes this kind of plot as possibly the most insidious.

"The better ones are the most infuriating, for often they are only a step away from being the exact kind of literature we'd like to see for girls *and* boys *about* girls. The actual cop-out may be only a crucial line, a paragraph, the last chapter. But somewhere a sexist compromise is made, somewhere the book adjusts to the stereotyped role of woman, often for the sake of social pressure and conformity. The compromise brings with it a change, and this change is not only disturbing but often distorts the logical development of the character herself. Suddenly her development is redirected—or, rather, stunted."

The most controversial tomboy-turned-lady was Jo March of *Little Women*. Many former child-readers remember that she was wondrously, inspiringly active, determined, and rebellious—while many adult critic-readers notice that she ended up tamer and more conventional. Elizabeth Janeway is enthusiastic (*Only Connect*, 1969): "Jo is a unique creation: the one young woman in nineteenth-century fiction who maintains her individual independence, who gives up no part of her autonomy as payment for being born a woman—and who gets away with it. Jo is the tomboy dream come true, the dream of growing up into full humanity with all its potentialities instead of into limited femininity: of looking after oneself and paying one's way and doing effective work in the real world instead of learning how to please a man who will look after you, as Meg and Amy both do with pious pleasure." In chapter 6 I will offer evidence that Janeway is partially wrong in her conclusion; Jo does make sacrifices to please a man, and does tame her wild manners, and does end up treating her writing career as secondary, almost a joke.

It is perhaps meaningful that several men writing on this subject—who are possibly more objective than former girls about this most loved of girls' books—recognize how much Jo gave up and how much she changed over the course of her story. Humphrey Carpenter in *Secret Gardens* (1985) says, "Although *Little Women* describes Jo's assumption of the masculine role, it is not an account of a battle won. The Jo-Louisa character loses out in the end"; he quotes various passages that show Jo's increasing obedience and humility. Bob Dixon also, in *Catching Them Young: Sex, Race and Class in Children's Fiction* (1977), describes Jo's drift into a conventionally limited woman's role. Male critics are not more insightful than female; perhaps the women for whom Jo was tremendously important continue to emphasize the ways in which she was a strong role model because they are glad to acknowledge that she has affected them in those ways. Does she also remain somewhere in their memories as a woman who gave up and compromised? I cannot be sure. But her tendency to reform started early on and was not limited to a brief, easily ignored, coda at the end of the book or the series.

Here are some of the other books in which a strong heroine eventually sold out:

• Heidi, free spirit of the Alps, settled down in her second and third books, written not by Johanna Spyri but by one of her translators. In *Heidi Grows Up*, she showed herself to be a brilliant and happy teacher, revitalizing the chaotic village school. But she didn't last long:

"YOU SEE WHAT YOU'VE DONE," PETER SCOLDED HER. "YOU'VE MADE YOURSELF SO INDISPENSABLE THAT YOU WON'T BE ALLOWED TO GIVE UP TEACHING AND WHEN UNCLE GETS TOO FEEBLE TO DO THINGS, HOW IS HE GOING TO MANAGE ALONE?" "THE GRANDFATHER NEEDS ME. NO, PETER, I SHALL NOT TEACH AGAIN IN THE FALL."

• Rebecca of Sunnybrook Farm, the young poet and scholar, was eager to start a challenging job but gave it up to tend her sick mother. THERE WAS A MUTINOUS LEAP OF THE HEART THEN. SHE FELT AS IF THE WIND OF DESTINY WERE BLOWING HER FLAME HITHER AND THITHER, BURNING, CONSUMING HER, BUT KINDLING NOTHING. BUT THE CLOUDS BLEW OVER, THE SUN SHONE AGAIN, A RAINBOW STRETCHED ACROSS THE SKY. THREADS OF JOY RAN IN AND OUT OF THE GRAY, TANGLED WEB OF DAILY LIVING. THERE WAS THE SATISFACTION OF BEING MISTRESS OF THE POOR DOMAIN; OF PLANNING, GOVERNING, DECIDING, OF BRINGING ORDER OUT OF CHAOS; OF IMPLANTING GAIETY IN THE PLACE OF INERT RESIGNATION TO THE INEVITABLE.

• Rebecca's creator, Kate Douglas Wiggin, at least permitted the girl "a mutinous leap of the heart," which is more than L. M. Montgomery allowed to Anne of Green Gables (1908). When Anne learned that Marilla—the spinster who took her in as an orphan—might be losing her sight, she gave up her university scholarship without a pang. In fact, there were several other people who could have been enlisted to care for Marilla so the sacrifice was not necessary. Anne's conviction grew even stronger in later life (described in *Anne of Ingleside*), after six children crushed the writing career she had started:

"OCCASIONALLY I DO WRITE A LITTLE STORY," ADMITTED ANNE. "BUT A BUSY MOTHER HASN'T MUCH TIME FOR THAT. I HAD WONDERFUL DREAMS ONCE BUT NOW I'M AFRAID I'LL NEVER BE IN WHO'S WHO." A former girlfriend of Anne's husband asked, "DO YOU REALLY NEVER FEEL THAT YOU WANT A BROADER LIFE? DIDN'T YOU WRITE SOME RATHER CLEVER LITTLE THINGS WHEN YOU WERE AT REDMOND? AND YOU'VE QUITE GIVEN IT UP?" "NOT ALTOGETHER. BUT I'M WRITING LIVING EPISTLES NOW," SAID ANNE, THINKING OF JEM AND CO. How could girls not revere these confident, smug matrons? They turned away from the outer world with no regrets, knowing their true career lay in sacrifice and service.

Recently, I have dipped into the current incarnation of Nancy Drew. Her world today has less sexism but also less personality than her original world of 1930. The Ur-Nancy Drew was quite lively. In *The Hidden Staircase* and *The Secret of the Old Clock*, "Carolyn Keene" (who at first was Mildred Wirt Benson) developed characters and situations somewhat more than the current formulaic authors. Because she was a fairly energetic character, one fact about Nancy's life is particularly striking. In these books, she was finished with school, intelligent, efficient, and enthusiastic. Yet she apparently planned to spend her life "running the house" for her widowed father. Even though there was a live-in housekeeper, it seemed to be a full-time job for Nancy to hang about, having luncheon and doing errands in her roadster. No wonder she had time to solve other people's mysteries.

Carson Drew, eminent lawyer, frequently said to his daughter that she had a brilliant legal mind, and citizens came from miles around to seek her detecting help. But no one suggested she go to law school or set up a detective business or even follow a more traditional female career. She seemed content with her amateur status.

The Nancy Drew books were second only to the Alcott books in the hearts of girls. A friend told me: "The reading passion of my youth was Nancy Drew books. They were probably the first books I encountered in which a girl was clever, resourceful, smart, pretty, etc. and didn't need a man or anybody to figure things out for her. She was independent and 'plucky' and nothing like the other female heroes. I knew that Nancy Drew was who I wanted to be—a life of excitement, intrigue, with both girls and boys looking up to you."

On the continuum of fictional girls from passive to active, Nancy's position is indeed at the active end, and women who say she was a strong model for them must be right. But she *did* depend on her father for a great deal of help and she *did* speak slightingly of her adventures and abilities. There was something apologetic in her attitude toward herself and something patronizing in the attitudes of others toward her. "IT WAS ONLY AN ACCIDENT THAT TOOK ME TO THE BUNGALOW AT THE CRITICAL MOMENT," SHE PROTESTED MODESTLY. "I DON'T DESERVE ANY CREDIT FOR THE ROUND-UP."

Juicier than Nancy Drew and more sentimental, was Betsy Allen's Connie Blair, another girl detective I liked. Perhaps the spunky quality many girls admired in Nancy was the reason I preferred Connie Blair. First appearing in the 1940s, Connie worked for an advertising agency. So in these books women were really allowed out into the world? But no, here is the kind of thing that happened. Connie and Georgia, her businesslike supervisor, went on a business trip.

NEVER BEFORE HAD CONNIE SEEN GEORGIA'S EYES SO BRIGHT. HER VERY MANNER WAS CHANGED. THE ADVERTISING EXECUTIVE HAD VANISHED COMPLETELY. SHE WAS THE COUNTERPART OF ANY PRETTY, ROMANTICALLY INVOLVED GIRL. When Georgia got engaged, SHE HAD LOST SOME OF HER BRISKNESS. SHE HAD LOST SOMETHING, BUT SHE HAD GAINED SOMETHING MORE IMPORTANT. THERE WAS A SWEETNESS AND GENTLENESS ABOUT HER THAT WAS DEFINITELY APPEALING AND NEW. AS MRS. PHILIP TREMONT, SHE WOULD BECOME RELAXED AND GRACIOUS, MORE THE YOUNG MATRON THAN THE BUSINESS EXECUTIVE, BUT STILL INTERESTED ENOUGH TO TAKE A HAND IN TREMONT SHOP'S AFFAIRS, SHOULD OCCASION DEMAND. Occasion will probably not demand, very often.

Once I drove a seventeen-year-old niece to Kennedy Airport. She was flying alone to Vienna. Her plans were organized but not rigid, her attitude toward strangers friendly but not gullible. It was in 1960 that I traveled through Europe on a bus with thirty-two other girls and two chaperones. At the age of 21?—and we did indeed call ourselves "girls." I had some common sense, could speak tolerable French, but I would no more have dared control my own European trip than I would have hiked the Himalayas. The travel was tedious, with much waiting for luggage and people; the restaurants' group fare was humdrum. But I loved the trip and was happy to pay the price of turning off my brain, in order to get total security. After twenty-one years I had no sense that I could plan and execute complicated maneuvers, and I was convinced that modesty was more important than self-assertion and self-respect. I knew Connie Blair was right:

"I'M TRAVELING WITH MISS CAMERON." SHE LOOKED ACROSS THE TABLE IN GEORGIA'S DIRECTION. "WE ARE GOING TO BERMUDA FOR THE ADVERTISING AGENCY WE WORK FOR, TO GET SOME ANGLES ON PRO- MOTING A NEW ACCOUNT." DAVID WHISTLED SOFTLY. "SOUNDS VERY IMPORTANT." CONNIE'S HAIR RIPPLED ON HER SHOULDERS AS SHE GAVE HER HEAD A FAINT SHAKE. "I'M JUST MISS CAMERON'S HELPER. THERE'S NOTHING IMPORTANT ABOUT ME."

An important study is summarized by M. K. Rudman in *Children's Literature: An Issues Approach* (1984): "One study by Broverman et. al. concludes that clinical psychologists have regularly defined anything but conventional gender role behavior as abnormal. . . . The study goes on to demonstrate that the concept of the healthy adult and the healthy male are congruent, while the concept of the healthy female differs from that of the healthy adult. Aggression, independence, objectivity, leadership, sense of adventure, ambition, self-confidence, and logic are among those valued male characteristics that are considered unhealthy for women to exhibit. The assigned female characteristics of being talkative, tactful, gentle, religious, neat, vain, quiet, and dependent on others for security are considered to be signs of emotional problems in males and in the generalized category of 'adult' when evidenced to any great extent." An *adult* woman, then, is a logical impossibility, a contradiction in terms.

School report, Fourth grade, December 1947: "Debby is cooperative and is well liked by the other children. They don't seem to resent her academic excellence. This is probably due to her fortunately casual attitude about her achievements." Achievement was acceptable in girls as long as they kept a fortunately casual attitude and didn't try too hard. Stress was not becoming, not graceful. Connie Blair knew: "There's nothing important about *me*."

Did my childhood reading tell me that girls are finally as competent and enterprising as boys? Look at Heidi's twins (*Heidi's Children*, 1939). THE BABIES HAD FINISHED THEIR NAP AND WERE DEMANDING ATTENTION. ALREADY TOBI REACHED FOR HIS SPOON WHEN HEIDI TRIED TO FEED HIM HIS GRUEL. HE WOULD LEARN TO HELP HIMSELF EARLY. MARTALI, HOWEVER, MADE NO EFFORT TO TAKE THE SPOON, BUT ONLY HELD HER MOUTH OPEN LIKE A FLEDGLING.

There's no doubt who would go through life getting the larger share of the gruel.

· 4 ·

Girls with Grownups: Loving Authority, Melting Hostility

Adults play a larger role in girls' fiction than boys'. Girls' books idealize adults, who represent comfortable stereotypes and urge conventional behavior. Fictional boys do not take grownups as seriously as fictional girls do; the girls and their authors exhibit less irony, distance, and rebellion. In girls' books, when adult characters do not conform to stereotypes, their deviations do not seriously challenge convention. Strong women must also be feminine or domesticated; weak men must maintain a strong facade, often with the connivance of their women.

Girl characters respond to adults by obeying, enduring, sacrificing and, most interesting, by reforming the adults. When a boy character is opposed by difficult or hostile adults, he finds ways to escape or defeat them; when a girl is similarly opposed, she reforms the adults, revealing them as basically good after all. Girls deny aggression.

Motherly Women and Fatherly Men

LAURA LAY AWAKE A LITTLE WHILE, LISTENING TO PA'S FIDDLE SOFTLY
PLAYING. SHE LOOKED AT PA SITTING ON THE BENCH BY THE HEARTH.
SHE LOOKED AT MA, GENTLY ROCKING AND KNITTING. SHE WAS GLAD
THAT THE COSY HOUSE, AND PA AND MA AND THE FIRELIGHT AND THE
MUSIC, WERE NOW.

Adults take care of children, in predictably male and female
ways. Much of children's fiction deals in stereotyped characters—
presented glaringly in the more superficial books, more subtly in
the better books. The books I loved told me mothers always acted
like mothers and fathers like fathers and when they did not, they
were representing some deviant role that was also familiar and
thus bearable, like the stepmother or the unjust father. Incidents
ended with the child falling asleep in a safe, familiar place. Laura
Ingalls Wilder (from 1932 on) was especially good at making readers feel secure, protected from bears and blizzards.

I always wished I had a Mary Poppins to dissolve my fears; my
mother probably wished I had a Mary Poppins too. JANE WATCHED
HER, DRYING HER TEAR-STAINED FACE ON THE LARGE BLUE HANDKER-
CHIEF. SHE GLANCED ROUND THE WELL-KNOWN ROOM. SHE FELT SAFE
AND WARM AND COMFORTED. SHE LISTENED TO THE FAMILIAR SOUNDS
AS MARY POPPINS WENT ABOUT HER WORK, AND HER TERROR DIED
AWAY. (1934)

There were two stories that hideously overturned these simple
adult roles—the adventures of Alice (1865)—but I couldn't abide
them. Reading, for me, was not expansion but confirmation. Who
could enjoy an ugly Duchess both bad and good, bullying and
genial? The Duchess's unpredictable behavior was disturbing, too
much like real, complex people. So was the behavior of the Red
and White Queens. If consistency and convention were disrupted,
Alice might prove really to be bigger than her pawns and knights,
and grownups—authority—might prove to be "only a pack
of cards."

So I never re-read Alice, choosing instead female-grownups like
Kanga (who liked giving medicine to Baby Roo), and male-
grownups like Mr. Crewe in *A Little Princess* (who liked giving
Parisian dolls to his beloved Sara). It was greatly satisfying to see

a formula observed, even perfunctorily. For instance, Helen Wells, author of Cherry Ames's career, reassured her readers at the start that no surprises were ahead, when she introduced Cherry's parents as typical in appearance and posture. CHERRY'S FATHER WAS WAITING FOR THEM. CHERRY THOUGHT AFFECTIONATELY THAT SHE WOULD RECOGNIZE HIS TALL BUSINESS-LIKE FIGURE ON ANY RAILROAD STATION PLATFORM IN THE WORLD. It was natural that he should bestride the platform like a Colossus, while Cherry's mother was equally proper in her reclining posture: HER MOTHER ROSE FROM THE PORCH SWING. SHE WAS A YOUTHFUL, SWEET-FACED WOMAN, WITH THE MOST UNDERSTANDING EYES IN THE WORLD.

Adult characters were more static than children; they were emblematic of forces controlling the child's world, but were not people in the way other children were. Women embodied domestic virtues, of course, being warm but strict. Mothers went in for moral lectures, which drew vows of improvement from remorseful children. Alcott's mothers did these lectures perfectly, as did several mothers in the Little Colonel books. Amy March had to put up with this from her mother: "YOU ARE GETTING TO BE RATHER CONCEITED, MY DEAR, AND IT IS QUITE TIME YOU SET ABOUT CORRECTING IT. YOU HAVE A GOOD MANY LITTLE GIFTS AND VIRTUES, BUT THERE IS NO NEED OF PARADING THEM, FOR CONCEIT SPOILS THE FINEST GENIUS. THE GREAT CHARM OF ALL POWER IS MODESTY."

Caddie Woodlawn's pioneer mother passed on stories and manners from the civilized world back in Boston. Laura Ingalls's mother corrected grammar as well as manners. Mothers taught and nice teachers mothered, and girls took seriously the exhortations of mothers and teachers. The aunt-type was more frivolous, purveying fun rather than rules, but even they gave girls moral and social advice, helping to slide them smoothly into society, and never urged independent thought or action. Miss Allison in the Little Colonel books was like this.

When I was a child, it seemed right that I should be on the receiving end of female exhortation. I enjoyed living up to expectations and did not fear criticism and punishment so much as I dreaded disappointing my mother or other mother-type people. Lest I give the impression that my mother fussed about rules, I should say that her daughter-rearing was casual and avoided the disturbing emphasis on manners and appearance many mothers believed in. Nonetheless, any sign of disapproval or disappointment would devastate me, any suggestion that I wasn't doing things right. To this day my stomach churns when I enter a highway and see a big red sign "WRONG WAY GO BACK": The sign certainly *looks* to be directed at other lanes, not my own; but I have, always, a strong conviction that at any moment I may make a wrong move and somebody will get hurt or angry or—heaven forbid—*disappointed* in me.

While women in children's fiction always represented civilized virtues, girls' and boys' stories viewed them differently. Girls' books described them straight, seldom with irony. Compare civilizing women in *Little Women* and *Huckleberry Finn*—one, the ultimate girls' book, the other a book that came to be considered the ultimate boys' book though not written for children—and note the reactions of their child characters to the civilizing efforts.

"I THOUGHT I WOULD SHOW YOU WHAT HAPPENS WHEN EVERYONE THINKS ONLY OF HERSELF. DON'T YOU FEEL THAT IT IS PLEASANTER TO HELP ONE ANOTHER, TO HAVE DAILY DUTIES WHICH MAKE LEISURE SWEET WHEN IT COMES, AND TO BEAR AND FORBEAR, THAT HOME MAY BE COMFORTABLE AND LOVELY TO US ALL?" "WE DO, MOTHER!" CRIED THE GIRLS. "WE'LL WORK LIKE BEES, AND LOVE IT TOO, SEE IF WE DON'T!"

THE WIDOW DOUGLAS SHE TOOK ME FOR HER SON, AND ALLOWED SHE WOULD SIVILIZE ME; BUT IT WAS ROUGH LIVING IN THE HOUSE ALL THE TIME, CONSIDERING HOW DISMAL REGULAR AND DECENT THE WIDOW WAS IN ALL HER WAYS; AND SO WHEN I COULDN'T STAND IT NO LONGER I LIT OUT. THE WIDOW SHE CRIED OVER ME, AND CALLED ME A POOR LOST LAMB, BUT SHE NEVER MEANT NO HARM BY IT.

As a little girl, I found Huck Finn annoying and I knew others who could not understand his yearning for freedom. Tom Sawyer was better, as Tom's "scrapes" were more containable within ordinary domestic life, but Tom also viewed female teachings with suspicion. This skepticism appeared not only in a great writer for adults like Mark Twain, whose view of life was inevitably complex, but in the most superficial boys' fiction as well.

Fictional boys did share with girls a taste for warm, loving care: They were tucked in bed at night, fed hot soup when they were sick, soothed when they were in trouble. But boys' books also insisted on distance from the mother; they declared independence even as they acknowledged a degree of dependence. Girls identified with the nurturing mother and did not question her position. They knew they would become mothers and they practiced being mothers now. They also knew that they would continue to be dependent girls even when they were mothers. Their lives were seamless, without rebellion. Girls do not make the break that boys do, when they leave the women's house and go into the men's lodge.

"DON'T FEEL THAT I AM SEPARATED FROM YOU, MARMEE DEAR, OR THAT I LOVE YOU ANY THE LESS FOR LOVING JOHN SO MUCH," SHE SAID, CLINGING TO HER MOTHER, WITH FULL EYES. "I SHALL COME EVERY DAY, FATHER, AND EXPECT TO KEEP MY OLD PLACE IN ALL YOUR HEARTS, THOUGH I *AM* MARRIED. THANK YOU ALL FOR MY HAPPY WEDDING DAY." A fictional daughter (like Meg from *Little Women*, in this passage) never felt separate from her mother, never was an independent individual even when adult; while the son never felt totally tied to the mother even when a child. There was the nineteenth-century Henry Esmond tradition, in which a boy worshipped his mother as a saint, but that tradition weakened in boys' books, leaving only the girls to take their mothers seriously. In books where the boy character's view predominated, the mother was generally seen as trivial and irrelevant.

Another boy in the Huck Finn tradition was Booth Tarkington's Penrod (1914). For him, coping with a mother involved hiding, ignoring, defying. Penrod's father inspired fear, his mother, only irritation. In one scene Penrod and his mother enacted a travesty of the sanctified custom of ministrations to the sick. Mrs. Scofield decided that Penrod—a distressingly healthy youth—was wasting away and needed motherly attention.

THAT NIGHT PENROD AWOKE FROM A SWEET-CONSCIENCELESS SLUMBER—OR, RATHER, HE WAS AWAKENED. A WRAPPERED FORM LURKED OVER HIM IN THE GLOOM. "UFF—OW—" HE MUTTERED. HE SIGHED AND SOUGHT THE DEPTHS OF SLEEP AGAIN. "GAWN LEA'ME

'LONE," HE MUTTERED. "IT'S JUST A NICE LITTLE PILL, PENROD. COME, DEAR, IT'S GOING TO DO YOU LOTS OF GOOD." SOME HOURS LATER HE BEGAN TO DREAM THAT HIS FEET AND LEGS WERE BECOMING UNCOM-FORTABLE. "YOU *QUIT* THAT!" HE SAID ALOUD, AND AWOKE INDIG-NANTLY. AGAIN A DARK, WRAPPERED FIGURE HOVERED OVER THE BED. "IT'S ONLY A HOT-WATER BAG, DEAR," MRS. SCHOFIELD SAID. "PUT YOUR FEET DOWN ON IT." "OW, MURDER!" HE EXCLAIMED CONVULSIVELY, "WHAT YOU TRYIN' TO DO? SCALD ME TO DEATH?"

You would never talk that way to Marmee. This scene under-cuts all those scenes in other books in which a motherly form near the sickbed represented the height of love and care and unselfish-ness. Readers of girls' books felt awe and respect at the "wrap-pered" figure, the cool hand on a fevered brow, the sad yet brave lullaby. But readers of *Penrod*, mostly boys, might modify with a corner of skepticism their devotion to shadowy, comforting mother-figures.

Fathers were stereotypes too. In *The Railway Children* (1906), FA-THER WAS MOST WONDERFULLY CLEVER WITH HIS FINGERS. FATHER MENDED THE DOLL'S CRADLE WHEN NO ONE ELSE COULD, AND WITH A LITTLE GLUE AND SOME BITS OF WOOD AND A PEN-KNIFE MADE ALL THE NOAH'S ARK BEASTS AS STRONG ON THEIR PINS AS EVER THEY WERE. The difference was hierarchical: fathers were to mothers as mothers were to children. In J. D. Wyss's *The Swiss Family Robinson* (1813), although the mother was as clever as her husband in mak-ing contrivances for their island life, she was frightened and sub-servient. She dreaded her husband's foraging trips to the wrecked ship in the bay: "OH DEAR!" SHE EXCLAIMED, "THAT DREADFUL SHIP! I AM IN AGONIES ALL THE WHILE YOU AND THE BOYS ARE AWAY." "BUT MY DEAR," I REPLIED, "THERE IS NO NECESSITY FOR SUCH EXCESSIVE FEAR." As long as Frau Robinson stuck to her own sphere she was able to cope. VERY SOON MY WIFE CALLED US TO DINNER. WE TRULY ENJOYED THE EXCELLENT SOUP, AND THE FLESH OF THE PORCUPINE SHE HAD BOILED FOR US. The chief delight of *The Swiss Family Robinson* came from the Robinsons' ability to perpetuate in a wilderness the stereotyped roles and customs of civilization.

Another instance of the father's ascendency over the mother appeared in *Little Women*. In one scene, Marmee revealed that over the years her husband had taught her to control her temper, just as Marmee was trying to teach her girls. "HE HELPED AND COMFORTED ME, AND SHOWED ME THAT I MUST TRY TO PRACTISE ALL THE VIRTUES I WOULD HAVE MY LITTLE GIRLS POSSESS." Jo responded, "I USED TO SEE FATHER SOMETIMES PUT HIS FINGER ON HIS LIPS, AND LOOK AT YOU WITH A VERY KIND, BUT SOBER FACE. WAS HE REMINDING YOU THEN?"

When the father, law-giver and decision-maker, was absent the mother had to cope alone. The toy-mending father of the Railway Children was sent to prison on a false charge, leaving their mother to run the household cheerfully with a breaking heart. She turned the struggles of poverty into games and wrote popular stories that supported the family. It took courage to endure, but always Mother—and the reader—knew the mystery would be solved and her husband honorably cleared. The woman might have to wait and suffer but almost always she would be rewarded by being released from this unnatural responsibility for herself and her family. Ma in the Little House books could wait out the blizzard or face the Indians alone with the children, because she knew that Pa would soon make it through.

Other lone mothers had a harder time. The widowed mother of *The Five Little Peppers* (1881) couldn't make the old stove work or pay for medicine. Without a man around, MRS. PEPPER HAD HAD HARD WORK TO SCRAPE TOGETHER MONEY ENOUGH TO PUT BREAD INTO HER CHILDREN'S MOUTHS AND TO PAY THE RENT. WITH A STOUT HEART AND A CHEERY FACE, SHE HAD WORKED DAY AFTER DAY AT MAKING COATS, AND TAILORING AND MENDING OF ALL DESCRIPTIONS.

Though her life was close to the edge, she came up with not one but three male rescuers. Rich old Mr. King took such a fancy to the Pepper children that he invited the whole bunch to live with him, with Mrs. P. to be his housekeeper. Then, to relieve the ambiguity of her social class, Mr. King's son-in-law Whitney appeared, revealing that Mrs. Pepper was his long-lost cousin. In the second book we see her once again rescued and this time married, to the good Dr. Fisher who tended her family back in the poor days.

Such an excess of chivalric attention sweetened for the Peppers and for the reader any bitter memories of life in the Little Brown

House. A final scene in the mansion showed the Pepper children describing to their new cousins, with total lack of irony, those good times back in the Little Brown House. They did not mention living on watered milk and stale brown bread, and never celebrating Thanksgiving. "LET'S TALK OF THE LITTLE BROWN HOUSE, ALL THE NICE TIMES YOU USED TO HAVE IN IT!" "OH, THE LITTLE BROWN HOUSE!" CRIED DICKY, HIS CHEEKS ALL AFLAME. "THE *DEAREST* LITTLE BROWN HOUSE, MAMMA! I WISH I COULD LIVE IN ONE!" "AND THEY HAD SUCH PERFECTLY *ELEGANT* TIMES."

A mother like Mrs. Pepper, if she suffered patiently and kept her children virtuous and clean, would be rewarded. Girls learned that they did not need to *solve* problems, just live through them uncomplainingly, after which they would eventually be saved by a man. Thus women were glorified children, closer to the child's level but able to intercede. Men inspired awe not only through their power but through their distance, their incomprehensible and exalted concerns. They were frightening and titillating.

I was never good at problem-solving. We had a number of dogs who eventually were hit by cars. After our beloved mutt Wizard died, my parents were persuaded to buy from a friend a purebred Kerry Blue Terrier, a snappish and highstrung breed. Called "Secundus" in honor of his predecessor, Seccy was an unpleasant, scowling beast. While his preliminary bites usually did not break the skin, they caused sad bruises on my calf or arm and a permanent state of terror in my soul. I would snivel a little to my mother and complain, but she merely placated me, denial being one of her stronger habits. So for several years of my middle childhood I couldn't get from the living room to the kitchen. I would stare at Seccy through the glass doors to the dining room, where he would be snarling in his sleep or crouched in the shadows peering at me, and then I would journey through the front hall, out the door, all around the big house, and in at the kitchen door—even at night, even in rain or snow. While I could endure a lot, I could not stand up for myself or figure out how to fix things. I could only wait for an outside rescuer—finally, the Dugan Bakery delivery man, who was thoroughly bitten one day and caused Seccy to be sent "to a nice farm."

A mother might have secrets but she was not herself mysterious, as a father-figure usually was. Children in books like *The Secret Garden* and *The Bastables* had only the vaguest sense that the head of the family had some problem or sorrow. Sometimes this remoteness had a dramatic cause, as in *The Chestry Oak*, Kate Seredy's 1948 story about wartime Hungary. Michael gradually learned that his brave father, Prince Chestry, was pretending to be a Nazi collaborator in order to develop an underground network and help free the world from tyranny. The Prince was depicted as a noble suffering father to his son and his people, who didn't understand him. He was an emblematic figure: LIKE A SILVER-TIPPED BLACK ARROW HE STOOD ON THE HALF-LANDING OF THE STAIRWAY, TALL, SILENT, AND STRAIGHT.

A Little Princess (1905) contained exquisitely one of the basic patterns—father-worship, father-deprivation, and father-restoration. It presented the fantasy situation where a little girl could adore her father with no interference from a mother. Before her father's departure for India, SARA SAT UPON HIS KNEE AND HELD THE LAPELS OF HIS COAT IN HER SMALL HANDS, AND LOOKED LONG AND HARD AT HIS FACE. "ARE YOU LEARNING ME BY HEART, LITTLE SARA," HE SAID, STROKING HER HAIR. "NO," SHE ANSWERED, "I KNOW YOU BY HEART. YOU ARE INSIDE MY HEART." AND THEY PUT THEIR ARMS ROUND EACH OTHER AND KISSED AS IF THEY WOULD NEVER LET EACH OTHER GO.

Sara's misery at her father's absence was as nothing to her pain when she heard of his death. Her sudden descent then, from heiress to scullery maid, increased her wretchedness. But after she suffered with brave dignity through months of hunger and humiliation, she was rescued by her father's old partner and restored to true Princesshood. At the end, it seemed as if any kind, rich gentleman would do, to give fatherly protection and receive daughterly adoration. Sara's new father was even described in much the same terms as the old one. SHE WENT AND SAT ON THE STOOL, AND THE INDIAN GENTLEMAN DREW HER SMALL DARK HEAD DOWN UPON HIS KNEE AND STROKED HER HAIR.

If you speak of girls and fathers to someone familiar with nineteenth-century girls' fiction, she will roll her eyes heavenward and murmur "Elsie Dinsmore." The dozen or so Elsie books (from 1868 on, by Martha Finley) were the apotheosis of traditional female masochism, an appallingly extended sick joke in which pale little girls felt transports of pleasure when chastised or mistreated by their fathers. There is a horrid fascination in reading about Elsie, as the emotional energy in her story is high. Elsie and her gang presented in an extreme version a very common kind of fictional relationship.

Elsie, another motherless child, had two great needs: to be loved and to be punished. Indeed, the two are connected, as apparently a girl could only earn love by suffering punishment. When the father who had never seen her finally returned to his parents' house, where Elsie was living, we find that she and her father were well matched: he was only too happy to bully her. As he told a family friend, "COST WHAT IT MAY, I *MUST* SUBDUE HER; SHE WILL HAVE TO LEARN THAT MY WILL IS LAW." . . .

"ELSIE," SAID MR. DINSMORE, "WHAT ARE YOU DOING THERE? DID I NOT FORBID YOU TO BE OUT IN THE EVENING AIR?" "I DID NOT KNOW YOU MEANT THE DOORSTEP, PAPA. I THOUGHT I WAS ONLY NOT TO GO DOWN INTO THE GARDEN," REPLIED THE LITTLE GIRL, RISING TO GO IN. "I SEE YOU INTEND TO MAKE AS NEAR AN APPROACH TO DISOBEDIENCE AS YOU DARE," SAID HER FATHER. "GO IMMEDIATELY TO YOUR ROOM, AND TELL MAMMY TO PUT YOU TO BED." "OH!" SHE MURMURED AS SHE COVERED HER FACE WITH HER HANDS, AND THE TEARS TRICKLED THROUGH HER FINGERS, "I DON'T DESERVE THAT HE SHOULD LOVE ME OR BE KIND AND INDULGENT, WHEN I AM SO REBELLIOUS." She was so submissive that she could only offend by accident.

Elsie would do anything (except disobey the teachings of Jesus) to win the caresses she yearned for. "I'M SURE PAPA WAS GOING TO TAKE ME ON HIS KNEE. DEAR, DEAR PAPA, IF YOU COULD ONLY KNOW HOW I LONG TO SIT THERE." In his first months at home, Elsie hovered around her father with no such reward. HE SELDOM NOTICED HER, UNLESS TO GIVE A COMMAND OR ADMINISTER A REBUKE, WHILE HE LAVISHED MANY A CARESS UPON HIS LITTLE SISTER, ENNA. OFTEN ELSIE WOULD WATCH HIM FONDLING HER, UNTIL, UNABLE ANY LONGER TO CONTROL HER FEELINGS, SHE WOULD RUSH AWAY TO HER OWN ROOM TO WEEP.

Elsie's misery was matched by her sense of unworthiness. She thought and talked constantly of not deserving good things, of wanting punishment to make her better. Her punishments were not beatings but humiliation, deprivation of love, and immobilization. A girl might be forgiven if she sat still long enough to certify her abasement. One time she was guilty of setting free a little bird that she did not know had been captured by her father as a rare specimen.

"I SHALL TIE THIS HAND UP, ELSIE," HE SAID. "THOSE WHO DO NOT USE THEIR HANDS ARIGHT MUST BE DEPRIVED OF THE USE OF THEM." Later, he said, "BRING THAT STOOL AND SET YOURSELF DOWN HERE CLOSE AT MY KNEE, AND LET ME SEE IF I CAN KEEP YOU OUT OF MISCHIEF FOR AN HOUR OR TWO." "MAY I GET A BOOK, PAPA?" SHE ASKED TIMIDLY. "NO," SAID HE SHORTLY. "YOU MAY JUST DO WHAT I BID YOU, AND NOTHING MORE OR LESS." SHE SAT DOWN AS HE DIRECTED, WITH HER FACE TURNED TOWARD HIM, AND TRIED TO AMUSE HERSELF WITH HER OWN THOUGHTS. "HOW HANDSOME MY PAPA IS!" THOUGHT THE LITTLE GIRL, GAZING WITH AFFECTIONATE ADMIRATION INTO HIS FACE.

In her moments of high misery Elsie was always still, frozen like a statue of a saint. Her finest hour came when she had to sit still at the piano all day in front of company, because she would not break the Sabbath and sing for guests. After sitting up straight in the hot parlor without food for hours, she not surprisingly keeled over. The horrified guests peered at ELSIE'S LITTLE FACE, GHASTLY AS THAT OF A CORPSE, WHILE A STREAM OF BLOOD WAS FLOWING FROM A WOUND IN THE TEMPLE, MADE BY STRIKING AGAINST SOME SHARP CORNER OF THE FURNITURE AS SHE FELL. SHE WAS A PITIABLE SIGHT INDEED, WITH HER FAIR FACE, HER CURLS, AND HER WHITE DRESS ALL DABBLED IN BLOOD.

Mr. Dinsmore eventually softened toward his daughter, won by all this satisfactory interaction. He then provided Elsie and the reader with a great deal of lapsitting, caressing, fondling, entwining, and embracing—rather more than anyone this side of pathology would care to hear about. There were rosy lips, heaving bosoms, breathless whispers, little trembling, clinging, soft hands. But even after she won his love, Elsie could never tell when she would once again commit an unconscious but punishable crime.

There would always be a chance to renew his love by enduring more punishment.

I describe Elsie at length because her hysterical tale contains so many elements of girl-grownup relations that appear more subtly in other books. I cannot, even in this much space, convey the hypnotic quality of Dinsmore's tyranny, the relentless repetition in his scoldings, or the obsessional quality of Elsie's self-flagellation.

It is easy to be patronizing about Elsie's pitiful guilts and misdemeanors, but I remember feeling similarly overwrought emotions on an occasion which to any sane adult must seem as ludicrous as Elsie's torments. I was in sixth grade—not a baby. My teacher, annoyed that supplies were being lost and wasted, announced that every Wednesday she would check each pupil's equipment. Then she started afresh, handing out pencils, rulers, whatever—and elegant pink erasers, the neat kind with sloping ends. I received my supplies reverently. I was a good girl, never in trouble.

But I had some odd nervous habits. (I still possess Alcott books with bits of the inside paper lining peeled off. These tiny injuries to my beloved books caused me enormous guilt.) In a fit of abstraction I took a sharp pencil and drilled a hole in my new eraser, turning and turning the point so that pinkish-black shavings bubbled up from the deepening hole, until the hole went all the way through in a perfect round. I became aware of what I had done on about Saturday, and dragged through the next days in a wretched trance. I tried to be sick on Wednesday morning but was nudged out the door toward the bus. I knew I would be shamed and punished; I deserved no forgiveness.

The public humiliation did not come: when I muttered a confession to Joan who sat behind me, she offered to hand me her virginal eraser under the desk as soon as Mrs. Morris checked it off, so I could show the same one, pretending it was my own. It worked, but I felt like throwing up. I knew I was very bad, and I knew that even the enormity of eraser-rape was surpassed by the act of lying to avoid punishment. I was a child with shy and modest tendencies, but not an extreme case. Extrapolating from my own experience, I suspect that my generation produced a good supply of seemingly confident women who were and are full of weird self-laceration and guilt.

Strong Women and Weak Men

Men characters were uncles, grandfathers, teachers, old family retainers, workmen, doctors, or preachers, as well as fathers. A character might exhibit a father's authority, or his competence, or his courage or strength or shrewdness, or his susceptibility to cute little girls, or any combination. A woman character—aunt, grandmother, teacher, nurse, housekeeper, neighbor, nice old lady—might have a mother's warmth or charity or domestic talents or social know-how or culture or piety. Such characters represented variations on sex-linked behavior, not denial of it.

In a few cases, though, the stereotype was definitely reversed—books where a woman was especially strong or a man especially weak. In only a few books was the most powerful person a women, and even in those cases the woman was still "feminine." In the Oz books the most powerful character was Glinda the Good, the sorceress whose magic powers supported the ruler, Princess Ozma. Most motherly characters were like martyred saints, strong in suffering; Glinda was more like a goddess, strong in power and action. Some other women verged on this goddess category, like Mrs. Brown in *National Velvet*, the Amazon who once swam the English Channel. And of course Mary Poppins was the supreme priestess of children's fiction.

Such women as these had unusual powers but exercised them in ordinary roles, disguised as ordinary conventional females. Women could properly be regal and superb like Glinda, as long as they were also gentle and unobtrusive. Velvet's mother was heroically strong and determined as an athlete, but in middle age she allowed obesity to immobilize her, forcing her to sit still like lesser females. And Mary Poppins—before whom the king of the sea bowed, the sun stooped for a kiss, the springtime agreed to blossom—never ceased to be the Nanny who ran baths and pushed prams.

A few of the women, then, were strong in unusual ways but camouflaged, like a Superman who never shed his Clark Kent disguise. Some of the younger girl characters, too, had potential beyond conventional limits. Most such heroines, the ones with more gumption and ambition than their peers, were urged in this direction by a male mentor. As a child, Alcott's Rose Campbell was a wispy, orphaned heiress with a supposedly weak constitution and not much more backbone than Elsie Dinsmore. In *Eight Cousins* and *Rose in Bloom* (1875 and 76), she grew into a sensible and independent young woman. Most of the credit was due to her guardian, Uncle Alec, who gave eccentric orders as to her care: when she first came to live with the Campbell clan, she was in bad condition. "I AM SO TIRED AND POORLY ALL THE TIME, I CAN'T DO ANY THING I WANT TO, AND IT MAKES ME CROSS," SIGHED ROSE, RUBBING THE ACHING HEAD LIKE A FRETFUL CHILD.

But Dr. Alec insisted that she replace her coffee and "hot bread and fried stuff" with milk and porridge, her tight belt with a soft sash. He made her run. She turned into a young lady robust in mind and body. When female weakness was seen as a bad thing (and that was not often), it was generally presented as the girl's own fault or the fault of women around her. "AUNT MYRA SAYS I HAVE NO CONSTITUTION AND NEVER SHALL BE STRONG," OBSERVED ROSE, IN A PENSIVE TONE, AS IF IT WAS RATHER A NICE THING TO BE AN INVALID.

Caddie Woodlawn (1935, by Carol Ryrie Brink) was another delightful girl who was delightful precisely because of her father's influence. Mr. Woodlawn took pride in telling people about it, HOW FRAIL SHE AND LITTLE MARY HAD BEEN AND HOW, AFTER LITTLE MARY HAD DIED, HE HAD BEGGED HIS WIFE TO LET HIM TRY AN EXPERIMENT. "I WANT YOU TO LET CADDIE RUN WILD WITH THE BOYS. I WOULD RATHER SEE HER LEARN TO PLOW THAN MAKE SAMPLERS, IF SHE CAN GET HER HEALTH BY DOING SO. BRING THE OTHER GIRLS UP AS YOU LIKE, BUT LET ME HAVE CADDIE." After seven years of running wild, Caddie was strong and active. SHE WAS NO LONGER PALE OR DELICATE. HER MOTHER AND SISTERS LOOKED AT HER AND SIGHED, BUT FATHER SMILED AND KNEW HE HAD BEEN A GOOD DOCTOR.

This book shows ambivalence: when Caddie tormented a visiting cousin for being prim and civilized, her father lectured her on the state of womanhood. A WOMAN'S WORK IS SOMETHING FINE AND NOBLE TO GROW UP TO, AND IT IS JUST AS IMPORTANT AS A MAN'S. I DON'T WANT YOU TO BE THE SILLY, AFFECTED PERSON WITH FINE CLOTHES AND MANNERS, WHOM FOLKS SOMETIMES CALL A LADY. I WANT YOU TO BE A WOMAN WITH A WISE AND UNDERSTANDING HEART, HEALTHY IN BODY AND HONEST IN MIND." Mr. Woodlawn admired sensible womanhood. But the whole book showed that women's behavior and values were insufferable unless modified by the man's wiser perspective. Caddie's mother and older sister, cultured and sedate, sat around stitching and reading *Godey's Lady's Book*. Caddie's younger sister was arch and whiny. We are meant to see that Caddie was superior to the other females in sense, humor, courage, and integrity—primarily because she spent those years with her brothers. She was reconciled to becoming a woman now, having had the advantages of being an honorary boy.

Some of the girls I discuss here as conventional must have seemed shockingly unconventional to their original readers. (One critic was scandalized at *Eight Cousins* because Uncle Alec seized Rose's medicine bottles and heaved them into the shrubbery.) But often outer changes in the lives of fictional girls were not accompanied by inner changes in their attitudes. Adventurous "career" books for girls burgeoned in my childhood, proudly describing nurses, airline hostesses, businesswomen, and girl detectives. The activities of these young women would seem alien to readers of the last century, but I suspect that their attitudes toward themselves and authority would not.

There was Cherry Ames, for instance—Student Nurse, Visiting Nurse, Cruise Nurse, even Army Nurse. This was not a stay-at-home girl obsessed with suitors, but a competent and independent young woman. The catch was that the ambitions of young women like Cherry Ames fit so easily into the old stereotypes. Careers described in books like these were authoritarian, hierarchical ones, where men were at the top (often young, lean, and tanned), giving beneficent orders to the women below them. The hospital was like a family; the nurse was an obedient wife or grown daughter to the doctor, and a mother to her patients. Cherry's school song shows the nurses' image of themselves:

ALL O'ER THE EARTH
ANGELS IN WHITE,
IN SICKNESS, AGE, AND BIRTH,
BRING LIGHT.

These exciting careers were clearly to be scrapped when the heroine decided to settle down with a man. Cherry was hardly a New Woman, with her dreary and laborious fuss over clothes—a scarlet angora sweater set, a ruffled bathing suit, a nurse's cap that was A DAINTY CHARLOTTE RUSSE AFFAIR OF FLUTED ORGANDY, a dress of DIAPHANOUS BLACK CHIFFON, AIRY AS SMOKE, NARROW BLACK LACE AT THE EDGE OF THE PERT SHORT SKIRT. Her concerns were familiar feminine ones, and her moral decisions were too: they were choices about the right kind of obedience to authority in confusing situations.

So even though Cherry was sincere in her ambitions (SHE HONEST-TO-GOODNESS CARED ABOUT PEOPLE AND SHE WANTED TO HELP THEM ON A GRAND SCALE), the main impression was of a sheltered world—where, for instance, the head nurse suggested she take an extra month of vacation from nursing school because she looked peaked. Cherry was surrounded by father figures, kind or critical doctor-mentors.

The best example of Cherry's reliance on male authority was in *Cherry Ames—Visiting Nurse* (1947). Six friends took jobs as visiting nurses in New York and rented an apartment in Greenwich Village. Tenements, poor ethnic neighborhoods—a girl must be self-reliant to cope with the city. But note one curious incident. The muttering janitor of their brownstone building frightened the young women with predictions that the landlord would punish their repainting efforts by kicking them out of the apartment. Six healthy, sane, employed RN's spent the next month or so shivering with terror, hiding from the janitor. No one could think of what to do, until Cherry saved them with her great idea: call in a man. She telephoned their married friend, Ann, who agreed to lend her husband so he could talk to the landlord. The landlord turned out to be a jolly Italian who didn't mind the paint at all. Everyone was grateful to Jack; no one thought (nor did the author) that one of the *women* could have called the landlord. This pattern is typical of the "modern" young women in my girls' stories—

their progress took them three steps forward and two steps back. (Or sometimes two forward and three back.)

Fans of Nancy Drew may be offended at my opinion of her relation to her father and to the world, but it's right there in the books. Carson Drew, famous lawyer and detective, taught Nancy how to think logically and act decisively, that is, not like a girl. As a a result, she was able to solve many rather drab mysteries. Nonetheless, she often depended on her father for help, showing surprisingly little confidence and pride. "OH, YOU LAWYERS ARE SO PARTICULAR ABOUT FACTS," NANCY SIGHED." And, "IF WE FIND THE WILL, THEY WON'T BE ABLE TO KEEP THE MONEY," NANCY DECLARED. "FATHER WILL SEE TO IT THAT YOU GIRLS GET YOUR JUST DUE."

If Nancy viewed her own role as being of limited importance, it is not surprising to hear her father's tone, as she came into his office to ask advice about a case: "NOW WHAT?" HER FATHER ASKED, SMILING AS SHE BURST IN UPON HIM. "IS IT A NEW DRESS YOU WANT?" (This is not the kind of question the Hardy Boys' detective father would ask them.) And it seems natural to hear this reaction from an unfamiliar sheriff: "IF MY FATHER WERE HERE, HE'D CONVINCE YOU ALL RIGHT," NANCY SAID, WITH RISING TEMPER. "YOUR FATHER? YOU DON'T MEAN CARSON DREW? YOU'RE HIS DAUGHTER?" "I AM." "WELL, THAT'S DIFFERENT. WHY DIDN'T YOU SAY SO?"

When you compare early Nancy Drew with early Hardy Boy books, you can see differences. Frank and Joe Hardy were also sons of a well-known detective. They became involved in their father's cases; occasionally he helped with a solution. But in general it was assumed that, though they got their inherited talents and their inspiration from their father, they were now responsible for themselves. They viewed their relation to Fenton Hardy matter-of-factly, and so did the people they encountered. When Nancy's father went away in the middle of her adventures, there was an uneasy feeling, until he returned, that she had no resource in an emergency. The detective work of Frank and Joe was depicted as adventurous, as fun, as dangerous, but not as inappropriate or startling—certainly not as cute.

In my girls' books there were some cases of unusually weak males as well as unusually strong females. These deviations from the typical might be surprising, even funny, but they were contained within ordinary definitions of male and female behavior. This is the George Banks syndrome. The father in *Mary Poppins* was one of those men who blustered and preened but were really silly and ineffectual. The women of his household formed a conspiracy to ignore his real nature, uphold his dignity, and soothe his ego. Author and readers knew the truth, but they knew also that no one would dare puncture the pretensions of a paterfamilias.

We glimpse Mr. Banks's professional life in the City: HE SAT ON A LARGE CHAIR IN FRONT OF A LARGE DESK AND MADE MONEY. ALL DAY LONG HE WORKED, CUTTING OUT PENNIES AND SHILLINGS AND HALF-CROWNS AND THREEPENNY-BITS. HE BROUGHT THEM HOME IN HIS LITTLE BLACK BAG. He was an overgrown boy, terrified when his old governess came to visit; still harboring comfortable childish tastes. "MY DEAR, IF IT DOESN'T RAIN I THINK JANE AND MICHAEL MIGHT CALL FOR ME AT THE OFFICE TODAY. I SHOULD LIKE TO BE TAKEN OUT TO TEA AND SHORTBREAD FINGERS AND IT'S NOT OFTEN I HAVE A TREAT."

Mr. Banks's tyrannical fussing was only an act, so his wife and children did not mind humoring him. "WHERE IS MY *BAG*?" SHOUTED MR. BANKS, TURNING ROUND AND ROUND IN THE HALL LIKE A DOG CHASING ITS TAIL. AT LAST MR. BANKS DISCOVERED THE BAG HIMSELF IN HIS STUDY. "NOW" HE SAID, AS THOUGH DELIVERING A SERMON, "MY BAG IS ALWAYS KEPT IN ONE PLACE. HERE. ON THE UMBRELLA-STAND. WHO PUT IT IN THE STUDY?" HE ROARED. "YOU DID, MY DEAR, WHEN YOU TOOK THE INCOME TAX PAPERS OUT," SAID MRS. BANKS. MR. BANKS GAVE HER SUCH A HURT LOOK THAT SHE WISHED SHE HAD BEEN LESS TACTLESS AND SAID SHE HAD PUT IT THERE HERSELF.

A wild version of this Foolish Father theme appeared in *Peter Pan*. From the start Mr. Darling was described in terms both loving and condescending. HE WAS ONE OF THOSE DEEP ONES WHO KNOW ABOUT STOCKS AND SHARES. OF COURSE NO ONE REALLY KNOWS, BUT HE QUITE SEEMED TO KNOW AND HE OFTEN SAID STOCKS WERE UP AND SHARES WERE DOWN IN A WAY THAT WOULD HAVE MADE ANY WOMAN RESPECT HIM. Mr. Darling was full of rhetoric, but acted like a little boy. When the children called his bluff about taking medicine—"MICHAEL, WHEN I WAS YOUR AGE I TOOK MEDI-

CINE WITHOUT A MURMUR. I SAID, 'THANK YOU, KIND PARENTS, FOR GIVING ME BOTTLES TO MAKE ME WELL' "—demanding that he take some foul medicine now with Michael, their father poured his instead into Nana's drinking bowl. Nana, the protective shaggy dog, was the children's nurse. As the ensuing fracas about the medicine led Mr. Darling to chain Nana in the front yard instead of letting her guard the nursery, he made it possible for Peter Pan to enter and bewitch the children. When they flew away with Peter, Mr. Darling was devastated with a self-centered and childish grief. He crawled into the doghouse in penance, vowing he would not emerge until the children came home. Every day a cab carried the doghouse to work in the City and home again, attracting much attention. Mr. Darling admitted that his head might have been turned by all the sympathy, "IF I HAD BEEN A WEAK MAN!"

The traditional definition of the father, the man in charge, can stretch to include his weaknesses, but the expose is not radical. Instead of suggesting a coup to overthrow his rule, the family shore up his ego and cover up his mistakes. Did anyone tell Owl in the Milne books that he was not a scholar, that in fact he couldn't even spell Happy Birthday? Did anyone respect the Wizard of Oz less, in later books, after he was revealed as a fraud?

Even Alice, generally skeptical about the strange "adults" around her, was tolerant of the pretentious Tweedledum and Tweedledee as they prepared for battle. SHE HAD NEVER SEEN SUCH A FUSS IN ALL HER LIFE—THE WAY THOSE TWO BUSTLED ABOUT, AND THE QUANTITY OF THINGS THEY PUT ON, AND THE TROUBLE THEY GAVE HER IN TYING STRINGS AND FASTENING BUTTONS. She was amused at the militaristic swagger, and laughed—BUT SHE MANAGED TO TURN IT INTO A COUGH, FOR FEAR OF HURTING HIS FEELINGS. She knew that these gentlemen had a place in her world; in fact she could predict all their actions from the nursery rhyme she already knew about them. Masculine behavior, it seems, is a given of the universe. Girls must accept and respect its oddities.

Books starting in the 1960s seriously challenge old assumptions about male and female roles; but earlier books contained only the kind of deviation that confirms rather than challenges the assumptions. Men are stronger, women are weaker; and if they aren't, then we will all act as if they were and that will amount to the same thing.

What Girls Do about Grownups

What exactly do girls do, in their relations with adults, with more powerful beings? Mostly, they depend; they expect their elders to guide and protect them much more than fictional boys do at the same age. A little girl may have adventures without the usual disadvantages, because a wandering girl character often has strong allies as protection. Once Dorothy (1900) was out of her flying house (the scariest part of *The Wizard of Oz*), she picked up a comforting number of indestructible "adult" companions. Her friends may have had drawbacks, like a tendency to rust, but Dorothy never seemed in danger as Jim Hawkins was on the island, or Tom Sawyer in the cave. The Oz books made a distinction between beings like the Tin Woodman and Scarecrow, who could not know hunger, exhaustion, or pain, and "meat people," with their strange bodily needs. This distinction, which might seem alarming, was actually reassuring: it emphasized the superhuman powers of Dorothy's protectors. Many a child went to sleep comforted by the knowledge that those odd, clumsy chaps were guarding the sleeping Dorothy—standing there unblinking through the night. And Jane and Michael Banks could journey to the depths of the ocean and the heights of the constellations without fear, because they knew the beady eyes of Mary Poppins were always upon them.

Some of the fictional girls were not lucky enough to have someone to depend on; they were forced to go in for endurance. Sara Crewe, the "Little Princess," was perhaps the one who suffered the most, but scores of others practiced the time-honored female virtue of hanging on until help comes—not finding solutions, only suffering until someone else found solutions. Heidi couldn't have gotten back to her beloved mountain from the horrible city on her own. Her author found an ingenious way out, though: in Heidi's case, an unconscious action—sleepwalking—led people to discover how miserable she was and send her home. A girl could not exhibit the kind of positive behavior that would result directly in a change in her state. It was simply the weight of her passive yearning that caused Heidi's sleepwalking and then her rescue.

Mostly, girls did nothing so dramatic. They merely endured and waited for the invalid to get better; for the father to come home; for the crime to be cleared up and the money found; for the lover to discover that the quarrel was just a misunderstanding. In some cases, before rescue arrived, the heroine had to make some kind of sacrifice. It might be a sacrifice easy to endure, like Cherry Ames's leaving a Christmas dance to help with an emergency, or Rose's giving up a wonderful excursion in *Eight Cousins* so her protegée, the servant girl Phoebe, could take her place.

Or it might be a sacrifice that continued to sting, like Rebecca's giving up her teaching job in *Rebecca of Sunnybrook Farm*, and Anne's giving up her scholarship in *Anne of Green Gables*, both to go back to their isolated farms and nurse their invalid relatives. As for Connie in *Midnight Moon*, when her mother was sick and medical bills were crushing, she voluntarily sold the horse she had tamed and adored. (This being the kind of book it is, her mother got well and Connie got the horse back.) In most books a heroine suffered passively rather than taking action. When she did take action, it meant giving up something rather than getting or deciding or building or organizing.

Depending, enduring, and sacrificing are familiar female habits. What startled me as an adult, looking through my array of children's books, was the enormous amount of *reforming* that was also going on. When I started remembering cases where children reformed their elders, fifteen came to mind immediately and I know there were more. This is not a trivial question because the books were so popular. If this plot pattern was pernicious—hostility of the powerful vanished when faced with sweetness of the weak—it was absorbed by many girls over the years.

In the typical situation, a child (full of innocence, vitality, and love) encountered a middle-aged or old person who was in bad shape (lonely, depressed, grouchy). The disagreeable grownup had given up on people, often because of a death or disappointment. But the child's sweet and affectionate character, all by itself, melted the icy heart and turned the town grump into a Santa

Claus. This is the Silas Marner motif: I wonder how many authors of children's books read at an impressionable age that over-wrought story of a miser who learned to love the golden curls of a little girl better than his golden coins.

Some of these reformed grumps were women; more were men. Some were mildly irritable souls easily softened. Others were truly mean and required a longer exposure to the innocent child's virtue-vibrations before being transformed.

• In *Penny*, a gentle little book, the heroine was frightened of visiting her stiff great-aunt, with her formal parlor manners. Soon she discovered Granny making fudge and licking her fingers in the kitchen, and of course joined her for a summer of fudge-making and other happy activities.

• In *Anne of Green Gables*, the grouchy adult was more recalci-trant, wanting at first to return Anne to the orphanage, as she was not the expected boy. Marilla was not mean but strict and shy and narrow. Fortunately, behind her sarcasm she had affection and a sense of humor. She became devoted to Anne.

• In *A Little Maid of Philadelphia*, Ruth felt that her Quaker aunt didn't love her; she tried harder to be obedient and made Aunt Deborah sorry for seeming harsh.

The tougher cases are more interesting; a grouch who reforms easily is an unworthy opponent for an earnest child.

• In *Rebecca of Sunnybrook Farm*, Miranda Sawyer, an aging spin-ster, decided it was her duty to take in and educate her poor sister's daughter. Miranda, censorious and penny-pinching, was an excellent candidate for conversion. Her creator, Kate Douglas Wiggin, showed restraint in producing a modest rather than a sensational conversion.

IT WOULD BE PLEASANT TO STATE THAT MIRANDA SAWYER WAS AN ENTIRELY CHANGED WOMAN AFTERWARD, BUT THAT IS NOT THE FACT. THE TREE THAT HAS BEEN GETTING A TWIST FOR TWENTY YEARS CAN-NOT BE STRAIGHTENED IN THE TWINKLING OF AN EYE. IT IS CERTAIN, HOWEVER, THAT ALTHOUGH THE DIFFERENCE TO THE OUTWARD EYE WAS VERY SMALL, IT NEVERTHELESS EXISTED, AND SHE WAS LESS CEN-SORIOUS IN HER TREATMENT OF REBECCA, LESS HARSH IN HER JUDG-MENTS, MORE HOPEFUL OF FINAL SALVATION FOR HER.

• In *A Girl of the Limberlost*, we have a truly sensational conversion. Elnora's mother, noted for rage, neglect, sadism, finally came round because her daughter was so good and accomplished and forgiving; exchanged her black depression for a sunny and tolerant view of life; and got a new hairdo.

• If the Limberlost books gave us a conversion of the most intense (and most implausible) quality, *Pollyanna* may well have provided the greatest quantity of conversions. Most notably, Pollyanna reformed Aunt Polly, who first gave her an attic bedroom that was bare and claustrophobic but later moved her to a pretty, carpeted room below. As the maid told Pollyanna, "IT'S LITTLE WAYS SHE HAS, THAT SHOWS HOW YOU'VE BEEN SOFTENING HER UP AN' MELLERIN' HER DOWN—THE CAT, AND THE DOG, AND THE WAY SHE SPEAKS TER ME."

In case this conversion didn't prove Pollyanna to be saintly enough, the author had her also reviving a gloomy rich recluse and inspiring a depressive minister. In fact, Pollyanna, with her easily-parodied game of always finding something to be glad for, reformed three-quarters of the town of Beldingsville. Pollyanna's power to improve the world around her merely by her radiance and her uplifting chatter used to amaze and terrify me. I was given to chattering myself, but no one seemed uplifted; no poor washerwomen blessed me for bringing sunshine into their lives.

In books where the child's influence reformed a woman character, the woman was usually a relative or guardian with whom the girl was living on close, homely terms. While the girl's simple good nature played a large role in the adult's transformation, her practical helpfulness usually contributed also. The older woman could see the girl as a protegée, who would inherit and perpetuate her own customs and values. These transformations were rather mundane, requiring compromise and understanding on both sides.

The more exciting transformations were those in which a girl conquered a man. More chutzpah was involved, more distance, than in simply convincing your aunt that you were a good girl after all. The reformation of a man character had wider social implications than the merely domestic softening of a woman—more of the sense that a breach in the community was being healed. The power of female virtue was at its most triumphant in these relationships.

This sense that hostility is easily defused and does not really exist was a consistent and crucial theme in girls' books. Sometimes it was the main movement of the book; sometimes it was one incident, as when Jane Moffatt, after hiding in the bread bin all day to avoid the dread Chief of Police, found that he was not an ogre but a jolly fat man who thought she was hilarious. The most memorable embodiments of this theme, though, were solemn and sentimental, not funny. The man was usually old and rich, the girl poor and weak.

• In *The Littlest Rebel* (1914), a tearjerking Civil War tale by Edward Peple, implacable General Grant was about to have two men executed, the Southern Captain Cary for spying, the Northern Colonel Morrison for letting Cary escape. But angelic Virgie, Cary's daughter, softened Grant's tough old heart and saved them both by innocently describing their actions in a new, forgivable light. She had also saved her father earlier, by showing Colonel Morrison that her father was sneaking around enemy lines only to bring her provisions. That counts as another conversion, and a pretty good one when you can get an enemy to help a captured officer escape.

In canceling the execution, Grant not only had to give in to a barefoot moppet, he had to endure one of those mushy scenes that always resolved a situation like this: THERE WAS A RUSH OF BARE, CHILDISH FEET AND BEFORE HE COULD ESCAPE, VIRGIE'S BROWN LITTLE ARMS WERE ROUND HIM AND HER DIMPLED CHIN WAS PRESSED AGAINST HIS WAIST. THE GENERAL MADE NO EFFORT TO RELEASE HIMSELF BUT LOOKED DOWN ON HER WITH A SOFTER LIGHT IN HIS FACE THAN ANY OF HIS MEN HAD SEEN THERE IN MANY MONTHS. "AND AS FOR YOU, YOUNG LADY, THE NEXT TIME YOU PERVERT MY OFFICERS AND UPSET THE DISCIPLINE OF THE FEDERAL ARMY—WELL, I DON'T KNOW *WHAT* I'LL DO WITH YOU." HE LOOKED DOWN INTO HER FACE AND READ THERE A WISTFUL FEMININE APPEAL FOR OUTWARD AND VISIBLE RECONCILIATION. "OH WELL," HE SAID WITH MOCK RESIGNATION, "I SUPPOSE I'VE GOT TO DO IT," AND HE STOOPED AND KISSED HER. As if this weren't enough, the book ended with the irresistible Virgie now in the arms of Robert E. Lee. Perverting the officers, indeed!

• In *Heidi* one of the best-loved conversions took place. Everyone remembers the kind old grandfather up on the mountain, giving goat's milk to his little Heidi. He became so benign that it is easy to forget he had been for years a hermit brooding over his wicked past, a misanthrope who frightened the townspeople. Heidi's secondary conversion was to inspire with new life the lonely, despairing doctor from Frankfurt. After meeting and visiting Heidi, he retired from his practice, moved to her mountain, and made her his heir.

• In *The Secret Garden*, horrid Mr. Craven came to forget his tragic loss and share the vitality of his niece. Mary had so much magical power that she transformed herself from a sour weakling into a pretty, healthy girl, her cousin Colin from a neurotic invalid into a normal boy, Ben from a grim old gardener into a sentimental admirer, and Archibald Craven from a suicidal isolate into a loving father.

• In *Little Women* Beth, though morbidly shy, won the heart of the gruff old codger next door, Mr. Laurence, to the point where he gave her his dead granddaughter's piano. REMEMBERING THAT HE HAD LOST THE LITTLE GIRL HE LOVED, SHE PUT BOTH ARMS ROUND HIS NECK, AND KISSED HIM. IF THE ROOF OF THE HOUSE HAD SUDDENLY FLOWN OFF, THE OLD GENTLEMAN WOULDN'T HAVE BEEN MORE ASTONISHED; BUT HE LIKED IT—OH DEAR, YES! HE LIKED IT AMAZINGLY; AND WAS SO TOUCHED AND PLEASED BY THAT CONFIDING LITTLE KISS THAT ALL HIS CRUSTINESS VANISHED.

• In *Pollyanna* John Pendleton, the millionaire recluse, described his own conversion: "FOR LONG YEARS I HAVE BEEN A CROSS, CRABBED, UNLOVABLE, UNLOVED OLD MAN—THOUGH I'M NOT NEARLY SIXTY, YET, POLLYANNA. THEN ONE DAY, LIKE ONE OF THE PRISMS THAT YOU LOVE SO WELL, YOU DANCED INTO MY LIFE, AND FLECKED MY DREARY OLD WORLD WITH DASHES OF THE PURPLE AND GOLD AND SCARLET OF YOUR OWN BRIGHT CHEERINESS."

• In *The Five Little Peppers* old Mr. King was an irritable gentleman, WHOSE WHOLE BEARING SHOWED PLAINLY THAT PERSONAL COMFORT HAD ALWAYS BEEN HIS, AND WAS, THEREFORE, NEITHER A

MATTER OF SURPRISE NOR THANKFULNESS. But all Phronsie Pepper had to do was bake him a crooked gingerbread boy with wild raisin eyes, and his formality collapsed. NOWADAYS, NO ONE EVER SAW THE OLD GENTLEMAN GOING OUT OF A MORNING WITHOUT PHRONSIE BY HIS SIDE, AND MANY PEOPLE TURNED TO SEE THE PORTLY FIGURE WITH THE HANDSOME HEAD BENT TO CATCH THE PRATTLE OF A LITTLE SUNNY-HAIRED CHILD, WHO TROTTED ALONG, CLASPING HIS HAND CONFIDINGLY.

• In *Elsie Dinsmore,* as we have seen, the tyrannical Horace Dinsmore, moved by Elsie's innocence and abject submission, learned to love his daughter and give her those unsavory caresses she yearned for.

• The reforming child was not always a girl. *Little Lord Fauntleroy* showed the old Earl forgiving and acknowledging his hated American daughter-in-law just because of her little boy's moral and physical beauty. *Little Lord Fauntleroy,* though about a boy, was certainly more of a girls' book (written by Burnett for the same audience that read *Secret Garden* and *A Little Princess*), and thus shows the characteristic pattern of these other girls' books. But it's interesting to see one difference: the old Earl was consciously testing his grandson to see if he would be a worthy heir. He watched Cedric's behavior for signs of weakness or cowardice; he noticed Cedric's treatment of the tenants that he would eventually be responsible for. His softening attitude toward the boy was more a conscious choice than a spontaneous release from curmudgeonry. Cedric had to earn his grandfather's favor. Only a girl could win an old man's heart merely by sending forth rays of joy and purity.

• So the typical agent of infant conversion-power remains the little girl who is unconscious of her strength. *The Little Colonel,* to give a final example, described the capitulation of old Colonel Lloyd, known for being as dictatorial as Napoleon, to his equally stubborn granddaughter. No one thought he would forgive his daughter, who had married a Yankee, but when the fair-haired daughter of that marriage toddled into his life, A VERY UN-NAPOLEON-LIKE MIST BLURRED HIS SIGHT. IT HAD BEEN SO LONG SINCE SUCH A TOUCH HAD THRILLED HIM, SO LONG SINCE ANY CARESS HAD BEEN GIVEN HIM. Eventually all lived happily together—the

Colonel getting thrilling caresses out of the arrangement, and the Little Colonel getting admiration and money.

I have listed many examples because this theme is not only common in girls' fiction, it is very revealing. The idea that a girl can entirely change a hostile adult without really doing anything is one of the most dangerous notions in these books. It's not bad for girls to learn that they should be loving and helpful, but it's disastrous for them to learn that there is no way to cope with hostility except by sitting around exuding virtue and good cheer.

The remarkable thing in these books is that so few people are really bad. The few instances of real aggression are extreme, almost caricatures: Miss Minchin, the schoolmistress in *A Little Princess*; Fraulein Rottenmeier, the nasty housekeeper in *Heidi*; the Wicked Witch of the West. Such thorough wickedness could possibly be destroyed (though only by accident, as Dorothy destroyed witches), or could more likely be ultimately escaped, as Sara Crewe and Heidi escaped their tormenters. But aside from these few extreme cases, most girl characters did not have to deal with truly bad people. As soon as someone seemed to show real badness, it started dissolving into good. Women may well be harmed less by their desire to help and cooperate than by their inability to cope with aggression.

Boys' books contained bad guys as a given. The boys found some way to outwit or overpower their enemies, without being traumatized at the very existence of enemies. Fictional girls did not have enemies: enemies were really friends. What is a reader of *Pollyanna* going to think if she grows up and finds that someone's hostility does not melt when confronted with sweetness? She is going to think that she wasn't sweet and pure enough, that it was really her fault, for everyone is good inside. You can get a certain mileage out of that attitude, but if you are trying to function in the world it doesn't help to fall apart whenever hostility stays hostile.

The Oz books, on the whole, presented action adventures rather than personal dilemmas; but one book, *The Emerald City of Oz* (1910), showed an interesting moment of decision. Ozma, the benevolent ruler, learned that the Nome King was tunneling under the desert and planned to attack the Emerald City with thousands of evil, grotesque creatures. Ozma's friends were nervous, knowing the enemy were digging closer each day. Ozma, though, did not worry or form any plan. It took the Scarecrow (male) to realize that a storm of magic dust in the tunnel would cause the attackers to look for water, and once out of the tunnel, to drink from the Fountain of Oblivion nearby. This scheme succeeded, and the creatures were rendered harmless, forgetting all evil purposes.

What role did Ozma, the devoted ruler, take in saving her people? None at all, except in using her limited magic powers to raise the duststorm, at the Scarecrow's suggestion. Earlier, when her subjects looked to her for advice, she expressed only that catatonic, serene passivity so familiar to readers of girls' books. "OH, OZMA, OZMA! I'M *SO* SORRY FOR ALL YOUR TROUBLE ABOUT THE NOME KING." OZMA LAUGHED WITH GENUINE AMUSEMENT. "WHY, THAT HAS NOT TROUBLED ME A BIT," SHE REPLIED. "HAVE YOU ALL BEEN WORRYING ABOUT THIS TUNNEL?" "WE HAVE!" THEY EXCLAIMED IN A CHORUS. "WELL, PERHAPS IT IS MORE SERIOUS THAN I IMAGINED," ADMITTED THE FRAIL RULER; "BUT I HAVEN'T GIVEN THE MATTER MUCH THOUGHT."

At this point the reader wondered if Ozma had a secret solution that made her so confident. In fact she had none, and the Oz-ians sadly discussed what would happen when the land was destroyed. It was fortunate that the Scarecrow thought of his plan, as the supposedly wise Princess Ozma offered only one solution. Her solution didn't seem stupid to me when I was a child, because my ears were ringing with the endearing prattle of Pollyanna and the Little Colonel; my eyes were dazzled with the riches and caresses that those girls charmed out of their rich old men by just such behavior as Ozma was exhibiting. Ozma explained in a cheerful and reasonable manner: "I'LL GET UP EARLY TOMORROW MORNING AND BE THERE WHEN THE FIERCE WARRIORS BREAK THROUGH THE CRUST OF THE EARTH. I WILL SPEAK TO THEM PLEASANTLY AND PERHAPS THEY WON'T BE SO VERY BAD, AFTER ALL." The only method I learned of reducing grownup aggression was to Speak to the Aggressors Pleasantly, and hope they wouldn't be so very bad, after all.

When I was five years old, my parents went away on a trip. I liked writing even then, and made a checklist of instructions for myself while they were gone. Here are the items on my list, which was preserved by my mother and still exists today.

BEGOOD AND HELPFUL
KEEPCLM
pikuprum
MAKBED
TAKMDASN
BRSTEEH
WRITMUMMANDDADDY
BRS HAR
TAK BTH
OBA

A girl will do fine as long as she remembers to keepclm and always oba her elders and betters.

· 5 ·

Girls and Their Friends:
Civilized by the Group

THE LIVING ROOM PRESENTED A LIVELY SCENE. ALL THE NINE LINGER-NOTS WERE COMFORTABLY SQUEEZED INTO IT, FOR NOBODY MINDED A LITTLE CROWDING IN AN IMPORTANT CAUSE. THE GIRLS DISTRIBUTED THEMSELVES COSILY ON THE COUCH, IN THE WINDOW-SEATS, ON HASSOCKS AND ON THE FLOOR, LAUGHING AND CHATTERING MERRILY. . . .

IT WAS A VERY SMALL BOWER—JUST BIG ENOUGH TO HOLD THEM, AND THE BASKETS, AND THE KITTEN. OH, HOW GOOD EVERYTHING TASTED IN THAT BOWER, WITH THE FRESH WIND RUSTLING THE POPLAR LEAVES, AND BIRDS SINGING OVERHEAD! . . .

AT SEVEN O'CLOCK, THE FOUR MEMBERS ASCENDED TO THE CLUB-ROOM, TIED THEIR BADGES ROUND THEIR HEADS, AND TOOK THEIR SEATS WITH GREAT SOLEMNITY. . . .

My fictional girls clustered in groups. They liked to do things together but doing things was not as important as simply being together. Three patterns emerge in stories about girls' groups: (1) Being in a group helped a girl—flawed and feeble as an individual on her own—find completion, support, and vicarious perfection. This allowed her to be slightly different from the others yet still fit in smoothly. (2) Being in a group helped a girl change and improve herself. She learned to eliminate any sour notes in her personality that might threaten the harmony of the circle. This allowed her to become more similar to the others. (3) The group served as an inspiration to its members, another kind of superego fostering good girlish qualities like duty, cooperation, and guilt. It might seem that girls' informal groups would probably be subversive—a protection against all the mothers, teachers, and other adult mentors who smothered their girls in wholesome messages. But girls' stories of the mid-twentieth century and earlier periods didn't work that way. Most of them, most of the time, described girls' groups that simply, happily, reinforced the teachings of the elders.

Books describing children in groups included adventure stories full of action but these (except for the Nancy Drew mysteries) were not much read by girls. In plot-centered books the group of friends was incidental, part of the local color and setting. In true group stories, plot was secondary. Instead of embarking on elaborate adventures, children spent their time celebrating their own group, or defending it from some outside threat, or ironing out problems within it. Sometimes the children were members of a family—the kind of group you didn't choose, you just belonged to. In other books children joined with friends in choosing or creating a nonfamily group that became important in their lives. While group life in children's fiction sometimes supported a girl's efforts to become an independent, strong person, in many cases it deftly, comfortably undermined such efforts.

Girls and Boys, Groups and Pairs

Boys at mid-century liked books about a single hero with or without a buddy-sidekick; girls liked books about a girl hero closely entangled with at least two other children. The sociologist Georg Simmel pointed out in 1908 that a group of two is different from a group of three or more: A pair, a dyad, he says, is not really a group—the two members are aware of each other, but there is no super-personal collectivity existing beyond those two individuals.

A dyad no longer survives if one drops out of the pair, but a group of three or more continues even if one member leaves. In

a dyad, responsibility is shared by both members; no higher element controls or influences individuals. In a triad, of course, a
majority can overrule an individual member. David Balfour and
Alan Breck Stewart in *Kidnapped*, read mostly by boys, formed a
dyad; so did Robinson Crusoe and Friday, the two Hardy Boys,
Sherlock Holmes and Dr. Watson, and others. Mary in *The Secret
Garden*, read by girls, formed a triad with Colin and Dickon. Look
through the favorite stories of girls up to the mid-twentieth century: the typical girls' story features at least three children who
created and celebrated a marked group mystique.

Some boys did read stories about a group of characters: King
Arthur's knights, for instance, or team players in John Tunis's
sports books. Boys' groups have always been more conspicuous
in British children's fiction than American, in keeping with the
tradition that an American hero is a loner—perhaps a cowboy,
explorer, or private eye. While American boys of the mid-
twentieth century apparently liked *some* cooperative effort and hierarchical structure, as with a Team or Round Table, they did not
enjoy stories about groups of chums. *Treasure Island*, one of the
books most loved by American boys, concerns a male group acting more or less together, but it is no tale of devotion to the group;
each sailor was interested in saving his skin and his fortune; they
banded together only temporarily, out of self-interest.

When boys' stories did present characters in a group, it was a
group with a specific, concrete goal and a clear hierarchy, like a
baseball team. If the group's goal was abstract, as with the Round
Table, the story soon dropped the organizing abstraction to focus
on a particular adventure of individual characters or pairs. Of
course, when male characters form an alliance for a practical reason, they may also forge a personal bond. Men are not supposed
to be emotional but are allowed intense relationships within a
platoon or gang. The rituals of membership, coming of age, and
bonding are important to boys of a tribe. Huck and Tom and Jim
on the raft were not just escaping various kinds of slavery, they
were forming a magic band; Mowgli and his *Jungle Book* friends
swore loyalty to the death.

These male alliances differed from female groups because they
pointed outward, to action: self-defense or self-aggrandizement in

the outside world. Fictional girls' groups went in rather for celebrating themselves—activities and practical goals were secondary, an excuse. Even though the March sisters matured during *Little Women* and moved into separate spheres, the idea of the family group persisted for each as inspiration and guide. Their development was circular, shaped by departure and return, by quarrel and resolution—less linear than a boys' adventure.

This difference in plot pattern grew out of the different ways girls and boys related to the group. Boys, in these stories, sought power and achievement; for them a group was an alliance which could help or hinder progress. Girls sought community, connection; for them a group was a goal in itself. Often the group provided personal completion for its girl members—they knew themselves to be so incomplete, such partial, inadequate human beings, that they could find a whole identity only by joining together in a larger design.

Books about mixed boy and girl groups in this period were mostly matter-of-fact and plot oriented, like Enid Blyton's dreary, predictable series. I preferred the all-girl books, with minimal plots, where a girl could bask in the warmth and solidarity of the characters' relations. I was in the minority in disliking the adventurous Nancy Drew stories.

Nancy and her friends bored me, I now realize, because they did *not* subscribe to an emotional group mystique—they simply went about their business solving mysteries and having fun. No girlish guilt? No yearning for approval from others? No devoting the self to a higher cause? To me and my type of girl, this lacked excitement. Perhaps Nancy's bland stories, written in a pedestrian style, were important to many young women because they avoided both the "feminine" selflessness of the usual girls' story and the "heroic" selfishness of the boys' story. Though she spent most of her time with her two chums, Nancy was unlike heroines who defined themselves through their group of friends and accepted the group's conventions. Nancy Drew lacked subtlety; what she did offer was wholeness, the possibility that a girl hero could be independent and active, and still close to a circle of friends. So nonchalant and so knowledgeable, Nancy struck sheltered little girls as a major revelation.

WITH A LAST COUGH THE ENGINE STOPPED. "OH, PSHAW!" NANCY EXCLAIMED, "I GUESS THE DISTRIBUTER GOT WET. . . . HEEDLESS OF RUST AND DIRT SHE CLIMBED OVER THE EDGE [of the roof] AND DREW HER- SELF ERECT. Lines like these made it seem that anything was pos- sible. (Nancy did a good deal of drawing herself erect, an interesting image.) As Bobbie Ann Mason observed, "Nancy is so accomplished that she can lie bound and gagged in a dank base- ment or snowed-in cabin for as much as twenty-four hours with- out freezing to death or wetting her pants." At an extreme, plot-driven stories are a series of meaningless physical actions, as witless as today's action movies composed of a karate fight, a gun fight, and a car chase. Nancy Drew's adventures were better than that. She had "male" qualities like courage and initiative, while remaining thoughtful, cooperative, and "feminine." But hers are definitely plot rather than character stories—in the leader-and- followers genre like boys' books rather than the harmonious- group-of-girls genre. Apparently there were many girls who yearned for the action found in boys' adventures but rejected the arrogance. They found what they wanted in Nancy Drew.

Family: The Group You Didn't Choose

Books about families evoked comfort and passivity because, what- ever problems threatened the family group from without or within, the child's membership was automatic; she didn't have to invent or discover her group. Some family stories were mild and episodic, like Laura Lee Hope's beloved *Bobbsey Twins* books for very small children. These described ordinary activities, small fes- tivities, little expeditions to farm or shore—the normal days of well-to-do boys, girls, and parents. Plot and character were minimal; there were no individualized characters, just middle-class stereotypes. I always disliked the stupid Bobbsey Twins, older boy and girl twins Nan and Bert, and the younger set Flossie and Freddy, but many of my contemporaries in their youngest years seem to have been reassured by the predictability, the safety.

The Saturdays (1944), a more sophisticated episodic book by Elizabeth Enright, seems at first to celebrate a nice balance of group and individual: the four Melendy children decided to pool their weekly allowance so one child could get the total sum each Saturday afternoon and spend it as he or she wished. Four chapters described individual outings, in which Randy went to an art gallery, Oliver went to the circus, Rush went to the opera, and Mona went to a beauty salon to have her long hair cut off. However, the children finally decided it was more fun to do things together; they abandoned the system of separate expeditions and just played in Central Park, an unoriginal way to spend a good Saturday. Even the individual adventures themselves pointed back to the primary importance of the group: Rush brought back a stray puppy for everyone to enjoy, and Randy struck up a friendship with a rich old lady who became a benefactor to the family. The separate individual turned out to be lonelier and feebler than the group together—a popular theme in these stories about groups, which were read mainly by girls even though some of the groups also included boys.

Usually in family-survival stories, a sudden threat or a chronic problem hung over the family. The children were expected to endure, sacrifice, and obey rather than solve the family problem. At least these stories described difficult times, so there was some plausible reason for girls to put the family group ahead of their individual wishes. But their help generally was limited to comforting, enduring, and housekeeping rather than anything more strenuous.

There were a few better family books like *The Moffats*, with more complex worlds to survive in and more convincing characters. Rufus, Jane, Joey, and Sylvie knew that their widowed mother had to work hard at sewing to support the family in Depression-era Connecticut. They knew that it was disastrous to lose the family's last five dollars when they were sent to buy coal in January, and that it was futile to cry when forced to move out of the family house. I liked seeing how the children behaved in adversity, and I cared about Jane's run-in with the Superintendent of Schools and Rufus's running away on the trolley—in other words, I cared about who was good and who was bad. Eleanor Estes created the Moffats in 1941, when the ideal girl was still depicted as shy and submissive but a few authors were providing more solid characters. Jane Moffat was an unusual character because she didn't become a conventionally noble family prop—she simply helped when she could and put up with things when she couldn't help, with no self-consciousness or whining.

The more sentimental family survival story is typified by the Five Little Peppers books, beloved since 1881. Margaret Sidney wins the all-time prize for rhetoric about a bunch of Loving, Plucky, Poor Children. In treacly prose Polly struggled with the old broken stove, Joel got deathly ill, Phronsie was kidnapped by a swarthy tramp. The family ended up rich and happy because (the author implies) the children were industrious and loyal, and above all charming. This kind of family-survival book was read because its glow of self-congratulation spilled over to the young reader and made her feel virtuous too. The Peppers showed that you can be as self-sacrificing as a girl should be and still, if you follow the rules of your society, after the problems disappear, you will magically end up with everything you want.

Family-survival books before the mid-century period tended to be like the Pepper books—they taught that children could help their family endure troubled times and they told a story in such fantastic, fairy tale terms that no young reader would find the trouble very troubling. Even *The Railway Children* by E. Nesbit (1908), a better book about a family in trouble, dealt in magical coincidences and solutions. At the lowest point, when the children knew their father was disgraced but not why or how, their faith and solidarity and the author's intimate style still provided a soft cushion of comfort. Girl readers learned that in a storm you were safe if you all huddled together and tried to be good. The *practical* problems of a group were usually not as emotionally compelling as its interpersonal relations. In *Little Women*, for instance, the worries were enormous—poverty and sickness in the family—but the greatest emotion surrounds questions of guilt, duty, and loyalty.

Along with survival and the threat from outside, another important theme in the family story described the threat from within:

the behavior of a lively but misguided sister. This character learned, eventually, to merge her self and her wishes into the larger importance of the group. The book would focus on her, the one interesting character, as she settled into her proper role—while surrounding characters were generally faceless and uninteresting. *Caddie Woodlawn* is this sort of book, and so is *What Katy Did. Trudy and the Tree House,* written by Elizabeth Coatsworth in 1944, is a perfect example of this type—delightful but depressing in its implications. Trudy was the rebellious and spoiled youngest child in a family of seven girls. Gradually she realized that her pranks and her desire to be alone had a bad effect on the family group and also made her feel lonely. So she modified her independent behavior and even let her sisters come into her private treehouse. The creepiest part of this book is that the seven girls were named alphabetically, like hurricanes: first Ann, then Barbara, Claire, and on down to Gertrude. This gimmick confirms that the girls were just part of a set, not real people. They had a few minor differences in personality but not enough to make them individuals. Each was important only because she filled that particular alphabetical niche. Trudy was the only one to challenge her proper position in the hierarchy with a nickname that did *not* begin with her own letter. But by the end of the book she had settled down; they probably started calling her Gertrude, the "G" girl, instead of Trudy.

The girl-family book we all remember best is *Little Women,* which characterized and revered the whole group, not just the main character. While Alcott followed the familiar pattern of taming the wild hoyden sister, she didn't slight the other three. This kind of book was appealing because it offered a choice, but the choice had comforting limits. If you were not a heroine like Jo or a saint like Beth, you could still be a domestic Meg or an artistic Amy. You could be a Piglet or an Eeyore or a Rabbit or an Owl. The group embraced all sorts and considered each worthy of individual attention, a notion that made child readers feel good.

Characters in *boys'* group stories just happened to be of different types and abilities. They used their different qualities as best they could in pursuing individual and group goals—the strong lad and the clever one, the leader and the clown. Girls used their different personalities and skills more self-consciously to complete the circle. A girl character felt safe knowing that she contributed her mite to the larger whole and was supported by the contributions of others. It was all right for her to be small and lacking, because others provided what she lacked. The smart girl was interdependent with the beauty and the athlete and the motherly one and the naughty one and so on.

If children's stories generally assumed that females cared about the community more than about their individual selves, it is not surprising that many a girl character found her wholeness as a cog in the communal wheel. This snug and smug type-casting occurred frequently in books about girl families. In *Little Women* we were reminded of the sisters' contrasting personalities in hundreds of details such as the letter each one sent to their mother: Meg addressed her as "MY DEAREST MOTHER," Jo wrote "MY PRECIOUS MARMEE," Beth wrote "DEAR MOTHER," and Amy wrote "MA CHÈRE MAMMA." Once Beth watched the little gray sand-birds on the beach and mused, "MOTHER SAID THEY REMINDED HER OF ME, BUSY CREATURES, ALWAYS NEAR THE SHORE, AND ALWAYS CHIRPING THAT CONTENTED LITTLE SONG. YOU ARE THE GULL, JO, STRONG AND WILD, FLYING FAR OUT TO SEA. MEG IS THE TURTLE-DOVE, AND AMY IS LIKE THE LARK, TRYING TO GET UP AMONG THE CLOUDS, BUT ALWAYS DROPPING DOWN INTO ITS NEST AGAIN." Such type-casting was also popular in books about girl groups outside the family, and was even more thrilling there because of the element of choice in the group's membership.

Friends: Their Clubs and Mentors

The purest type of girls' group story does not concern a family. A sense of possibility arises when girls choose each other and band together outside the family. But the same patterns appear here: the individuals-conform-to-the-group story and the group-solidarity-in-the-face-of-danger story. Here, away from permanent, messy family loyalties, a character could answer questions about her position in a group, her relation to other members, her ability to contribute. The answers were usually reassuring and traditional.

In most of my own favorite tales, a bunch of non-related children spent the most significant part of their childhood in a group or club. The most significant part of that group experience was not activities; it was working out who and what the group was, and making it even more so. Jim Hawkins on Treasure Island was not at all exciting to me—exciting was the Little Colonel's house-party of girls, or Maida's little shop full of her buddies, or the mounted Girl Scout troop in *Silver Birch*. Exciting was how and whether they all got along, who fit in where, and what everybody thought of everybody else. That was a real group, and that was what a girl needed to know—at least up through the 1940s: What must she do to be accepted and approved? Because, for her, success was not winning the race or the treasure or the goal, it was winning the approval of her circle.

As Carol Gilligan, Mary Pipher, and others have shown in their writings about female development, most girls in our culture lose some of their childhood confidence and vitality as they enter adolescence. Like their brothers, little girls feel exhilarated at first as they grow bigger, stronger and smarter. The boys continue on toward independent maturity, but at puberty the girls receive strong signals to stop moving in that direction: signals announcing that the female type of "maturity" involves deference, passivity, conformity, and silence. Girls today at the end of the century face horrible physical and emotional dangers that we mid-century girls were not even aware of. But they also have more resources and choices than we did. There are more various voices being heard now, some of them urging teenage girls to hold on to their childhood strengths. The question here is which kind of message pre-adolescent girl readers of my generation and earlier got from stories of group solidarity. Did these fictional groups support their members as they tried to grow, or did they offer a comfortable way *not* to grow? Were the groups subversive or conservative? Most of these books written before 1950 were essentially conservative.

The nature of a fictional girls' group was determined by its members and also by its mentors. Some stories included a strong adult—a parent, or aunt or teacher who provided the superego's viewpoint. Others presented the girls directly without much outside perspective One simple 1940s series called *Betsy, Tacy and Tib*, by Maud Hart Lovelace, appealed to younger readers, who enjoyed watching the three little girls discover they were similar but also a bit different. Brunette Betsy was imaginative and impetuous and bossy, redhaired Tacy was shy and romantic and docile, and blonde Tib was cute and practical and independent. They worked out these identities in relation to each other through small escapades like trying to fly off a roof, cutting each other's hair, and venturing to the poor, "ethnic" side of town. Books like this are about what you *are*, and how that relates to what everyone else is—they are not about what you *do*.

Betsy, Tacy, and Tib set up a club self-consciously with rules and goals and secrets: they decided they were all three in love with the young King of Spain; they all agreed to use grownup expressions like "indeed"; and so on. Betsy had the most forceful personality and was something of a leader, but her status was challenged easily and often. They all respected the *idea* of their group, not any special member within it. The girls had no particular mentor, but clearly had ingested the teachings of the adult world around them: they formed the TCKC, "The Christian Kindness Club." "IT'S ABOUT BEING GOOD," SAID TACY. "AND WE'LL NEVER GET TO BE GOOD IF WE DON'T PUNISH OURSELVES FOR BEING BAD." Each wore a little bag on a string around her neck and put in a stone every time she did something bad, as a punishment. Soon they were competing to do bad things, each hoping to get the most punishment. The author in 1941 thought this scene was a great joke. In the 1990s, it seems a particularly horrid masochistic example of girls who knew just what was expected of them, first in play and then more seriously in later life.

Some group stories were as elaborately patterned as the *Mystery Stories for Girls, Four Complete Books* in one volume that I read numerous times as a middle-sized girl. The emphasis on character and connectedness in these books is especially noticeable when they are compared with the companion volume put out by the same publisher at the same period: *Mystery and Adventure Stories for Boys*. Each volume contains four 200-page novels but the boys' volume, written by three different authors, presents four sets of characters in different settings while the girls' volume, written by a single author, Agnes Miller, describes one set of girls together in four different adventures.

In these two companion books, the writing style fit the content: The boys' stories went in for fast-paced, disconnected actions described in an unsubtle factual style, while the girls' mysteries, written in a more emotional style, always wove things together—relationships were strengthened, past and present were linked, and clues were connected to explain the unknown. Coincidence and luck played a large part in much girls' fiction. The easy solutions in these books were often preposterous but seemed all right because the whole texture of the girls' stories was so interwoven with connections. Living in such a world, the characters solved mysteries by discovering hidden links among seemingly separate people and events. Along with logic and observation, they used intuition.

Thus, in one of these stories, members of the Linger-Not Club discovered that an orphan girl was the heir to a merchant drowned in a nineteenth-century clipper ship; and in another they restored a lost family necklace to a poor Russian immigrant girl. The Linger-Not stories I liked best took place near the girls' New York neighborhood. In one they discovered a military secret from the Revolutionary War by finding the secret message sewn into a sampler by a girl of the eighteenth century. The other story told the romantic tale of a link from the historic chain spread over the Hudson River below West Point to stop the British; the Linger-Not girls encountered a feud between two local families whose ancestors had forged the original chain and had received a link from the chain in honor of their contribution. When the partnership turned into a feud, each family had kept one half of the broken link. Now the Linger-Not girls came along, had the two pieces forged anew into one link, and persuaded the families to end their quarrel. You couldn't get a clearer metaphor for what girls do: they mend and create links among themselves and other people.

A child reading these linked stories was perhaps pleased to know that everything connected and there was an important place in the circle for every kind of girl. Evelyn the writer and Rose the studious one solved the first mystery; Priscilla the gracious leader and Dorothy the down-to-earth athlete solved the second; Helena the sophisticated, musical one and Aline the motherly one solved the third; and the trio of younger girl buddies solved the fourth—quiet, clever Muriel, sensible Joyce, and mischievous Virginia. The members helped outsiders with their problems and, even more important, they helped each other improve their personalities and relationships. Rose became less withdrawn, Virginia became more responsible and, as convention always dictated, Helena became less snobbish and selfish.

Most characters in girl-group stories exhibited some such personality flaw; they tended toward an extreme and, in the view of the author, needed to be pushed toward the socially accepted mean. It was fine to have an individual talent—to be scholarly or athletic or literary—as long as you didn't go too far. Individual talents must not challenge the primary value of the Club; rather, they must contribute to it. Any member who put her own selfish whims first, like Helena, must be shown her error. This selfish character type appeared in every girl-group book I can think of. It's a variant on the situation in books like *What Katy Did* where the influence of an adult, usually a mother or other family member, taught a girl to subordinate her wishes to the needs of others. Here the social coercion was more subtle and more attractive: her own *peers* were working to socialize her through their group, not an older authority figure. The force of the superego is muted when embodied in a girl group like the Linger-Nots, but it's still the superego.

I especially liked books that had explicit, hovering, adult superego figures as well as girl group members. Dorothy Lyons's *Silver Birch* (1939), like the *Mystery Stories for Girls*, described a girls' group created by the girls themselves; it also presented loudly the voice of the girls' mentor and Girl Scout leader. Aunt Lou provided practical help, advice, and praise. She also provided a good scolding when necessary: "I'M ASHAMED OF BOTH YOU GIRLS! TO THINK WE SHOULD HAVE SUCH A SCENE AT THE PATROL'S FIRST CAMP. REMEMBER THAT THE SCOUT LAWS ARE MADE FOR YOU TO LIVE BY. THEY ARE TEN SOUND RULES THAT OUGHT TO GOVERN YOU EVERY

MINUTE THROUGHOUT YOUR WHOLE LIFE." So the Pegasus Patrol was watched over by a diligent Aunt-type and also by the wondrous standards of the whole Girl Scout organization.

Girls like me, eager for approval, found books like this especially titillating because they created, on top of the supportive girls' group, several layers of adult opinion—perhaps several different mentor characters backed up by a judging narrator or by some disembodied ideal such as that of the Girl Scouts. The girls in *Silver Birch* had this typical kind of adult support and they themselves covered the typical spectrum of club members: spunky Connie and reserved Di and impulsive Bing and sickly Martha and so on, all learning to conform so as to be more worthy of their little society. And of course there was snobbish Ann, who had to be chastened through the trauma of a near-tragedy.

This group of girls was typical but had an unusual goal: living in farm country they all loved to ride and several owned horses, so they decided to form a mounted Girl Scout patrol. On top of bonding together and improving their individual selves, they had to find horses for everybody and even learn to ride together, in formation. Just as the Linger-Not members embodied their ideal of connection in the metaphor of the Revolutionary War chain, the Pegasus Patrol acted out their relationships in their riding demonstrations at parades and horse shows. Their synchronized riding reinforced and displayed the harmonious relations within the group; it also won them approval from their leader, parents, neighbors, and no doubt the Girl Scouts of America. The sequel, *Midnight Moon*, showed the girls at the height of their glory riding with a drill team: SIXTEEN HORSES SWUNG INTO A DIFFERENT MOVEMENT LIKE MECHANICAL MOUNTS. THEY DISCOVERED THE JOY OF PERFECTION AND THE FUN OF BEING ONE PART OF A HARMONIOUS WHOLE.

For a few summers, at my pleasant summer camp in Maine, I was actually part of a Group of Chums. Jo (yes, she really was called Jo) was athletic and rebellious, Sally was fun and cute and nice, Susie was competent and sensible and witty, Debby was smart and imaginative. We felt a real, comfortable balance completing each other. When I humiliated myself at some activity like tennis, I could forgive myself because my roommate was Jo, the camp's top athlete. It was a little embarrassing for me, though, as we got older: One summer we became Counselors-in-Training, each CIT being assigned to work with some camp activity. Where to put Debby? They came up with a satisfactory answer—Put her in the kitchen. I became helper to two sweet old-lady cooks, learned the fastest, tidiest way to peel forty-five potatoes, and supervised camper dishwashing crews. It's true that I also handled the Camp Log that held the summer's history, and ran the little theatricals, so I was not totally a Cinderella Wimp. But I especially liked the safe, non-competitive kitchen work, and took full advantage of my opportunities to sneak into the walk-in refrigerator and eat leftover pie.

The Alcott books and the Little Colonel books by Annie Fellows Johnston offered the best examples of girls together hearing multiple voices explaining how to be good. The first Little Colonel short stories (1896) merely told simple stories of Lloyd Sherman, the little girl who had the stubbornness of her grandfather, the fierce Old Colonel, and also the charm of her lovely grandmother. But starting with the full-length *The Little Colonel's House Party* (1900) the books were infused with a heavy sense of moral and social duty, and the focus broadened from one little girl to a whole bunch of girl characters. Each girl had to learn to make moral choices, and the setting for those choices was the small world of friends and mentors who encouraged and challenged her. Their world was Lloydsboro Valley, a Kentucky town full of gracious plantations and happy darkies; a paradise for its privileged (white) children, but a paradise where bad actions brought terrible consequences.

Thus, *The Little Colonel's House Party* is not just another episodic bunch of childhood anecdotes: it is a succulent stew of praise and blame, selfishness and humility and duty and forgiveness—all those interpersonal issues so fascinating to group-oriented girls. I was a serious child but my serious thoughts were not religious; church was only a pleasant place we went on Easter. The sort of preaching I found in the Little Colonel Books, *that* was my scripture, my code of ideals transcending but guiding the group. Curious about these books that were formative in my development, my husband tried to read *The Little Colonel's House Party*. To him it was not boring or silly but incomprehensible—he literally could not figure out what those girls were talking and worrying about. There may be an analogy in my own reaction, then and now, to *Treasure Island*—I have never been able to fathom the relations among Jim and the pirates, why they were as they were and why they were interesting. Their moral issues are not mine. Perhaps a well-balanced person of either gender could appreciate both traditionally female issues that involve community *and* traditionally male ones that involve competition.

What I did understand was Lloyd and Betty and Eugenia and Joyce, all together for a summer month at "The Locusts." Eugenia, Lloyd's motherless cousin from New York, had the most to learn from this newly-formed group. A typical bad girl character—spoiled, vain, supercilious—she did great harm by ignoring her duty to the group and its mentor. Eugenia insisted that the girls visit a Gypsy camp, even though Lloyd's mother had refused permission. She violated the group code by disobeying and lying and putting her whims ahead of the good of the group, and she caused them all to catch measles from the Gypsies. (Swarthy ethnic people in these books were depicted as dirty and diseased.)

At the other end of the moral spectrum from mischievous Eugenia was Betty, saintly like *Little Women*'s Beth. A poor orphan who did housework for a farm family, Betty was overjoyed when Mrs. Sherman, her mother's childhood friend, invited her to the house party. Betty was a docile, selfless girl but in spite of her desire to please she would never do what she knew was wrong; she therefore refused to join Eugenia's trip to the Gypsies. The innocent one always suffered most, so when Betty caught the measles from the other girls it was a serious case and she almost went blind. Selfish Eugenia was transformed by remorse and became a worthy member of the group. Betty couldn't improve much, being close to perfect, but did become less shy, more confident, and more willing to accept help. The third guest, Joyce, came from a hearty middle-class family in the west. She learned to be herself, a sensible cheerful girl, and to ignore pretensions of snobs like

Eugenia. Lloyd's lesson was to be more considerate, less willful: as a rich only child, beautiful and clever, she had never thought about the needs of others.

In this series, whenever the girls were involved in a moral crisis someone told them or read them an uplifting legend or parable. In the house party book, Betty's illness made her particularly unhappy because she didn't want to be a burden to Lloyd's family: she was trying to build a "Road of the Loving Heart" like the one built by Samoans for their beloved leader, Robert Louis Stevenson. Betty showed her friends her tattered magazine clipping about Stevenson's last years, which he devoted to helping the Samoans. In gratitude the old chieftains undertook the backbreaking task of building a road that he needed, through the jungle. The four Lloydsboro girls took this tale as their inspiration; each one vowed to build a smooth Road of the Loving Heart for everyone around her, with no stones or unpleasant memories. Eugenia realized, "EVERY DAY I'VE LIVED I'VE LEFT A WHOLE ROAD FULL OF STONES FOR SOMEBODY TO JOLT OVER," and as a reminder she bought each of the girls a gold ring engraved with the word "Tusitala," Stevenson's Samoan name. Betty confessed, "IT WILL BE HARDER TO DO NOW THAT I AM BLIND, BECAUSE I CAN'T HELP BEING A CARE TO EVERYBODY, BUT GODMOTHER SAYS PEOPLE WON'T MIND IF I'LL ONLY BE PLEASANT AND CHEERFUL ABOUT MY MISFORTUNE." She regained her sight, and never lost her cheerfulness.

This cloying fervor for moral improvement pervades all the Little Colonel books. At Lloyd's house party there were picnics and magic lantern festivals and lounging on the lawn, puppies and ponies for everyone—but most of all, each girl treasured the group bond and her own role within the group. The safety of belonging was central; the greatest satisfaction was becoming more worthy of membership and being recognized as worthy. You could have it both ways, a comfortable sense of one's virtue along with lesser satisfactions like a private bedroom with crystal candlesticks, white Angora rugs, and dainty toilet articles of gold and ivory, or a party like this one: GAY BUTTERFLIES WERE POISED EVERYWHERE, ON THE FLOWERS, THE CANDLE-SHADES, THE CURTAINS. THE MENU CARDS WERE DECORATED WITH THEM, THE FINE HAND-PAINTED CHINA BORE SWARMS OF THEM AROUND THEIR DAINTY RIMS, AND EVEN THE

ICES WERE MOULDED TO REPRESENT THEM. THE LITTLE HOSTESS HER-
SELF WORE A GAUZY DRESS OF PALEST BLUE, EMBROIDERED IN BUTTER-
FLIES AND BUTTERFLIES WERE CAUGHT HERE AND THERE IN HER
GOLDEN CURLS. I tormented my mother about birthday parties—
why couldn't she reproduce this one?

Once Lloyd's core group was established in *House Party*, its
membership expanded or shifted slightly in later books, but a
group was always central. Each story featured its own setting.
There were two boarding schools, a tour of Europe, a ranch in
Arizona, several seasons in Lloydsboro Valley. In each location
Lloyd and her friends were shown moving into some new phase
of moral and social development, with common themes elabo-
rated in different ways—sympathy, loyalty, responsibility, self-
denial, kindness (the patronizing sort) to outsiders. Group stories
like this gave each character and each reader a haven between the
past (with its family group all-important to small children) and
the future (with the outside world adolescents move into). The
girls' group strengthened its members and helped them meet that
world. The danger was that the group would also constrict its
members, requiring them to suppress their selves and their wishes
and grow only in conventional directions.

It's true that Joyce wanted to be an artist and Betty a writer,
but not for personal fulfillment—only in order to support and
honor their loved ones. At the age of fourteen Lloyd told her father (in her saccharine accent) about her own ambition: to "NOT
DO ANY MOAH THAN JUST GATHAH UP EACH DAY'S HONEY AS IT COMES
AND LAY UP A HIVE FULL OF SWEET MEMORIES FOR MYSELF AND OTHAH
PEOPLE." And that's what she did. After boarding school and a
debutante season she wed her childhood chum and settled down
to gather honey and radiate joy throughout the Valley. Any self-
sacrifices required in these books were not too painful because a
reward usually followed that was more delightful than whatever
you gave up.

For readability's sake it's fortunate that the Little Colonel books
described so much girlish fun, because the bombardment of in-
spirational messages was enormous. There were always pills under the sugarcoating. Along with the Tusitala story there were
allegories of the would-be knight Ederyn faithfully "Keeping the

Tryst," of Shapur with his lame camel patiently toiling in the Desert of Waiting, of Hildegarde refusing to give away the golden mantle (of virginity) until it was certain to fit a worthy prince. One of the girls or the elders would read or recite these legends to the group, thus binding the members together more firmly with a secular version of saints' lives. There were quotations from *Pilgrim's Progress* and *The Vicar of Wakefield*, scenes from *Idylls of the King*, accounts of Clara Barton's exemplary life. Dozens of mentors' voices urged the girls on to a life of self-improvement—mothers, aunts, teachers, occasionally a father or kindly male doctor.

This was an unusually hypnotic, satisfying series because it showed virtue to be often easy, usually rewarded, and always picturesque; and because individual effort toward virtue was guided by kindly mentors and supported by devoted friends. If I had to name one author whose influence most pervaded and perverted my childhood, it would have to be Annie Fellows Johnston. Her world was softer and more sustained than Alcott's and there was more of it (I read nine Little Colonel books, while Alcott wrote only three about the March family). I was too obtuse to notice Johnston's racism and the gross Negro dialect she invented.

Although their social perspective was distorted, the girls in the Little Colonel books seemed real and their struggles seemed important—learning to get along with each other and earn the praise of their elders. Another series presented a circle of privileged children in a more simplistic way that seemed silly even to my tolerant taste. Nonetheless, I found it irresistible. *Maida's Little Shop* (1909) introduced a sweet, wan, rich little invalid who had been cured of her physical malady but was still wasting away because she didn't know how to live or what to live for. Only when she was given a tiny shop to run in a lower-middle-class Boston neighborhood did she become energetic and cheerful.

Selling toys and candies and pencils to the neighborhood, Maida made friends with real children. They formed a club of three girls and three boys, the Big Six, and allowed the younger children in as a satellite gang, the Little Six. The actions and relationships of this group were bland and boring, merely demonstrating old stereotypes—one girl was charming and smart, one energetic, one artistic; the boys were an explorer, a scholar, and a military sort. When Rosie the tomboy said, "I HATE EVERY SINGLE THING YOU LIKE, LAURA. BUT I'M GLAD YOU LIKE IT BECAUSE THEN I DON'T HAVE TO DO IT," she was referring to more than household chores—she was articulating the notion that a girl is incomplete and becomes a whole person only through her group. The Maida books may have described an equal number of boys and girls but they were unquestionably girls' books, depicting girls who must join together in order to amount to anything at all. It's a rehearsal for the next stage, when each must join with a husband in order to amount to anything.

The main thing worth noting about the Maida series is the amazing role of the children's mentors: the children by themselves seemed to have no ability to think or act, almost no volition. Benevolent adults (in this series, almost always men) arranged all the fun. Maida's father was a billionaire financier who once gave her her weight in silver dollars. When she was convalescing he bought her the little shop she admired; in each later book he planned and executed some grand enterprise for the whole bunch of children such as building or buying them a houseboat, a camp, and a whole historic village. In the second book they took over the "little" house behind his mansion for the summer. The idea was that the children would learn housekeeping, gardening, and responsibility; the presence of four nurturing adults living in the little house, however, and the authority of Maida's father behind the whole project made it clear that everything was being managed by grownups. The children had little opportunity for responsibility and less inclination.

Many scenes in many of the books started out with the children lounging about on the grass moaning that they didn't know what to do with themselves—and then Maida would appear with the news that her amazing father (called "Buffalo" Westabrook by the press) had come up with another way to entertain her and her friends. Other times the father's protegé, a strange, elfin writer with unlimited time to play with the children, would come up with a plan. The fatuity of the children was so great that any tiny sign of initiative brought an awed response: on a nice summer day Laura suggested a picnic and

Maida replied, "OH LAURA! WHAT A WONDERFUL IDEA! I LOVE PIC-NICS TOO! HOW DID YOU COME TO THINK OF IT?" The Maida books were the apotheosis of passivity.

As I reread these girls' stories recently to see how they treated girls in groups, I was not surprised to see how dependent the characters were on each other. What I had not realized was how deeply and obviously the girls, supposedly playing their own games together, were controlled by their world and its expectations—how dependent they were on the powers around and above them. Maida's feeble bunch of friends is only the most blatant example; The Little Colonel, Betsy and Tacy and Tib, the girls of the Pegasus Patrol, the Little Peppers, and most of the others were constantly manipulated by their loving mentors in small matters and large. In books about groups for boys, an authority figure like King Arthur or a football coach may have supervised the proceedings but such figures were not so prominent or so interfering. In girls' groups the autonomy of the individual was greatly restricted: by her loyal peers and her loving elders and particularly by the code of behavior constantly drilled into her by those elders. Most of the girls welcomed these restrictions, endorsing them in playful versions of the adult code—as in this passage from *What Katy Did At School*:

KATY WAS CHOSEN PRESIDENT, AND PROCEEDED TO READ THE BY-LAWS, WHICH HAD BEEN COPIED ON AN IMMENSE SHEET OF BLUE PA-PER. THEY RAN THUS:—CONSTITUTION OF THE SOCIETY FOR THE SUPPRESSION OF UNLADYLIKE CONDUCT. THE OBJECT OF THIS SOCIETY IS TWOFOLD: IT COMBINES HAVING A GOOD TIME WITH THE PURSUIT OF VIRTUE. VIRTUE IS TO BE PURSUED AT ALL TIMES AND IN ALL SEASONS, BY THE MEMBERS OF THE SOCIETY SETTING THEIR FACES AGAINST THE PRACTICE OF BOWING AND SPEAKING TO YOUNG GENTLEMEN WHO ARE NOT ACQUAINTANCES; WAVING OF POCKET-HANDKERCHIEFS, SIGNALS FROM WINDOWS, AND ANY SPECIES OF CONDUCT WHICH WOULD BE THOUGHT UNLADYLIKE BY NICE PEOPLE ANYWHERE, AND ESPECIALLY BY THE MAMMAS OF THE SOCIETY.

In the English Swallows and Amazons series of the 1930s and 1940s, Arthur Ransome created a world where both boys and girls showed imagination and initiative in creating adventures, an anti-Maida sort of world. These books described a bold, competent gang of individuals in which girls outnumbered boys, five to three. (There's a kind of affirmative action here—because boys in children's fiction have dominated girls for so long, you need a larger number of girls than boys in order to give an impression of equal weight.) The only American series I know from the first half of this century with such a balance of male and female power, and with more than one strong female character, was Walter R. Brooks's Freddy the Pig series (1940s). At that time the idea of independent, forceful women was so alien that it appeared mostly in a few fantasy worlds. In Freddy's stories the large, sensible cow became mayor of the barnyard and every animal was encouraged to do what he or she could do best. But *realistic* series about children's groups couldn't handle such radical notions.

Complications in the Self and in the Group

Group stories for girls, then, pushed a distinctly conservative viewpoint about the relations of girls' groups to the adult world. It is not surprising that relations among the girls themselves were also conservative: the challenge faced by a typical girl, learning to deal with her peers, was to subdue her individuality, not to develop it. It's the process described by Gilligan whereby the adolescent girl gradually loses confidence and voice, the opposite of empowerment. Katy and the Little Colonel and Maida and the Pegasus Girl Scouts and the Peppers and the Linger-Nots Club and other sociable young women wanted to become better listeners, not better speakers. When a few girls had individual goals, like Connie taming the wild horse Silver Birch or the Little Colonel's Betty writing a novel, their goals (since they were good girls) were the kind that supported the group and did not threaten it in any way.

Meanness and quarrelling were seldom seen among the nice members of a fictional girls' group; these were reserved for the scapegoat character, the conceited one who ultimately learned to think of others before herself. Brown and Gilligan's *Meeting at the Crossroads* describes the serious, painful work real-life girls must do (in the 1990s as in earlier periods) to resolve the tension between respect for themselves and respect for their friends. Most girls and women have experienced the teasing and whispering and cruelty that occur in these years of intense negotiation, as victim or aggressor or both. But in the stories I read and reread as a child, such meanness was not acknowledged; it was considered unusual and curable. Competition was not recognized as important or normal. No one questioned that the desirable pattern of a girl's development involved abandoning an immature "selfishness" in favor of gracefully integrating into her peer group and then into the larger world.

I used to like how clearcut the problems were in these stories, how obvious the solutions. I read them over and over, reassuring myself that the complexities in my own friendships didn't really exist. In fact, my real-life classmates went in for Byzantine, shifting alliances. They badgered nonconformists and shy girls; minor victims would join in tormenting major victims. I tried to be inoffensive, but many recess periods I spent crouching in the big wooden box where rubber balls were kept, while the top girls who put me there for some unknown crime sat on the lid and laughed. I never learned to stand up to bullies—certainly my books didn't show me how. I used indirect methods to placate my peers, like lowering my grades with deliberate mistakes on math tests. Girls like me expected to reduce aggression through passive pleasantness.

In the stories I liked best, meanness was rare and quickly regretted. One time Lloyd, the Little Colonel, was haughty to a spoiled, lonely girl in a hotel but soon realized how insensitive she had been: "OH, IF I HAD ONLY KNOWN! I FEEL TOO MEAN FOR ANYTHING! MOTHAH TOLD ME I OUGHT TO PUT MYSELF IN HER PLACE, AND MAKE ALLOWANCES FOR HER, BUT I DIDN'T WANT TO EVEN TRY. I'M GOIN' TO WRITE TO HER THE MINUTE I FINISH POLISHIN' MY NAILS, AND TELL HER HOW SORRY I AM THAT I DIDN'T LEAVE A KINDAH MEMORY BEHIND ME." Lloyd's remorse was sincere, but not so excessive as to prevent her from polishing her nails properly.

So fictional girls who were friendly and flexible worked out their differences easily. Storybook girls didn't learn to cope with aggression and competition in themselves or others, children or adults. They could remain admirably weak as individuals—not needing to accomplish anything on their own—and could still absorb strength from their collectivity.

The better, more complex, books, went beyond assigning simple labels to different kinds of girl characters; they revealed unresolved tensions between a girl's allegiance to her society and her need to develop a self of her own. In the girls' books that were most interesting and perhaps most popular, the central girl was ambivalent—active and passive, competent and confused, strong and weak, at once, in a single character. My contemporaries and I read children's books in a transitional period when women were becoming less certain that they should lead passive lives following society's expectations, but weren't yet completely certain that they shouldn't. Our favorite stories reflected this doubleness.

I am thinking, for instance, of Heidi, well loved since 1880. A nice child but not cloyingly sweet, she spoke abruptly and did unexpected things. Heidi at the age of five climbed the mountain with her aunt, who had bundled her up in two heavy dresses. Going unafraid to live with a grandfather she had never met, she responded to the bright, wild landscape by removing her shoes and dresses and capering about in her underwear. Presumably nineteenth-century Swiss underwear involved a substantial amount of discreet cloth; even so, this was a bold thing to do. But Heidi's stay in Frankfurt revealed the other side of her character— depressingly soppy. Her posture of Christian submissiveness was alarming, as were effusions like "OH, HOW GLAD I AM THAT THE DEAR LORD DID NOT GRANT WHAT I ASKED AND LONGED FOR!" By the end of the book, Heidi's brusque independence was less conspicuous than her pious, vapid docility.

Nancy Drew was another two-sided girl, both daring and cautious; independent and conventional. Sometimes her ideas and actions were really dumb ("PERHAPS A BIRD FLEW IN AN OPEN WINDOW AND TOOK THE PIN"), while other times her competence and courage were staggering, as when she saved an unconscious captain in a shipwreck. A villain soon found that she STOOD HER GROUND; HE WAS NOT DEALING WITH A GIRL WHO COULD BE BLUFFED. She would zip about town in her roadster, stirring up adventure. But she also loved lunching and shopping with her buddies (flow-

ered crepe gowns, high-heeled slippers). NANCY SPENT A RESTLESS
DAY IDLING ABOUT THE HOUSE. SHE CLEANED THE ATTIC, ACCOM-
PLISHED A LITTLE SEWING AND PRACTICED ON THE PIANO, YET TIME
HUNG HEAVY UPON HER HANDS. Nancy's fans learned that young
women could be smart, stubborn, and skillful. They also learned
young women could live comfortably at home with no plans or
goals, indulged by a father and a housekeeper. Nancy never
changed or developed herself. At least she had a self, shallow and
elitist though it was.

Even Lewis Carroll's Alice, whom we remember as so cool and
bold in her adventures, worried terribly about politeness and tact
and rules. She tried not to give offence or hurt anyone's feelings
(like the ridiculous Tweedledum and Tweedledee); she scolded
her kittens for misbehavior ("SIT UP A LITTLE MORE STIFFLY, DEAR!"
"CURTSEY WHILE YOU'RE THINKING WHAT TO PURR"); she went in for
moralizing words like "rude," "fault," "disgrace," and "reproach-
ful." Yet her toughness in an unmanageable universe was heroic.
Even when she could not stop things from happening, like a drink
making her bigger and a cake making her smaller, Alice tried to
understand what caused the change and use the knowledge to
help herself. She tried to make rational plans, which is not easy
in a world where you run the opposite way to get where you
want to go and you are ordered about by animals. "THE FIRST
THING I'VE GOT TO DO IS TO GROW TO MY RIGHT SIZE AGAIN, AND THE
SECOND THING IS TO FIND MY WAY INTO THAT LOVELY GARDEN. THAT
WILL BE THE BEST PLAN."

She stood up for herself, literally: ALICE WAS DOUBTFUL WHETHER
SHE OUGHT NOT TO LIE DOWN ON HER FACE LIKE THE GARDENERS, BUT
SHE COULD NOT REMEMBER HAVING HEARD OF SUCH A RULE AT PRO-
CESSIONS; "AND BESIDES, WHAT WOULD BE THE USE OF A PROCESSION,"
THOUGHT SHE, "IF PEOPLE HAD TO LIE DOWN SO THEY COULDN'T SEE
IT?" SO SHE STOOD WHERE SHE WAS. Alice persisted until she reached
her goal of becoming a queen—"I DON'T WANT TO BE ANYBODY'S
PRISONER"—but she always acted polite, concealed her true feel-
ings, and curtsied a lot.

This mixture of propriety and strength appeared in its most
extreme form in Mary Poppins—a young nanny who tidied the
nursery and ran errands, *and* an ancient sorceress who climbed

stairs by sliding up the banister. From Mary Poppins girls learned to resist bullies and help outsiders and ride through the air on peppermint-stick horses. And girls learned to admire themselves instead of seeking admiration from others: Mary liked to look at herself and her new blouse in store windows not out of uncertainty but out of an overflow of self-satisfaction. SHE THOUGHT THAT, ON THE WHOLE, SHE HAD NEVER SEEN ANYBODY LOOKING QUITE SO SMART AND DISTINGUISHED.

It's splendid that a nanny might really be a powerful wise-woman, but this can be seen the other way round: a wisewoman must hide her identity and take on the disguise of a nanny. It's a complicated image of female strength. Before she left at the end of the second book (*Mary Poppins Comes Back*, 1935), whirling into the dusk on a flying merry-go-round, Mary Poppins said, "JANE! TAKE CARE OF MICHAEL AND THE TWINS!" AND SHE LIFTED JANE'S HAND AND PUT IT GENTLY ON THE HANDLE OF THE PERAMBULATOR. She was passing on to Jane her skill in caring for people. Will Jane also conquer tyrants and dance with the Sun, like Mary Poppins? Jane will grow up responsible, but will she be able to fly? The children shared Mary's adventures in a context of conventional propriety; Mary denied all the magical events the children knew really happened. Even with her own Jane and Michael, Mary Poppins maintained the façade of ordinary propriety. "NO MORE NON-SENSE!" "SPIT SPOT INTO BED!" "SIT STILL, PLEASE—YOU'RE NOT PERFORMING MICE!" Mary Poppins gave her protegée a gift Jane would never forget—the swirling dance of the universe; she also gave Jane the gift of civilized hypocrisy and lies.

The saddest case of ambivalence is Mary Lennox in *The Secret Garden* (1911), because the ambivalence lies not in Mary's character but in her author: Mary herself never weakened but her creator "disappeared" her at the end of the book, so her position in her world weakened terribly. The grumpy little orphan from India, transported to a lonely Yorkshire mansion, stayed clever and stubborn. With no governness or school, she also became resourceful and independent and thoughtful.

She was actually growing up. At one point Mary discovered the door not only into the secret garden but also, unconsciously, into her sexual nature: Gazing at the garden wall, Mary spied something under tendrils of ivy—A ROUND KNOB WHICH HAD BEEN COVERED BY THE LEAVES HANGING OVER IT. SHE PUT HER HANDS UNDER THE LEAVES AND BEGAN TO PULL AND PUSH THEM ASIDE. MARY'S HEART BEGAN TO THUMP AND HER HANDS TO SHAKE A LITTLE IN HER DELIGHT AND EXCITEMENT. WHAT WAS THIS UNDER HER HANDS WHICH HER FINGERS FOUND A HOLE IN? (Bobbie Ann Mason noticed a similar scene in Nancy Drew and I found another: FLASHING HER LIGHT INTO THE CLOSET, SHE FOCUSED IT UPON THE KNOB. IT WAS A TINY THING AND APPEARED TO HAVE NO SPECIAL PURPOSE. CURIOUSLY, NANCY TWISTED THE KNOB. IN THE DIM LIGHT SHE COULD MAKE OUT A LONG CRACK. "I BELIEVE I'VE STUMBLED UPON SOMETHING IMPORTANT," NANCY THOUGHT EXCITEDLY.)

Mary and her invalid cousin Colin expanded and found their true shapes, by sharing the magic of springtime in the garden. She brought the wretched youth out from his dark sickroom into the sunlight. When Colin's brooding father came home and found his crippled son running about, however, Mary moved to the edge of the scene while everyone admired Colin: he would be strong enough to grow into a true, bullying master of Mistlethwaite Manor. Mary appears hardly at all in the last thirty pages, and is not mentioned in the last four pages (as Shirley Foster and Judy Simons have noted). *The Secret Garden* created a wonderful group of equals supporting one another—Mary, Colin, the nature boy Dickon, Dickon's wholesome mother and sister, and the old gardener—until Burnett's devotion to the male aristocracy caused her to destroy the nurturing group, deify Colin, and abandon Mary.

Speaking of tensions between the self and the group, my own favorite emotion was guilt. Girls constantly worried about what might be wrong in their behavior, speech, or appearance, and suspected that anything wrong in their world was their fault. Not all girls were like this—my sister certainly wasn't—but I felt guilty all the time. Feeling wretchedly guilty about reading my father's memoirs of Casanova on the sly, skipping piano practice, listening to the Lux Radio Theatre under the blanket when I was supposed to be asleep?—these sins were dumb and dreary, not worth such fear and shame.

The high priestess of guilt was Jo March, whose guilts were of a much more serious order. Many readers remember only her independent side: At sixteen she proclaimed, "I WANT TO DO SOMETHING SPLENDID—SOMETHING HEROIC, OR WONDERFUL. I MEAN TO ASTONISH YOU ALL SOME DAY." Jo's split character was aggressive but eager to please, bold but anxious. Marmee and Father knew exactly what was bad in Jo, telling her so in little sermons; and the narrator knew they were right. (WRONG-DOING ALWAYS BRINGS ITS OWN PUNISHMENT; AND, WHEN JO MOST NEEDED HERS, SHE GOT IT, said the narrating voice smugly when Jo was writing sleazy stories for money; SHE WAS BEGINNING TO DESECRATE SOME OF THE WOMANLIEST ATTRIBUTES OF A WOMAN'S CHARACTER.)

Jo herself knew those kindly critics were right, she was deeply wicked. Her family newsletter contained a Weekly Report: "MEG—GOOD. JO—BAD. BETH—VERY GOOD. AMY—MIDDLING." A reader could admire Jo's blunt, unladylike behavior but would also hear and perhaps believe the constant, despairing wail of her self-flagellation: "IT'S MY DREADFUL TEMPER! I TRY TO CURE IT; AND THEN IT BREAKS OUT WORSE THAN EVER. I'M AFRAID I SHALL DO SOMETHING DREADFUL SOME DAY, AND MAKE EVERYBODY HATE ME." She yearned to be boyish and free but even more she wanted to be good, and her efforts gradually paid off. She worked on keeping her temper, paying social calls politely, doing chores without complaint.

If you read *Little Women* carefully, you realize Jo was painfully torn, often thoroughly wretched. Why should jolly, "virile" Jo be depressed, tormented by guilt, pitifully dependent on the group—the approval of others? As Jerry Griswold points out (in *The Classic American Children's Story*, 1992), "Alcott hunts for and delivers the cloud in every silver lining that ensures that her characters will be left miserable." Many incidents explain Jo's chronic sense of unworthiness—little acts of rudeness, selfishness, disobedience. But the stain of her guilt ran deeper and could never be washed away. Within her general guiltiness there lay a specific, terrible offense. She knew that her penance must be everlasting: *for she knew that she herself killed her sister Beth.* Jo's youthful insistence on getting her own way led eventually to Beth's death—after which Jo renounced the idea of fulfilling herself, embracing instead the traditional role of the Good Girl loyal to the group or family.

It's right there in the text, as I recently noticed while rereading *Little Women* once again. Beth was the sister so lovable in childhood, so angelic in her final years, whose life was FULL OF THE SELF-FORGETFULNESS THAT MAKES THE HUMBLEST ON EARTH REMEMBERED SOONEST IN HEAVEN. (When reading this book I still find myself sobbing just about every time Beth is mentioned.) In the beginning Beth was not unhealthy, just timid. When Marmee went to Washington to tend the sick Father, a Civil War chaplain, the four healthy sisters stayed home being virtuous. Beth had been visiting the poor German family who were the Marches' pet charity. One day she begged Jo to go in her place, as the baby was sick and she didn't know what to do. Jo had already had scarlet fever and believed herself immune but she refused on feeble, selfish pretexts. So Beth went again herself, caught the disease, and began her journey toward death.

When Beth told her sister about the baby dying of scarlet fever, Jo moaned, "HOW DREADFUL FOR YOU! I OUGHT TO HAVE GONE. IF YOU SHOULD BE SICK I NEVER COULD FORGIVE MYSELF!" Beth did get sick and Jo insisted on nursing Beth herself "*BECAUSE IT'S MY FAULT SHE IS SICK;* I TOLD MOTHER I'D DO THE ERRANDS AND I HAVEN'T." After that Beth was DELICATE, NOT AN INVALID EXACTLY, BUT NEVER AGAIN THE HEALTHY CREATURE SHE HAD BEEN. Four years passed in which Beth wasted away and then she sweetly died. Jo was the most adoring nurse in her final days and the most heartbroken mourner at her death. But there was something deeply uncomfortable in Jo's sorrow about Beth. It is downright creepy the way Jo, in a terrible depression, tried to take Beth's place with the housework, humming among brooms and dishcloths. (SOMETHING OF HER HOUSEWIFELY SPIRIT SEEMED TO LINGER ROUND THE LITTLE MOP.)

No one in the story admitted why Jo was so devastated; but I am convinced Alcott wanted us to see Jo's responsibility and agree that her guilt could never be washed away. While a bad girl like Jo could improve her behavior and conformity to the group, she could not outgrow her strong will, her self. *Self* became a permanent danger, threatening harm to others. (A strong, willful girl can kill without meaning to, as when Dorothy's flying house landed in Oz and squashed the Wicked Witch.)

Years earlier Jo almost caused Amy to drown, an incident fore-shadowing her role in Beth's sickness: Jo was furious about something and failed to warn Amy that the ice was too thin to skate on. Amy crashed through and Jo COULD ONLY STAND MOTIONLESS, STARING AT THE LITTLE BLUE HOOD ABOVE THE BLACK WATER, while Laurie pulled her out. Later Jo sobbed to her mother, "IF SHE *SHOULD* DIE, IT WOULD BE MY FAULT. IT SEEMS AS IF I COULD DO ANYTHING WHEN I'M IN A PASSION; I COULD HURT ANY ONE, AND ENJOY IT." Only a continuing remorse, an acceptance of guilt and inadequacy, could partly atone for the awful things Jo did and might do when she insisted on her own needs, when she did such an antisocial thing as getting into a passion. She must always be vigilant. I understood this instinctively, in my early readings of *Little Women*. A girl could easily be guilty of all sorts of monstrous infractions.

At the end of *Little Women*, Jo rejected the heroic dreams that were so lovable in the young girl Jo. When Amy asked "DO YOU REMEMBER OUR CASTLES IN THE AIR?" Jo answered, "YES, I REMEMBER; BUT THE LIFE I WANTED THEN SEEMS SELFISH, LONELY AND COLD TO ME NOW." Jo March remains a wonderful hero for girls to admire. It's just that she was a more ambivalent, tormented hero than is usually recognized, and a sadder one. She developed a fine, quirky self until it tormented her, and she denied it—convinced that development of the self meant betrayal of the group.

· 6 ·

Girls and Boys—Conservative Romance

We knew, girls in the 1940s, that childhood work and play led straight to the one female goal—courtship and marriage. If some of us had ambitions to amount to something in the world outside the home, we never talked about it. I certainly had none. My mother, a social worker, worked before she married and after I reached junior high; but my own images and fantasies never went beyond the domestic scenes I admired in the *Ladies' Home Journal* and *Good Housekeeping*. Today the Martha Stewart kind of domestic dream serves as a piquant alternative to normal life— annoying to many people, nostalgically appealing to others. Back then when I was a sheltered WASP child, that was our world, a place where we learned how to knit argyle socks for men and how to color-coordinate ribbons and strawberries and cupcakes on Valentine's Day. Girls from prosperous families did go to college but many left to get married, or married soon after graduating. The perfect, romantic thing was a wedding the day after graduation in the white, chaste college chapel.

The books we read as young children aimed us at that wedding chapel. As we grew to puberty the message in our books became explicit, telling us exactly how and how not to behave, exactly what to think and feel, in the coming years. What action was a girl supposed to take in the serious courtship game? According to our books, only the most minimal, defensive, inactive sort of action. Yet we read them eagerly for hints and models.

My mother gave me embarrassing books of advice on teen behavior and sex—self-consciously cute sermons. The most vivid advice book was *Letters to Jane* (by Gladys Denny Shultz, 1947), in which troubled college girls corresponded with their friend Jane's understanding mother. By this period girls were less sheltered than in Alcott's time, even needing to fend off "wolves." One girl in *Letters to Jane* complained, "IT MAKES MY BLOOD BOIL WHEN BOYS GET SO FRESH WITH GIRLS WHO WANT TO BE DECENT. I'M NOT SAYING EVERY GIRL IS AN ANGEL. MANY OF US HAVE DONE THINGS WE'D GIVE AN ARM OR AN EYE TO SPONGE OUT, BUT IT WAS BECAUSE SOME FRESH WOLF TALKED US INTO IT." Jane's mother responded with gentle chiding, pointing out that usually girls are responsible for anything bad that happened to them: "YOUNG MEN OF THE AGE YOU ARE DEALING WITH ARE IN THE LUSTIEST FLOWER OF THE PROCREATIVE URGE. MANY GIRLS BRING UNPLEASANT EXPERIENCES ON THEMSELVES BY KISSING 'TOO LONG AND TOO EXPERTLY,' AS ONE MAN PUT IT, ON LONELY ROADSIDES. GIRLISH EBULLIENCE IS A THING SOME MEN MISCONSTRUE."

As late as the 1940s a girl could not do much to decide her fate—but more than ever she was to blame if things went wrong, even the most unforeseeable things. Consider, for instance, the dour maternal warning reported in a memoir by Beverly Cleary, author of the Ramona Quimby stories: " 'Never play leapfrog with boys,' she said. 'They might look up.' "

I respected the wise hints of my elders and vowed to avoid Fast Behavior. I agreed with the author that "Petting" was a terrible threat to a girl's happiness and "wholesome and lighthearted contacts" with boys were the key to a successful life. But Jane's story was obvious propaganda and focused too much on modern dangers we didn't want to think about. Identifying with lighthearted heroines like Judy in *Daddy-Long-Legs* and Laura in the *Little House* books, I entered their worlds and absorbed their ideals of female behavior.

Girls did take such stories seriously and read them voraciously. Books read by boys included virtually no scenes of courtship, while girls' books pullulated with romance. In many of the girls' series, a popular first book has no courtship plot but a later book gets the heroine married: notably, *Anne of Green Gables*, *Heidi*, *The Five Little Peppers*, and *Pollyanna*. Romances written for adults were also popular with girls at mid-century, novels such as *Gone with the Wind* and *Rebecca*.

A chorus of voices surrounded girls, guiding them toward marriage. I see now that the fictional suitors I liked best were bland characters. They were representative types, like those men I liked to make pictures of in my prepubescent years. In little rectangles I would draw men with permutations of clothes and hairstyles—striped, patterned, or dotted ties; solid or plaid jackets; dark or light hair sticking up in a crewcut or folding over to one side. They all had the same blank expression and squinty eyes. The variations did not disguise the fact that all these men were the same, merely pleasant instruments for fulfilling a girl's destiny. Women were not the only ones viewed as Objects in young people's minds and in their reading.

Courtship without Pain

Following her destiny, a girl was allowed only a few actions: she could *accept* a suitor, take subtle measures to *attract* a suitor, perhaps *select* from a group of suitors. Once the selection stage was passed, she could *help* him and she could *suffer* for him. Some popular courtship books described an easy, effortless drift into accepting marriage. Laura of the *Little House* books was an energetic girl who faced discomfort and danger bravely, yet her relations with the man who became her husband were amazingly passive. In *These Happy Golden Years* (1943) Laura, not yet sixteen, took a teaching job where she had to board with a crazy woman on an isolated farm. She disliked teaching and only took the job to help pay for her sister's school for the blind. The bright spot was going home on weekends. Laura was surprised and grateful when every Friday instead of her father a young neighbor farmer appeared at the school to fetch her home and when every Sunday he appeared at her home to take her back.

Gladly she let Almanzo Wilder rescue her without asking permission, swathe her in blankets, and carry her off in his sleigh. "IT'S LIKE FLYING!" LAURA SAID. THERE WAS NOT A JOLT NOR A JAR; THE LITTLE CUTTER SKIMMED THE SNOW AS SMOOTHLY AS A BIRD IN AIR. Their low-key courtship proceeded like that, as smoothly as a bird in air, with very little conversation or action. One ripple disturbed the smoothness: Another girl, vulgar and forward, tried to entice Wilder; but Laura knew there was no real threat.

During this brief spell of jealousy, Laura responded like most of the other girl characters I read about: passively. THE THOUGHT OF NELLIE OLESON JUST CROSSED HER MIND. BUT IF ALMANZO WANTED TO SEE HER AGAIN, HE KNEW WHERE SHE WAS. IT WAS NOT HER PLACE TO DO ANYTHING ABOUT IT, AND SHE DIDN'T INTEND TO. The two drifted peaceably for three years until one day Almanzo PICKED UP LAURA'S HAND AND HIS SUN-BROWNED HAND CLOSED GENTLY OVER IT. HE HAD NEVER DONE THAT BEFORE. "YOUR HAND IS SO SMALL," HE SAID. "I WAS WONDERING IF YOU WOULD LIKE AN ENGAGEMENT RING." "THAT WOULD DEPEND ON WHO OFFERED IT TO ME," LAURA TOLD HIM. After a week's pause and a few more bits of conversation, Laura finally said "IT IS A BEAUTIFUL RING. I THINK . . . I WOULD LIKE TO HAVE IT." "THEN LEAVE IT ON." She told him he could kiss her goodnight—for the first time—and went into the house while he drove away.

They had a simple wedding and moved right into the little cabin he had built for her. The mood was placid and loving, not intense. Laura's most passionate moment came when she said about Almanzo, "WE JUST SEEM TO BELONG TOGETHER." The reader comes away with a sense that Laura was extremely lucky such a good man happened to trot her way, because there was nothing she could have done about it except wait. She was a dutiful daughter and sister, a good friend, and a kindly teacher of small children; after learning to be this worthy person she received her reward. Laura's journey to marriage was as smooth as Almanzo's sleigh rides, NOT A JOLT NOR A JAR; and all the time she was pulled along happily while somebody else controlled the journey.

The courtship in *Heidi Grows Up* (1935) was briefer and even more primitive, and Heidi's role was even more passive. Teaching the village school, Heidi felt a yearning for something she couldn't quite identify: "SOMETIMES IN THE SCHOOLROOM I LONG TO BE UP ON THE MOUNTAIN WHERE I CAN STRETCH MY ARMS AND FEEL FREE." A few pages later, WHEN PETER, QUITE UNEXPECTEDLY, ASKED HEIDI TO MARRY HIM, SHE EXCLAIMED IN THE UTMOST SURPRISE, "WHY PETER! I THINK THAT MUST HAVE BEEN WHAT I WANTED." THEY PLANNED A STREET WEDDING SO THAT EVERYONE IN THE VILLAGE COULD TAKE PART IN THE BEAUTIFUL CEREMONY. And that was it.

Heidi's story and Laura's described the simplest kind of courtship, where the girl simply waited to be chosen. *Daddy-Long-Legs* (1912) showed another lively heroine falling happily into the arms of a wonderful suitor, but this is a more convoluted story—one with a weird, frightening perspective on relations between man and woman. The author, Jean Webster, was a great-niece of Mark Twain and had a bit of his humor and energy. In Judy Abbott she created a fine, saucy character: a teenage orphan sent to college by a Trustee of her orphanage. "Mr. Smith" announced through his man of business that Judy's expenses at Vassar would be taken care of; her only duties were to write Mr. Smith a monthly letter and respect his desire for anonymity.

His generous plan gave Judy freedom from drudgery and freedom to develop her talents as a person and a writer. The book is full of ambiguity about her freedom, however: it shows a young heroine controlled by a man (rich, wise, and considerably older) who knew what was best for her and who ended up marrying her. It is a twentieth-century version of uncomfortable Victorian plots where an older man raised a child ward to be his wife, but here the story was told from the viewpoint of the happy young girl. Judy's response to her new life was spirited and far from fawning. In her first letter she explained that a glimpse of her patron's shadow leaving the orphanage told her he was tall, and she would therefore address him as "Daddy-Long-Legs." She even teased him with guesses about his appearance: YOUR MOUTH IS A STRAIGHT LINE WITH A TENDENCY TO TURN DOWN AT THE CORNERS. OH, YOU SEE, I KNOW! YOU'RE A SNAPPY OLD THING WITH A TEMPER.

In college, joyously, she started to learn about herself and her world. In a letter to Daddy-Long-Legs she reported, THIS IS THE

FIRST CHANCE I'VE EVER HAD TO GET ACQUAINTED WITH JERUSHA AB-
BOTT. I THINK I'M GOING TO LIKE HER. She developed independent
opinions. By sophomore year she could say, I AM BEGINNING TO
FEEL AT HOME IN COLLEGE AND IN COMMAND OF THE SITUATION. Was
she really in command? She had not objected back when the orphanage matron announced that the Trustee was PLANNING TO
EDUCATE YOU TO BECOME A WRITER, but that had been the first clue
that this kindly gentleman thought he owned her life. Conflict
arose between her wishes and his orders. She was awarded a
scholarship which he instructed her to turn down. They clashed
over other decisions.

The reader gradually understands what Daddy-Long-Legs was
up to, because Judy's letters mentioned that the uncle of a rich
classmate began turning up on campus frequently, to take his
niece and Judy out for treats. Jervis Pendleton, a philanthropist
fourteen years older than Judy, had also (not coincidentally) been
a visitor since childhood at the farm where Mr. Smith sent her for
the summers; she became good friends with him there. The web
around Judy grew tighter, as Daddy-Long-Legs's orders were in-
creasingly influenced by jealousy—he refused to let her make a
visit, for instance, because a friend's Princeton brother was interested in her. Readers could see that Judy's mentor was a dog-in-
the-manger (as well as a spidery insect), but the author presented
his possessiveness as lovable rather than greedy.

In the end, the secretive suitor got his way without being revealed as a gross bully because Judy confessed her love for *Jervis*
in a letter to *Daddy-Long-Legs*. She did not know that her suitor
and her benefactor were one and the same, and thus he could not
be accused of buying her love and pressuring her into marriage.
Nonetheless, the whole relationship developed in a context of
smug manipulation. The man held the advantages of wealth and
power and experience and secret knowledge, while the woman
was innocently pursuing her life and education with no idea she
was dancing into his web.

Like Laura Ingalls with her farmer, Judy was enormously lucky
that such a man came to claim her. But the book's happy ending
failed to erase the creepy image of Daddy-Long-Legs in his shadowy appearance at the orphanage in Chapter One: She CAUGHT

ONLY A FLEETING IMPRESSION OF THE MAN. THE SHADOW PICTURED GROTESQUELY ELONGATED LEGS AND ARMS THAT RAN ALONG THE FLOOR AND UP THE WALL OF THE CORRIDOR. IT LOOKED, FOR ALL THE WORLD, LIKE A HUGE, WAVERING DADDY-LONG-LEGS. Of course a daddy-long-legs is a harmless bug and plenty of girls are willing to play with it; but this description is not benign. It came as no surprise that this huge figure—like an alien in science fiction— slowly, patiently, gathered Judy into the grasp of its grotesquely elongated legs and arms and promised to hold her there forever. And it came as no surprise by the end of the book that Judy was transcendently grateful at being clutched so tightly and so lovingly by her monstrous daddy-long-legs.

In the crucial letter where Judy told him about her love for Jervis, she made a revealing remark: WE THINK THE SAME ABOUT EVERYTHING—I AM AFRAID I HAVE A TENDENCY TO MAKE OVER MY IDEAS TO MATCH HIS! The author seems to have had no regrets that this bright, feisty girl would now make over her ideas to match her rich husband, and it didn't occur to the author that Judy might resent the fact that for four years this man had played with her ignorance and deceived her into revealing her private thoughts about him in unguarded letters. When I was a preteen reader around 1950, *Daddy-Long-Legs* was considered a happy fairy tale, and Judy a happy girl who would be happy ever after in her silken web.

We were taught, quite young, how to apply these lessons in waiting. Starting in fifth grade we attended dancing classes. Girls clustered in the lobby in soft, bright dresses and white gloves while the boys watched, until the dancing teacher clicked her hand clicker. Following a hierarchy we all understood, the popular boys strolled over and asked the popular girls to dance. Then the okay ones; then the last few pathetic ones. I was okay, somewhere in the lower-middle; my partners were nice enough, smart but short, with glasses and/or big ears. Although I wasn't treated badly I would get a stomachache lasting through each session, from the tension of waiting over and over again to be asked. There was nothing you could do but stand there smiling wanly, hoping your stocking seams were straight. When pushed around the floor in a stiff foxtrot or rumba, you could do nothing but follow your partner's lead and smile.

In sixth and seventh grade the waiting game got worse, because now boys would phone girls with invitations to little dances held in the gym or local country clubs. One time my social level seemed about to rise a notch: A popular boy (handsome but short) was turned down for a school dance by his first- and second-choice girls and asked me to go with him. I felt overjoyed, honored before my peers. Steve was coming down with the flu—ten minutes into the dance he threw up on the gym floor. I smiled wanly while waiting for his mother to arrive and drive us home. There was nothing I could do about anything but look nice and act pleasant.

The Proper Choice

In many stories the heroine chose from two or three suitors. Occasionally she ended up with an outsider, a beau who came from beyond her small circle of family and friends. We loved tales of a romantic stranger but seldom found them in books written for children. We found them instead in some adult novels that were popular with young girls—passionate books such as *Jane Eyre* and *Rebecca* and *Gone with the Wind*.

In stories that mid-century girls were *supposed* to read, the successful suitor was not the stranger but rather the comfortable, familiar chap who was more like a brother or father than a lover. The thrust of these stories was conservative: a girl would be safest and happiest staying within her own milieu and passing on the values and virtues of those she had grown up with. Adults writing for girl readers preferred to create suitors who seemed like family members, because they did not threaten the established social order and they did not reek of sexuality. Young readers got around such squeamishness by seeking out adult books with intense, sexual heroes like Rhett Butler and Heathcliff. But the wise fatherly lovers and jolly brotherly lovers in girls' stories had their own appeal too, and helped nudge a girl toward conventional behavior and sensible marriage.

When a girl chose to marry the older suitor, she chose to be cared for and protected in traditional style by a husband she acknowledged as wiser and better than she. In her childhood and teens Jo March of *Little Women* showed a bold, independent character. In her twenties, though, after trying a new life as governess and writer, Jo was beaten down by loneliness, homesickness, and sorrow (at her sister's death) into such a depression that only the proposal of kind, middle-aged Professor Bhaer restored her happiness and sense of purpose. The Professor, a scholarly sort who resembled Jo's father, cherished and guided her through two preachy sequels, *Little Men* and *Jo's Boys*. Jo was able to fulfill herself so beautifully (according to her author) because her husband was a fine teacher and father, praising her generously and, when she needed it, scolding her gently. Everyone was happy that the Professor took over the parental role so well. We young admirers had thought that Jo could run her own life and make her own mistakes; we found that we were wrong—and that she was thoroughly comfortable with her new circumscribed world. Jo, this girl who defied everyone at fifteen, at twenty-five was eager to obey three watchful fathers: her Heavenly and earthly fathers and her husband.

To post–Freudian adult readers these stories have odd and unsavory elements, but to earlier readers they followed a familiar pattern. Today it's hard to believe that the many masochistic Elsie Dinsmore books, about the little girl's unwholesome worship of a father and later a father-like husband, were immensely popular. In one book young Elsie joyfully married her father's best friend, "Mr. Travilla," as she called him, thus virtually managing to have sex with her father without raising eyebrows. Such tales satisfied some Victorian craving for women to undergo permanent paternal discipline, stern and captious.

Nineteenth-century assumptions underlie later books like *Daddy-Long-Legs*, where even ambitious girls got absorbed by husbands full of righteous authority and full of years. Women who enjoyed Louisa May Alcott's books as children remember, many years later, the charm and humor. They may think they forget the sermons and words of advice to sweethearts and wives, but some part of them remembers. Today I look at *Little Women*, *Jo's Boys*, and the rest with a suspicious eye, yet every sentence, every admonition, glistens for me with the absolute truth I found here as a child.

If the nineteenth century liked stories about a girl marrying a father-figure and this survived as a sub-theme into the twentieth, the most common choice of fictional girls in our century was marriage to a brother. Popular versions included the three Pollys: the heroine of *Pollyanna Grows Up* (1914) by Eleanor Porter, Polly Milton in Alcott's *An Old-Fashioned Girl* (1870), and Polly in *Five Little Peppers Grown-Up* (1893) by Margaret Sidney. Alcott's romances were lively enough, but Porter and Sidney, basically fatuous writers, became unusually fatuous when they described romantic situations.

Pollyanna's courtship included a ridiculous remnant of the Victorian father-marrying pattern. When Jimmy, the childhood chum who obviously should become her husband, proposed to her, he mentioned a suspicion that his middle-aged mentor, John Pendleton, also loved her. Then Pollyanna, who always had a close but unromantic friendship with Pendleton, decided that if he did indeed ask her to marry him she would be obliged to do so, giving up her love for Jimmy—because years ago her mother had broken his heart by spurning him and marrying Pollyanna's father. POLLYANNA GAVE A MOAN AND COVERED HER FACE WITH HER HANDS. HER EYES HAD THE HUNTED LOOK OF SOME WILD THING AT BAY. "YOU MEAN YOU'D *MARRY* HIM?" "OH, NO!—I MEAN—WHY—ER—Y-YES, I SUPPOSE SO," SHE ADMITTED FAINTLY. "POLLYANNA, YOU'RE BREAKING MY HEART." "I'M BREAKING MINE TOO. BUT I'LL HAVE TO DO IT. I'D BREAK YOUR HEART, I'D BREAK MINE—BUT I'D NEVER BREAK HIS!"

Because her *mother* had once made him unhappy, she must make it up to him? All ended well, because Pendleton actually wanted to marry a mature widow and Pollyanna could marry Jimmy with no guilt. A feebler plot device could not be imagined, but the author obviously felt she must show that Pollyanna would sacrifice love for duty and thus was certified a good-girl heroine. Basically, Pollyanna thought she ought to marry her father but then realized she didn't have to, so she married her brother and everyone was happy.

Alcott's Polly Milton did not share Pollyanna's notion that a girl was morally obliged to marry an older man to improve his life, but she shared the same itch for martyrdom. Polly felt affection but no love toward rich Arthur Sidney, a gentleman eight years older who appreciated her strength and simplicity. Old-fashioned Polly was a sensible country girl who had been taken up by some rich city relatives. Her values and habits startled her urban friends: she was not ashamed of poverty, not afraid of hard work, and not (except a little bit) tempted by the wasteful, frivolous social life of the Shaws' circle. Polly finally discouraged her fatherly lover Mr. Sidney and found fulfillment devoting herself to her lovable but immature brotherly lover, Tom Shaw. Tom was the actual brother of Polly's rich friend Fanny; he and Polly had been friends since her first visits when they were children.

Polly (unlike Jo March) would be the nobler spouse, helping Tom overcome his weaknesses. A hearty young woman, she was also angelic, inspiring the whole Shaw family and a number of their friends to discard crass ways and values. Like Jo March, Polly finally chose a man who was a comfortable family member rather than a romantic knight. These choices were very common in the books I am considering. Old-fashioned Polly's family-like relations with Tom are stressed to a grotesque extent. One whole chapter, entitled "Playing Grandmother," shows Polly taking the place of his dead *grandmother*. "I USED TO GO AND CONSULT GRANDMA, AND SHE ALWAYS HAD SOMETHING COMFORTABLE TO SAY TO ME. SHE'S GONE NOW, BUT POLLY, YOU SEEM TO TAKE HER PLACE. WOULD YOU MIND SITTING IN HER CHAIR, AND LETTING ME TELL YOU TWO OR THREE THINGS?" POLLY FELT THAT TOM HAD GIVEN HER THE MOST BEAUTIFUL COMPLIMENT HE COULD HAVE DEVISED. Tom says of his real sister, "FAN IS A GOOD SOUL, BUT SHE ISN'T PRACTICAL, SO WHO HAVE I BUT MY OTHER SISTER, POLLY?" Polly liked these familial games, saying to Tom even after they were engaged "BROTHERS AND SISTERS SHOULDN'T HAVE SECRETS FROM EACH OTHER." So Polly found a husband who was both brother and grandson, a striking incestuous coup.

As for the sacrifice theme, Polly (like Jo March) turned down the richer suitor and accepted the poorer. Tom's rich family had conveniently gone bankrupt, in time for Polly to marry him and show her contempt for materialism. That was one kind of sacrifice, to reject luxury and help your struggling mate face a life of hardship. The desire to put others' needs above your own took other forms too: Polly briefly wondered if she should sacrifice her love for Tom and marry Sidney, because his wealth would relieve her family's poverty. Even in romantic matters—*especially* in romantic matters—these heroines were constantly giving up their own desires, seeking the crown of martyrdom one way or another. The books our elders urged us to read showed girls who wanted to help; any girl characters who wanted to *be* helped and supported were scorned in these books. And we did read them, and we did believe them. The good girl's goal was usefulness not happiness—though she was taught that usefulness was the same as happiness.

The other Polly, Miss Pepper, easily wins the prize for most feeble engagement scene. (This is not surprising, for the Five Little Peppers series is probably the most saccharine, simplistic set of girls' books ever written.) From his first appearance Jasper King was clearly fated to become Polly's husband. In book one Jasper's rich father, old Mr. King, rescued the Pepper family from poverty and brought them to live in his mansion, whereupon it was discovered that the Peppers were actually cousins of the Kings. So Polly was related to her dear friend Jasper and called Jasper's father "Grandpapa" (which would make Jasper her uncle, a nice combination of brother *and* father figure). In *Five Little Peppers Grown Up* lovely Polly, now twenty years old, inspired marriage proposals from various young men with elegant names: Livingston Bayley, Jack Loughead, Pickering Dodge. She was somewhat dazed by this attention but had enough sense to know that none of these could meet her high standards or touch her heart. You would think, then, that Polly would realize what was going on when one evening as they all sat together Jasper asked her mother solemnly if he might "speak."

But no, Polly sat quietly in her childish stupor as Jasper continued: "LOOK AT ME, DO, DEAR!" POLLY LIFTED HER BROWN EYES QUIETLY. "WHY, JASPER?" "DO YOU THINK YOU COULD LOVE ME—I'VE LOVED YOU EVER SINCE THE LITTLE BROWN HOUSE DAYS, DEAR!" "OH JASPER!" POLLY CRIED, "HOW GOOD YOU ARE." "WILL YOU, POLLY?" CRIED JASPER, "TELL ME QUICKLY, DEAR." "WILL I WHAT?" ASKED POLLY

WONDERINGLY. "LOVE ME, POLLY." "OH! I DO—I DO," SHE CRIED. "YOU
KNOW IT. I LOVE YOU WITH ALL MY HEART." "POLLY, WILL YOU MARRY
ME? TELL HER, MRS. FISHER, DO, AND MAKE HER UNDERSTAND," BEGGED
JASPER, TURNING TO MOTHER FISHER IMPLORINGLY. "POLLY, CHILD,"
SAID MAMSIE, PUTTING BOTH ARMS AROUND HER, "JASPER WANTS YOU
TO BE HIS WIFE—DO YOU LOVE HIM ENOUGH FOR THAT?" POLLY, NOT
TAKING HER BROWN EYES FROM JASPER'S FACE, LAID HER OTHER HAND
UPON HIS. "I LOVE HIM ENOUGH," SHE SAID, "FOR THAT; OH, JASPER!"

Polly was not mentally disabled, just innocent. Apparently
sweet confusion was the proper response when your brother
asked you to marry him—erotic passion would be unseemly. She
was an outspoken young lady, a competent music teacher, but in
the marriage dance her role had to be merely receptive. You
couldn't expect anything better from an author who called the
mother "Mamsie"—a name even more repellent than Alcott's
"Marmee". You can't be surprised that this Polly who was leading a sweet, padded life as a maiden should slip so gently, with
so little change, into her role as a bride, especially when she had
been living in the same house with her husband since they were
children.

Some other popular heroines of nineteenth- and early twentieth-
century series, who also chose sensible, brotherly suitors, had
more gumption than Pollyanna and Old-Fashioned Polly and
Polly Pepper, and less martyrdom. It is relevant that Lloyd in the
Little Colonel books and Rose in Alcott's Eight Cousins series
were extremely rich, and Anne in the Green Gables books graduated from college, with high honors. Even conservative authors
acknowledged that such circumstances gave a girl a certain extra
freedom of choice that modest, stay-at-home girls and humble el-
ementary teachers would not have. Despite this extra freedom,
though, Lloyd and Rose and Anne all chose to marry men who
had been unromantic friends of theirs since childhood. They still
followed the rule that a girl should marry a good brother rather
than a passionate stranger.

A woman was less threatening to a patriarchal society if she
didn't grow up completely and become an independent, sexual
person. These literary examples of the desire to control female

behavior may seem trivial, in a world that also contains, for instance, the custom of female genital mutilation, but they express the same intention in genteel form. In marrying comfortable old friends, Lloyd and Rose and Anne and the Pollys confirmed the social and economic status quo. It's not surprising that in the post–World War II period, our parents and teachers wished us to read such stories, and that many of us read them devotedly and believed them absolutely.

I read these books over and over as a child, thrilled by romantic dangers and dilemmas, and I remember being pleased with the rightness of the endings. In Alcott's *Rose in Bloom* (1876), the heiress announced that she must do something with her life: "WE WANT TO LIVE AND LEARN AS WELL AS LOVE AND BE LOVED. I'M SICK OF BEING TOLD THAT IS ALL A WOMAN IS FIT FOR!" Rose sounds almost like Isabel in James's *Portrait of a Lady*, but since *Rose in Bloom* was a book for girls it is clear from the start that (a) her ambitious work would be limited to local charities and (b) her choice of a mate would be limited to the seven boy cousins she had grown up with. A strong-minded girl like Rose had to be carefully monitored in those yearnings to live and learn. Rose was ALL AGLOW WITH THE EARNESTNESS THAT MAKES ONE HOPE SUCH HUMAN FLOWERS MAY HAVE HEAVEN'S PUREST AIR AND WARMEST SUNSHINE TO BLOSSOM IN. Words like fresh, innocent, pure, and maidenly surrounded Rose so lushly that we are not surprised when handsome Charlie, her favorite cousin, proved insufficiently virtuous for her. He drank, in fact, and came to see her once in such a wobbly state that she rejected his love. Predictably, Charlie died after falling off a horse while drunk and Rose married the good cousin, Mac, an ugly duckling who had turned into a famous poet.

Rose's story was a cautionary tale reminding girls that it's not enough to exclude dangerous suitors who come from afar—even within the family circle there may be crude and shallow men who must be cast off. Rose at the start seemed to be looking outward to all that the world might offer and all that she might offer the world. By the end, her life was bundled up safely with a kind, bespectacled cousin. A GIRL'S FIRST THOUGHT OF LOVE, Alcott told us, IS AS DELICATE A THING AS THE ROSY MORNING-GLORY, THAT A BREATH OF AIR CAN SHATTER. Reading about Rose and the others, we learned to be cautious and fastidious. I should not be ironic about Rose's choice, because she did do the right thing in rejecting Charlie: he was not just a drunk, he was also selfish and overbearing. In choosing the good brother Mac over the bad one Charlie, she chose stability, permanence, continuity; she protected her developing self admirably—and she also protected her powerful, traditional family and society.

While Rose's story reminded girls that romantic heroes would break your heart, even lads within your social circle who should know better, the Little Colonel books were more reassuring. They made it seem painless to make the right choice: you might feel a little tender regret but no anguish. In *The Little Colonel's Knight Comes Riding* (1907), many beaux besieged Lloyd Sherman, because of her charm, beauty, social position, and money, but her careful parents had given her an ideal yardstick for suitors—they must measure up by being clean, honorable, and strong. Phil gambled and Lloyd dismissed him. "Impetuous and headstrong" Leland Harcourt captured her fancy but lost out by grumbling selfishly at her attentions to a needy child. Lloyd had liked having a strange Knight gallop into her life and demand her hand, but her involvement was so mild that readers could not be upset when she told Leland to ride off again. HIS WOOING WAS THE KIND ONE READS OF IN BOOKS. IT WAS SO DELIGHTFUL TO HAVE SOME ONE WRITE POEMS TO HER AND SING SONGS IN SUCH A WAY THAT EVERY TONE DEDICATED THEM TO HER ALONE. IF ONE COULD ONLY GO ON THAT WAY THROUGH ALL THE SUMMERS, BEING ADORED IN THAT FASHION, KNOWING SHE WAS CROWNED QUEEN IN SOMEBODY'S HEART, HOW DELIGHTFUL IT WOULD BE.

Lloyd's infatuation with this phony Knight, Leland, contrasted with her growing appreciation for her old buddy Rob, big and dependable (like Rose's cousin Mac). IT'S ROB WHO GETS UP THE RIDES AND PICNICS, AND STIRS US OUT OF OUR LAZINESS BY MAKING US GO FISHING AND TENNIS-PLAYING. So Rob shifts smoothly from big brother to lover: "I THINK I'VE ALWAYS HELD THE THOUGHT OF YOU IN MY HEART, LLOYD, BUT IT HAS COME TO SUCH FULL FLOWER NOW, DEAR, I COULDN'T HIDE IT FROM YOU. ALL MY LIFE MUST HAVE BEEN A GRADUAL GROWING UP FOR THIS ONE THING—TO LOVE YOU!" For all the appeal of a stranger Knight, Lloyd's emotion was reserved for people and places she had always loved. Finally engaged to Rob, whose family had lost their fortune, Lloyd discovered the truly romantic kind of sacrifice: devoting yourself to a poor, struggling husband. Once again, a girl reader was instructed to grasp the known, support the system, and obey a true knight who—once again—turned out to be both a lover and a brother.

Anne of Green Gables faced special challenges as she grew toward womanhood, because imagination and intelligence drew her toward more education than most of her peers wanted. Bright and competitive as a child, she quarreled with the boy who shared her status at the top of the class. At the end of the first book she came to regret her stubborn pride and made up with this schoolmate, Gilbert. He then took on the role of friendly, helpful teenage brother. So Anne had grown up some, understanding that a girl must be flexible and forgiving, not proud: "WHAT A STUBBORN LITTLE GOOSE I WAS!" she reminisced.

She still had to learn what Lloyd and Rose learned, and other girl heroines: You must resist romantic notions; embrace solid, homely values; resist handsome romantic strangers; and embrace brotherly friends from childhood. (Although you must not embrace them until you are engaged.) Such good sense did not come easily to Anne. Her instinct for the romantic cliché was unerring, and led her for example to haunt the grave of a local bride who had died of consumption in the garden her husband had made for her. Of the dead bride Anne said, "SHE HAD FOUR YEARS OF PERFECT HAPPINESS, SO I THINK SHE WAS TO BE ENVIED RATHER THAN PITIED. AND THEN TO SHUT YOUR EYES AND FALL ASLEEP AMONG ROSES, WITH THE ONE YOU LOVED BEST ON EARTH SMILING DOWN ON YOU . . . OH, IT WAS BEAUTIFUL!"

Anne's first beautiful romance (in *Anne of the Island*, 1915) was with Roy Gardner, a true Prince Charming—his full name was Royal and he had all the romantic qualifications. Eventually, in spite of Roy's flowers and sonnets, she realized he was stiff and humorless; she didn't love him. And she realized that her vision of an ideal hero was shallow. She now valued and accepted the simple, worthy vision that Gilbert offered her: "I HAVE A DREAM," HE SAID SLOWLY. "I PERSIST IN DREAMING IT. I DREAM OF A HOME WITH

A HEARTH-FIRE IN IT, A CAT AND DOG, THE FOOTSTEPS OF FRIENDS—
AND *YOU*!"

Attracting a Prince

Let young women stick to that hearth-fire and cat and dog and
they will be fine. As a preteen reader I felt safe hearing that I
wouldn't really want to marry someone exciting—Rhett Butler
and Heathcliff would probably use bad language and act crude.
To be happy, I just had to prepare to be a worthy bride and choose
the familiar, tame suitor over the exotic, passionate one. This rule
was still honored in the 1950s, but our world differed in one way
from the earlier worlds of Laura, Anne, Rose, and Lloyd: a society
less stable and less homogeneous, it couldn't promise that suitable, familiar grooms would appear as soon as we were marriage-
able. In the transitional era of mid-twentieth-century courtship, we
had to do more than stay pure and choose well—we had to make
an active, anxious effort to *attract*. After the 1920s, Depression, and
war years, elders accepted that girls could no longer lead the complacent life of the Little Colonel but did not much want them to
leave home and strike out on their own. In the 1940s heroines
were created who—in spite of restless energy and competence—
still assumed the future would contain husband and home; they
focused energy on ways to ensure that future. Popular series, like
those by Rosamond DuJardin and Maureen Daly, starred teenage
girls who worked diligently on appearance and behavior to attract
the right boys. A girl was still a prize to be won by a prince—
that had not changed—but now the prize had to do more than
wait to be won. She had to make herself highly desirable or no
true prince would want to win her. The prize had to work as hard
as the prince, though her efforts must be hidden.

Our courtship and dating books (written from the 1930s
through the 1950s) were founded on the Jo March/Anne of Green
Gables tradition, where a girl grew up by molding character, controlling selfish impulses, and developing useful skills. Our newer
books endorsed this tradition while also requiring that a success-

ful girl should entice and manipulate the boys she met. Jo March and her sisters struggled to be good, scorning the few frivolous girls who tried too hard to be admired; eighty years later Marcy Rhodes and Angie Morrow wanted to be good, sure, but most of all they wanted to be admired and popular.

If a fictional girl had the prerequisites—a respectable family, a last name that seemed prosperous and usually Protestant, and a first name that ended in an "ee" sound—she could start developing qualities that would attract desirable boyfriends. They would take you to THE DANCE IN THE BIG GYM AT HIGH, WITH PAPER FESTOONS AND THE LIGHTS SOFTENED AND ALL THE GIRLS AND THEIR DATES, WHIRLING AND SWAYING. Books like *Wait for Marcy* (1950), by Rosamond DuJardin, offered three guidelines: be beautiful, be manipulative, and be yourself. It was hard to be yourself and beautiful at the same time, and impossible to be yourself and also manipulative, but the contradictory nature of the rules was not acknowledged.

Rule One, Be Beautiful, involved self-conscious fussing and fretting. Marcy agonized over a date: WHAT TO WEAR WAS SETTLED. BUT—HOW TO DO HER HAIR? WHETHER IT WOULD BE BEST TO HAVE IT WASHED AND SET A DAY AHEAD OR ON SATURDAY MORNING? WHETHER TO WEAR HIGH HEELS OR LOW? Self-doubts played a large part in these stories: WHY HAD I EVER SAID I'D GO? WHY HAD I THOUGHT IT WOULD BE FUN TO COMPETE WITH BEAUTIFUL GLAMOUROUS GIRLS WITH GORGEOUS CLOTHES? I FELT THAT MY NOSE WAS SHINY AND MY LIPSTICK SMEARED AND PROBABLY MY STOCKING SEAMS WEREN'T EVEN STRAIGHT. OR MY SLIP COULD BE SHOWING.

DuJardin and her characters followed Rule Two with amusement rather than shame. According to Tobey in *Class Ring* (1951), MEN ARE SO EASY TO MANIPULATE, IF YOU GO AT IT IN THE RIGHT WAY. THERE ARE TIMES IN EVERY GIRL'S LIFE WHEN SHE FINDS IT NECESSARY—NOT TO LIE EXACTLY, BUT NOT TO TELL QUITE THE WHOLE TRUTH. IT NEVER PAYS TO LET A BOY THINK YOU'RE TOO FOND OF HIM, EVEN WHEN YOU'RE WEARING HIS CLASS RING. There was always a bad girl in these books, a predatory, insincere girl in jangly bracelets who showed the others how not to behave. But the bad girl was merely a good girl who wasn't subtle enough in her manipulation, and even heroine Marcy and her friends went in for "playing hard to get," "teaching them a lesson," "keeping them guessing," and "winding men around your finger."

Marmee in *Little Women* would have lectured these girls sharply. DuJardin's books included a superficial allegiance to Rule Three, Be Yourself, a few feeble instances where the boy liked the girl better for being natural and honest, but Rule Two was followed with much more conviction. By 1950 the practical cynicism of Scarlett O'Hara had entered into these thin, popular stories for pre-adolescents and the idealism of earlier stories had mostly fled. We were still instructed that the proper goal of a young girl was to marry well; we were just being encouraged to play a part in the process that was—in a sneaky, passive-aggressive way—more active.

Seventeenth Summer (1942), by Maureen Daly, painted a less shallow picture of young romance but its message was ultimately the same—catch a man and you will become Somebody, a real person. Even the heroine Angie Morrow, a sensible heroine, shared this belief: IT'S FUNNY WHAT A BOY CAN DO. ONE DAY YOU'RE NOBODY AND THE NEXT DAY YOU'RE THE GIRL THAT SOME FELLOW GOES WITH AND THE OTHER FELLOWS LOOK AT YOU HARDER AND WONDER WHAT YOU'VE GOT AND WISH THEY'D BEEN THE ONE TO TAKE YOU OUT FIRST. GOING WITH A BOY GIVES YOU A NEW IDENTITY. She was discovering social status and also sexual delight, innocently reporting such sensations as A WARM, CONTENTED FEELING WENT THROUGH ME LIKE WHEN YOU DRINK HOT MILK. As she picked flowers in the evening, A THROBBING WARMTH SURGED THROUGH MY WHOLE BODY. Sailing with her boyfriend she discovered SOMETHING IN ME WAS SUDDENLY ALIVE. IT WAS WARM, STRANGE, AND BEATING.

Angie harnessed these impulses in socially acceptable ways and avoided the mistakes of her friend Margie (engaged to someone she despised just for the security) and her sister Lorraine (a pitiful, man-crazy mess). Lorraine wore curlers all the time except when she went out, and put on lipstick with a brush. She was self-conscious and artificial and tried too hard to impress men. While Angie's friendly naturalness led to a romance with a nice football player, her sister spent the summer running after a sarcastic man who sneered at her, lied to her, failed to show up for dates, and broke her heart. Lorraine was a grisly example of the girl who couldn't be herself: "I WISH I KNEW WHAT KIND OF GIRLS HE LIKES— I DON'T KNOW IF I SHOULD PRETEND I'M THE INTELLIGENT TYPE OR PRETEND I'M SOPHISTICATED AND HAVE BEEN AROUND."

Angie could do nothing but watch her sister self-destruct. Lorraine HAD ON PURPLISH LIPSTICK AND WAS DANCING WITH HER HEAD BACK, LAUGHING VERY HARD AND HAVING A GAY TIME, BUT HE WAS LOOKING AT HER IN A SURPRISED SORT OF WAY, HOLDING HIS HEAD BACK AT A FUNNY ANGLE AS IF HIS NECK WERE STIFF. There is nothing pernicious about a story that tells girls not to be phony; the trouble with *Seventeenth Summer* is that Lorraine was condemned not for playing manipulative, dishonest games with her dates but for playing them badly. Angie herself FELT THAT WARM, POSSESSIVE POWER THAT COMES FROM KNOWING THAT YOU ARE ABLE TO WORRY A BOY, and worked deliberately to make the right impression on Jack and his friends. Being yourself was not enough.

Readers were supposed to like Angie and identify with her lack of confidence. IT DIDN'T SEEM THAT A BOY SO NICE COULD REALLY BE WITH ME. IT SEEMED AS IF MY FACE WAS STIFF WITH SCOWLING AND MY EYEBROWS MUST BE GROWING STRAIGHT ACROSS MY NOSE, DARK AND HEAVY. When she thought Jack did not like her, she sat numbly in their booth at the teen hangout, FEELING AS USELESS, AS HOLLOWED AS A SUCKED ORANGE. IF YOU DON'T MAKE THE GRADE AT PETE'S, YOU JUST DON'T MAKE IT. After becoming an insider she wasted no sympathy on others who didn't make the grade, as when two girls came into Pete's wearing flat black oxfords instead of saddle shoes and were icily ignored. Angie thought that ANY GIRL WHO DOES THAT ALMOST DESERVES NOT TO HAVE FELLOWS LOOK AT HER. Most teenagers of my generation shared Angie's ambivalence about the future: she went off to college at the end of the book and wanted to be smart, but her dream—as she explained it to Jack—was that "WE WOULD BE, MAYBE, GREAT PEOPLE WHEN WE GROW UP. I COULD BRUSH MY HAIR EVERY NIGHT AND YOU COULD READ A LOT SO WE WOULD REALLY BE SOMETHING."

I was a smart girl like Angie in those nice years after World War II and I too wasn't sure how to stop being a nobody; but I knew she was right, it required a man at your side, and it wouldn't hurt to brush your hair a lot. By seventh grade my friends and I were chanting "I must, I must, I must increase my bust," while flinging our elbows behind our backs in a futile bosom exercise. We analyzed lipstick colors like Cherries in the Snow and Fire and Ice. We were getting in shape for the biggest struggle of our lives, the effort to attract a husband—without any visible effort.

Grownup Romance: Schemers and Sufferers

We swallowed a lot of conservative advice in our girls' books, classics like Alcott's and contemporary ones like Maureen Daly's. Some girls scorned these books that told us to wait patiently, choose carefully, and attract cleverly—preferring romances written for adults. Even cautious girls sometimes read adult novels, which showed broader romantic possibilities but still preached a conservative moral. Adult romances popular with my generation perpetuated the old split in female characters: they were bad girls, enterprising but selfish, or else good girls, submissive but strong in suffering for others.

Bad-girl heroines were most appealing when they were safely distanced in time or space. Many girls liked cliché-laden historical novels such as *Forever Amber* and *Desirée*—about restless young women who became mistresses to rich, powerful men. *Gone with the Wind* (1936) was in this category; we loved Scarlett in nineteenth-century Georgia but knew we would not befriend her if she appeared now in our orderly world. (Melanie, of course, was the best of the good girls, and of course she died.) The women authors of these historical romances made it clear that ambivalence was the right attitude toward the racy young heroines. We empathized when they were taken advantage of and betrayed; we yearned to be as clever and beautiful and bold as they; but we realized that their restlessness turned too easily into ruthlessness. The naughty girl characters went too far, neglecting family, morality, and decency, and were punished. In reading about Amber, Desirée, and Scarlett, we indulged rebellious urges in a safe context.

We also liked other kinds of adult romance that reinforced only virtuous impulses. In these the heroine might be a girl-goddess, an airy supernatural being who got sacrificed; or a saint, a more earthy, humble creature who suffered for her man. Girl-goddess stories had a particular appeal: we comfortably adored characters like tragic Rima in *Green Mansions*, knowing their stories were only fantasy—while we could all too easily see ourselves as having the problems of more realistic heroines like Jo or Anne.

I read W. H. Hudson's *Green Mansions* (1916) with my friends at summer camp. Under the pines on a chilly lake in Maine we devoured this tale of jungle passion, awed by Rima's mysterious life and horrible death. Fantasy stories like *Green Mansions* mostly had male authors and narrators: Men imagined so beautifully the Otherness of these shadowy sprite-goddesses. Abel, an explorer in Guyana, escaped from a blood-thirsty savage tribe and came upon an elusive being hidden in the forest. I CAUGHT THE FAINT RUSTLE OF A LIGHT FOOTSTEP, A GLIMPSE OF A GREY, MISTY OBJECT MOVING IN THE DEEPER SHADOWS. Discovering this strange girl living in a remote hut with a rough Spanish foster-grandfather, Abel fell in love with her innocence, her various beauty, and her melodious voice: like the song of the flute-bird but PURE, MORE EXPRESSIVE; A SOFT WARBLING, INFINITELY TENDER, SINKING TO LISPING SOUNDS THAT SOON CEASED TO BE AUDIBLE. IT WAS A VOICE PURIFIED AND BRIGHTENED TO SOMETHING ALMOST ANGELIC. As for appearance, HER FACE AND FEATURES WERE SINGULARLY DELICATE, BUT IT WAS HER COLOUR THAT MADE HER DIFFER FROM ALL OTHER HUMAN BEINGS. Abel praised this shifting skin color as dim white, alabastrian, semi-pellucid, rosy purple, dim blue, pale grey, and other unlikely tints; and rhapsodized on her eyes and hair in equally overwrought terms.

Their spiritual love was heating up nicely (I LOVED HER AS I NEVER COULD LOVE ANY OTHER BEING, WITH A PASSION WHICH HAD CAUGHT SOMETHING OF HER OWN BRILLIANCE AND INTENSITY), when things got complicated. Rima announced she must journey in search of her dead mother's people, who might share her unique language, soften her isolation, and help her decide what to do about her love for Abel. After the fruitless journey to find her lost tribe with its warbling bird-language, Rima reconciled herself to living alone with her love and rushed back to the hut ahead of Abel, to prepare for their nuptuals. This separation gave the superstitious natives an opportunity to trap her in a tree and burn her up as an evil spirit. Like other dead maidens Rima turned into an icon for her lover to worship the rest of his life. The girl who had seemed so pure as to be immortal was gone: as one savage told the lover, "FROM THE TOP OF THE TREE CAME A GREAT CRY, LIKE THE CRY OF A BIRD, 'ABEL!' AND THEN WE SAW SOMETHING FALL INTO THE FLAMES BENEATH.

Abel located the tree and stuffed the bones and ashes into an urn, which sat for years in his parlor as he lamented—MEMORY OF ALL THE MYSTIC, UNIMAGINABLE GRACE AND LOVELINESS AND JOY THAT HAD VANISHED SMITES ON MY HEART WITH SUCH SUDDEN, INTENSE PAIN THAT I CAST MYSELF PRONE ON THE EARTH AND WEEP TEARS LIKE DROPS OF BLOOD—but found consolation in hopes of joining Rima one day in eternity. NO LONGER "YOU ARE YOU AND I AM I—WHY IS IT," THE QUESTION ASKED WHEN OUR SOULS WERE, LIKE TWO RAINDROPS SIDE BY SIDE, DRAWING EVER NEARER: NOW THEY HAD TOUCHED AND WERE NOT TWO, BUT ONE INSEPARABLE DROP, CRYSTALLISED BEYOND CHANGE, NOT TO BE DISINTEGRATED BY TIME, NOR SHATTERED BY DEATH'S BLOW.

We lapped this stuff up. *Green Mansions* was my favorite book the summer I was ten. Rima's death was even better than Carol's in that other bird-girl book, *The Birds' Christmas Carol*. Rima was an example to us girls in many ways, notably in showing how desirable it was to have a sweet voice so low it could hardly be heard, a voice that would SINK TO LISPING SOUNDS THAT SOON CEASED TO BE AUDIBLE. It was good for a girl-heroine to be misty, lisping, and inaudible, and even better for her to be dead.

Rima's sufferings were over faster than Ramona's, in that classic tale of Southern California in the early days. Her story seems endless, her nobility boundless. For years Señora Moreno scorned and tormented her foster-child Ramona, the orphaned daughter of a Scottish father and Indian mother. Ramona endured and obeyed until she fell in love with a proud young Indian. Enraged at such plebian behavior on the part of her ward, the Señora locked her up until she ran away with Alessandro. They escaped through hills and canyons, hiding from pursuers; found a fertile Indian settlement, married, bore a child, worked hard. Then Americans seized the Indian lands. Driven out, Ramona and Alessandro journeyed into the mountains and twice made a new start but the baby died, they almost starved, Alessandro went mad from the hardship and was killed in a dispute. Ramona bore a new baby, went into one of those pitiful heroine-type comas, and recovered when rescued by her foster brother who brought her home to a peaceful ranch now that the Señora was dead. She married him out of gratitude but forever mourned her only love, Alessandro.

The template for Helen Hunt Jackson's *Ramona* (1884) was the traditional, exemplary tale of saints' lives, strangely blending passive and active, strength and weakness. The girl WON THE AFFECTION OF ALL THE SISTERS at her own convent school, WHO SPOKE OF HER AS THE "BLESSED CHILD." SHE LOOKED MORE LIKE AN APPARITION OF AN ANGEL OR SAINT THAN LIKE A FLESH-AND-BLOOD MAIDEN. SHE WAS A SIMPLE, JOYOUS, GENTLE, CLINGING, FAITHFUL NATURE. This is the standard list of saintly adjectives. She was especially good at the clinging part: IT WAS STRANGE HOW RAMONA, WHO FELT HERSELF PRETERNATURALLY BRAVE SO LONG AS ALESSANDRO WAS BY HER SIDE, BECAME TIMOROUS AND WRETCHED THE INSTANT HE WAS LOST TO HER SIGHT. SHE WAS TRANSFORMED TO A TIMID, SHRINKING, DESPONDENT CHILD. Yet she found strength to defend and suffer for her husband and baby. "I AM STRONG. I CAN WORK, ALESSANDRO. I AM NOT AFRAID TO LIE ON THE EARTH; AND GOD WILL GIVE US FOOD."

Duty and love energized Ramona, and at the end it was the thought of new duties that roused her from her sickness: Though Alessandro was gone and happiness lost forever, she had to care for her new baby and her newly recovered foster-brother. As long as self-sacrifice was required, a woman like Ramona could keep going. In the words of the old lady from Tennessee who befriended her, "I DONNO BUT I SH'D COM TER BELIEVIN' IN SAINTS TEW, EF I WUZ TER LIVE 'LONG SIDE ER THET GAL. 'PEARS LIKE SHE WUZ SUTHIN' MORE 'N HUMAN." Fictional girls and women were less than fully human, since they were thought to lack male strength and intelligence, but they were also more than human in devotion and self-abnegation.

Innocent Ramona suffered in a cruel society. O-lan, the humble Chinese heroine of Pearl Buck's *The Good Earth* (1931), also suffered from her society, but she was even more martyred than Ramona because she was mistreated by the husband she served and reverenced. O-lan displayed typical traits of the female martyr: working long days in the house and fields, trudging with a basket to pick up animal dung from the road for fuel. Her husband, Wang Lung, felt she was a good bargain. AT NIGHT HE KNEW THE SOFT FIRMNESS OF HER BODY. BUT IN THE DAY SHE WAS LIKE A FAITHFUL, SPEECHLESS SERVING MAID, WHO IS ONLY A SERVING MAID AND NOTHING MORE. Everyone has heard about Chinese peasant women who returned to the field after giving birth—that was O-lan. THE DAY CAME WHEN SHE LAID DOWN HER HOE ONE MORNING AND CREPT INTO THE HOUSE. LATER BEFORE THE SUN SET SHE WAS BACK BESIDE HIM, HER BODY FLATTENED, SPENT, BUT HER FACE SILENT AND UNDAUNTED. HIS IMPULSE WAS TO SAY, "FOR THIS DAY YOU HAVE HAD ENOUGH. GO AND LIE UPON YOUR BED." But the work had to be done, so he picked up his scythe and they went on digging until dark.

O-lan beautifully combined the most desirable qualities—she seldom spoke and seemed stupid but was clever at solving terrible problems, even when the family was reduced to eating gruel made of dirt. After decades of hardship and then prosperity, she developed a tumor and drifted out of life without complaint. FOR THE FIRST TIME WANG LUNG AND HIS CHILDREN KNEW WHAT SHE HAD BEEN IN THE HOUSE AND HOW SHE MADE COMFORT FOR THEM ALL AND THEY HAD NOT KNOWN IT. (Like every woman's fantasy: "They'll appreciate me when I'm dead.") Wang Lung sat with her as she lay dying. HE LIT AN EARTHEN POT OF CHARCOAL AND SET IT BESIDE HER BED FOR WARMTH, AND SHE MURMURED EACH TIME FAINTLY, "WELL, AND IT IS TOO EXPENSIVE."

The author's attitude is revealing. While admiring O-lan's strength and dignity—such a fine, lowly, homely woman—Pearl Buck also extends enormous sympathy toward the husband who used her and never loved her. Wang Lung felt a vague guilt about rejecting her but concluded, "WELL, AND IT IS NOT MY FAULT IF I HAVE NOT LOVED HER AS ONE LOVES A CONCUBINE, SINCE MEN DO NOT. I HAVE NOT BEAT HER AND I HAVE GIVEN HER SILVER WHEN SHE ASKED FOR IT." We were supposed to read this as a tale of solid peasant life, a picturesque society where the husband brought a concubine into the house and the wife had no cause for complaint, where he took the one jewel his wife owned and loved and gave it to the concubine. Other characters play the villains; Wang Lung was misguided but sympathetic. The author seems to say that the husband's coldness enhanced the wife's nobility. WHEN HE TOOK HER HAND, DESIRING THAT SHE FEEL HIS TENDERNESS TOWARD HER, HE WAS ASHAMED BECAUSE HE COULD FEEL NO TENDERNESS. WHEN HE TOOK THIS STIFF DYING HAND HE DID NOT LOVE IT, AND EVEN HIS PITY WAS SPOILED WITH REPULSION TOWARDS IT. The author's forgiveness of Wang Lung contained irony, but she did forgive him as being a creature of his world and she seemed to admire herself for admiring him so tolerantly.

O-lan the earthbound HAD A SQUARE, HONEST FACE, A BROAD NOSE WITH LARGE BLACK NOSTRILS, AND A MOUTH WIDE AS A GASH IN HER FACE. HER EYES WERE SMALL AND DULL BLACK. She was the opposite extreme from Rima the jungle maiden, and I loved them both as a girl; I wanted to become both of them. At around this time I became infatuated with the recent musical *The King and I* and played the LP record over and over on our big chunky record player. My favorite song was "Something Wonderful," sung by the King's first wife who had been supplanted and humiliated:

> *This is a man you'll forgive and forgive*
> *And help and protect as long as you live. . . .*
> *He will not always say / What you would have him say,*
> *But now and then he'll say / Something wonderful.*
> *The thoughtless things he'll do / Will hurt and worry you*
> *Then all at once he'll do / Something wonderful,*
> *He'll always need your love / And so he'll get your love*
> *A man who needs your love / Can be—wonderful.*

Also, from *Carousel*, I admired: "What's the use of wond'rin' / If he's good or if he's bad— / He's your feller and you love him, / That's all there is to that."

These lines lodged in my heart and brain along with that seminal song from Disney's *Snow White*, "Some Day My Prince Will Come": "And how thrilling that moment will be, When the Prince of my dreams comes to me." I felt consciously that "The thoughtless things he'll do" were inextricably entwined with the wonderfulness, the thrill—that the heroine's putting up with the thoughtless things he'll do was the highest proof she deserved her heroine status. I doubt that I ever heard the word "assertiveness" in my youth; if I had I wouldn't have seen any value in such an unfemale quality. I yearned for an opportunity to show I was capable of self-sacrifice, at least self-abasement. It's not that we cringing types had a masochistic *enjoyment* of suffering, it was just that we knew suffering was the test of female excellence, the way a man might prove himself by going to war.

These adult romances, then, echoed the conservative, sacrificial patterns found in our wholesome stories of young girls finding a husband. Very seldom did a young heroine act honest and independent with her beloved, as well as loving. The only clear case I can think of was in *A Girl of the Limberlost* (1909), by Gene Stratton-Porter, in which a strange and passionate girl hero refused to be a victim or a clinging vine. The teenager living with her neurotic widowed mother in the Limberlost forest was a stunning beauty, a brilliant violinist, and a learned naturalist who financed her education by collecting rare moths. Elnora's virtues had a mythic flavor: SHE SEEMED TO POSSESS A LARGE SENSE OF BROTHERHOOD FOR ALL HUMAN AND ANIMATE CREATURES. SHE DID NOT SWERVE AN INCH WHEN A SNAKE SLID PAST HER, WHILE THE SQUIRRELS TOOK CORN FROM HER FINGERS. HER HEAD SHONE LIKE A SMALL DARK SUN.

A suitable hero came into the Limberlost, compared Elnora to his frivolous fiancée, rejoiced when the fiancée broke the engagement in a fit of pique. But Elnora did not go in for pliable heroine behavior: loving Philip, she sent him away, saying she would not listen to his suit until his former fiancée was convinced she could not win him back. In a way, this resembled the sacrificial, self-denying behavior of a traditional heroine—but Elnora's manner was proud and confident rather than pitiful. Considering Philip still bound to another, she refused his kisses and entreaties. When he whimpered, "PROMISE YOU WILL WRITE ONCE, ELNORA?" SHE LOOKED INTO HIS EYES, AND SMILED SERENELY. "IF THE TALKING TREES TELL ME THE SECRET OF HOW A MAN MAY GROW PERFECT, I WILL WRITE YOU WHAT IT IS, PHILIP. IN ALL THE TIME I HAVE KNOWN YOU I NEVER HAVE LIKED YOU SO LITTLE. GOOD-BYE."

When her snobbish, sneering rival attacked her, Elnora answered: "YOU INSULT MY BIRTH, EDUCATION, APPEARANCE, AND HOME. I ASSURE YOU I AM LEGITIMATE. I WILL PASS A TEST EXAMINATION ON ANY HIGH SCHOOL BRANCH OR FRENCH OR GERMAN. I WILL TAKE A PHYSICAL EXAMINATION BESIDE YOU. I WILL FACE ANY SOCIAL EMERGENCY WITH YOU. I AM ACQUAINTED WITH A WHOLE WORLD IN WHICH PHILIP AMMON IS KEENLY INTERESTED, THAT YOU SCARCELY KNOW EXISTS. I AM NOT AFRAID TO FACE ANY AUDIENCE WITH MY VIOLIN. I AM NOT REPULSIVE TO LOOK AT, AND I HAVE A WHOLESOME REGARD FOR THE PROPRIETIES AND CIVILITIES OF LIFE. PHILIP AMMON NEVER ASKED ANYTHING MORE OF ME, WHY SHOULD YOU?"

Elnora was more than refreshing; she was a whirlwind of energy and principle and wit. She stood alone, though. Next to her, Jo March was soft and whiny with men; Anne of Green Gables was feather-brained in her numerous stupid romances; Judy Abbott acted catatonic as she wandered into the web of Daddy-Long-Legs. Such lively girls these were, such good models for young readers—except that they crumpled so readily under the male gaze. Popular girls' fiction in the first half of the twentieth century produced no other characters as decisive in courtship as Elnora. Only late in the century did readers start to meet girls who were both eager to love and brimming with personal integrity.

I remember a little game which predicted your future relations with any boy: Cross out letters that match in his name and yours, then count remaining letters while repeating "Love, Marriage, Friendship, Hate." Thus, in the case of Debby Janney and John Smith (with a matching J and a matching N), *she* would find Love (nine letters remaining) and *he* would find Friendship (seven remaining). As a method for determining your fate, this was indeed paralysis rather than action.

By the age of six I had learned that boys were important and dangerous; girls should be tactful and devious. I admired a large, puffy boy named Jimmy, who told me he liked Valerie best but I could be his second girlfriend. That seemed all right, and once I even forgave him for torturing me when we were alone on a suburban train returning home from some activity (gas was scarce as

World War II came to a close): Bored by the trainride, Jimmy tore
up my ticket and told me the conductor would put me off at the
next stop because I had none. He also invented a boys' gang at
school to chase girls and lift their skirts to look at their underpants. The girls were not amused. I was one of the mousiest and
hated the constant threat; but I was clever and found a way to
avoid attacks. I told Jimmy I would be the nurse of the boys'
gang—a nominal post with no duties—if he would leave me out
of the attacks. I had learned to be responsive to the whims of boys,
even if that meant disloyalty to other girls. I never became one of
the popular girls invited first, but at least nobody saw my underpants. The whole situation seemed to me to be quite reasonable.
This is how things were.

· 7 ·

Today's Terrific New Girl
Heroes

One English school series written from the 1920s through the 1960s, critic Bob Dixon has pointed out, described a world where "the girls are so restricted in every way that, in order to create any activity at all, the author is forced to manufacture unlikely accidents and events. About all the girls can do is fall down." In one book, Dixon reports, "there are four falling or slipping incidents which lead to developments in the story."

I knew that comparing recent girls' stories with older ones like E. Brent-Dyer's school series would reveal major changes—presumably fictional girls after 1950 do something more than fall down. My tentative hypothesis was that some of the newer ones would present active, strong girl heroes but others, especially the popular formulaic series, would perpetuate old stereotypes that girls are flighty, flirty, fearful, and feeble. As I read more of these recent books, I was pleasantly surprised. Here are some glimpses:

. . . WHILE I WAS BUILDING THE FENCE AND THE HOUSE, I ATE SHELL-FISH WHICH I COOKED ON A FLAT ROCK. AFTERWARDS I MADE TWO UTENSILS. I WAS SHELTERED FROM THE WIND AND RAIN. I COULD COOK ANYTHING I WISHED TO EAT. IT WAS NOW TIME TO MAKE PLANS FOR GETTING RID OF THE WILD DOGS WHICH HAD KILLED MY BROTHER AND WOULD KILL ME SHOULD THEY EVER COME UPON ME UNARMED.

...I WONDERED HOW I COULD BE SO CALM—HOW I COULD JUST STAND THERE IN THE GRAY DARKNESS WITH THE COLD TREE MOISTURE DRIPPING DOWN ON ME AND THE DEAD BODY OF MY FATHER THERE BEFORE ME AND NOT BE AFRAID OF HOW GRISLY IT ALL WAS. IT'S BECAUSE I'M TOUGH, I THOUGHT, I'M SO TOUGH THAT IF A BEAR CAME OUT OF THE SIDE OF THE MOUNTAIN OVER THERE I COULD KNOCK HIM DEAD WITHOUT BREATHING HARD.

...BENGT HAD HOPED SHE WOULD GET MAD AND BEGIN TO CRY. WHEN NOTHING HAPPENED HE GAVE HER A PUSH. "I DON'T THINK YOU HAVE A VERY NICE WAY WITH LADIES," SAID PIPPI. AND SHE LIFTED HIM IN HER STRONG ARMS—HIGH IN THE AIR—AND CARRIED HIM TO A BIRCH TREE AND HUNG HIM OVER A BRANCH. THEN SHE TOOK THE NEXT BOY AND HUNG HIM OVER ANOTHER BRANCH, AND THE NEXT SHE THREW OVER A FENCE SO THAT HE LANDED IN A FLOWER BED.

The girls in these paragraphs were thirteen, fourteen, and nine years old. Karana of *Island of the Blue Dolphins*, Mary Call of *Where the Lilies Bloom*, and Pippi of *Pippi Longstocking* lived in a drastically different universe from the Little Colonel and Pollyanna and even Nancy Drew, for all the much-admired liveliness of those heroines.

Brave New Girls, 1950 to 1975

The new era of girls' fiction began—fittingly in 1950—with the explosion of Pippi Longstocking onto the scene. Despite a stilted translation from Astrid Lindgren's Swedish, the book was great fun. Nine-year-old Pippi lived on her own with a monkey and a horse, chatted with her mother in heaven, waited for her sea captain father to come home from being lost at sea, and did whatever she wanted. School she dismissed as worthless after one day. Housework she handled briskly: WHEN EVERYBODY HAD HAD ENOUGH, PIPPI TOOK HOLD OF ALL FOUR CORNERS OF THE TABLECLOTH AND LIFTED IT UP SO THAT THE CUPS AND PLATES TUMBLED OVER EACH OTHER AS IF THEY WERE IN A SACK. THEN SHE STUFFED THE WHOLE BUNDLE IN THE WOODBOX. "I ALWAYS LIKE TO TIDY UP AS SOON AS I HAVE EATEN," she said. Superstrong, she beat up an angry bull, and she lifted her horse to his bed on the porch.

This is not entirely a feminist world: it is implied that Pippi's strength came partly from the wonderful phallic shoes her father gave her, BLACK SHOES THAT WERE EXACTLY TWICE AS LONG AS HER FEET. And her friends were ridiculously stereotyped. But in the final chapter when Pippi gave sex-linked presents to her friends, a flute to Tommy and a jeweled brooch to Annika, she also transcended these roles by giving each one a pistol. She herself had a pistol and a sword, which she waved merrily about. When told she could not defeat the strong man at the circus because "HE'S THE STRONGEST MAN IN THE WORLD," Pippi answered, "MAN, YES, BUT I AM THE STRONGEST GIRL IN THE WORLD, REMEMBER THAT," before knocking him flat. In the book's last sentence, Pippi challenged her readers to follow her: "I'M GOING TO BE A PIRATE WHEN I GROW UP. ARE YOU?"

There were still transitional books with mixed messages, but more and more girls' stories with non-sexist plots and character types. From 1950 to 1975 some of the best books had girl heroes who were spectacular survivors or rescuers. Scott O'Dell based *Island of the Blue Dolphins* (1960) on the true story of a nineteenth-century Indian girl left behind when her tribe abandoned their island off Santa Barbara in order to avoid an enemy tribe. The real "lost woman of San Nicolas" lived alone eighteen years until a ship rescued her. With courage and intelligence, O'Dell's fictional Karana—as resourceful as Robinson Crusoe—built shelters, made tools, weapons, and clothes, caught and gathered food. She created elaborate plans: to kill hostile animals, to endure winter, to escape by repairing a ruined canoe.

Karana couldn't have been more different from traditional survivor heroines like brave-but-passive Sara Crewe in *The Little Princess*. You might think that Karana's actions were not particularly enterprising because she was in her home territory, exercising practical skills she already knew as a member of the tribe. But her actions went way beyond that. Her abandonment on the island came about by her own decision rather than chance or carelessness: As the white man's ship pulled out of the harbor to take her people to the mainland, Karana realized her six-year-old brother had been left ashore. The sailors would not turn back so she dove into the water and swam back to stay with him until the ship could return for them. A few days later he was killed by wild dogs and she began her eighteen-year vigil.

Her most frightening challenge was not coping with danger or loneliness or starvation; it was forcing herself to defy tribal taboos—the law that no female could make or use weapons. Karana overcame her conviction that A BOW IN THE HANDS OF A WOMAN WOULD BREAK IN A TIME OF DANGER. WOULD THE FOUR WINDS BLOW IN AND SMOTHER ME AS I MADE THE WEAPONS? OR WOULD THE EARTH TREMBLE, AS MANY SAID, AND BURY ME BENEATH ITS FALLING ROCKS? Pushing past the limits of her community, she invented and used weapons successfully. She also rejected tribal values when she tamed animals as friends and refused to kill any more for fur. All alone, she grew and changed.

This 1960 book is still popular. Karana's narrative voice is strong and memorable because it is so matter-of-fact. Far out from the island, I FOUND THAT THE CANOE WAS LEAKING. I FOUND THE PLACE WHERE THE WATER WAS SEEPING THROUGH A CRACK AS LONG AS MY HAND AND THE WIDTH OF A FINGER. I TORE A PIECE OF FIBER FROM MY SKIRT AND PRESSED IT INTO THE CRACK, WHICH HELD BACK THE WATER. Stubbornly paddling, bailing, and stuffing cloth in the crack, Karana made it back to shore. Much of her time on the island, though lonely, she was happy.

Another tale of survival appeared in 1972, Jean George's *Julie of the Wolves*, about a thirteen-year-old Eskimo girl. Animal friends helped Miyax to think and to act but her own strength and intelligence made the difference, in saving her from the northern waste. Miyax had run away onto the bare tundra to escape an arranged marriage. Her mother was dead, her father the hunter far away, and her real name buried under her new white name, Julie. Miyax was not stupid in getting lost on the Alaskan North Slope just before winter, she was merely ignorant: the island she grew up on offered compass signs in its plant and animal life, and she thought she could reach her destination by applying that knowledge. But the North Slope offered no such signs. She had a knife, pot, matches, and sleeping fur, but was lost and alone.

Miyax refused to panic (SHE HAD BEEN CERTAIN THAT TODAY SHE WOULD EAT—SO I WON'T, SHE SAID TO HERSELF, AND THAT'S THAT). Her meticulous observation won her a place in a wandering wolf pack. For days she studied the wolves' behavior until she knew enough to prance on all fours up to the enormous leader, make the right submissive grunting noise, and bite the wolf gently under the chin. Through sixty-six winter days with no sun she sent and understood messages in the wolves' howling language; she played with them and she shared their food. Finally finding a human settlement and her father, Miyax sadly left her wolf friends and went back to the Americanized world. When she first ran away she had planned to live with a San Francisco friend who sent letters about television and bikinis. Now she wanted only to stay close to her natural world and do all she could to preserve it from harm. She ended with a song to the wolf leader: AMAROQ, AMAROQ, YOU ARE MY ADOPTED FATHER. / MY FEET DANCE BECAUSE OF YOU. / MY MIND THINKS BECAUSE OF YOU.

Other girl heroes rescued and protected their families as well as themselves, notably Mary Call in *Where the Lilies Bloom* (by Vera and Bill Cleaver, 1969) and Meg in *A Wrinkle in Time* (1962). Earlier characters also helped their families in troubled times but those earlier girls stayed snugly within the family hierarchy, in a helping rather than a leading role. Mary Call Luther had no such comfort. As her father lay coughing his life away in their North Carolina mountain cabin, she promised she would take care of the two younger children and the eighteen-year-old sister who was slow and "cloudy-minded." So that the authorities would not split up the family, Mary Call and her brother kept their father's death a secret and dragged his body up to the grave he had dug for himself on the mountainside. Then she masterminded the family secret, ran the household, and slaved at earning money by selling herbs and making Christmas evergreen ropes. Her efforts could not support the family forever, but she managed to stall long enough that a solution was worked out and the family stayed together in their cabin.

At fourteen, to accomplish this, Mary Call Luther became a tyrant. The irascible landlord commented, "YOU'RE ENOUGH TO SKEER A MAN, STANDIN' THERE ALL SPRADDLE-LEGGED WITH YOUR JAW STUCK OUT UGLY. WHY CAN'T YOU BE SWEET AND NICE LIKE YOUR SIS-TER?" "BECAUSE SWEET, NICE GIRLS GET THEMSELVES RUN OVER BY PEO-PLE LIKE YOU." She told her sister she was mean and ugly because,

"IT TAKES TIME TO BE SWEET AND PRETTY AND I'M TOO BUSY SEEING TO IT THAT YOU AND THOSE OTHER TWO DON'T STARVE AND DON'T FREEZE TO DEATH AND THAT THE COUNTY PEOPLE DON'T COME AND HAUL YOU AWAY." Things got worse; storms caved in the roof so a crazed fox leaped into the room and attacked Mary Call until she whopped it to death with a board.

Eventually she got worn down and discouraged, thinking: I MUST HAVE MOSS GROWING WHERE MY BRAINS SHOULD BE. NOBODY BUT A POOR DEMENT WOULD DO WHAT I'M DOING, HIDING MY OLD DEAD DADDY OVER THERE. TAKING ME ON THREE SNOT-NOSED KIDS TO RAISE. IF I HAD THE SENSE OF A RABBIT I'D JUST TAKE OFF AND KEEP RIGHT ON WALKING. THEY'D MAKE OUT ALL RIGHT WITHOUT ME. She weakened but hung on until spring. BY THE GRACE OF THE LORD WE'RE HERE AND WHAT WE MAKE OF IT IS OUR OWN AFFAIR. MY NAME IS MARY CALL LUTHER, I THOUGHT, AND SOMEDAY I'M GOING TO BE A BIG SHOT.

In books published from 1950 to 1975, most of the powerful girl heroes inhabited worlds that were quite unlike the lives of their readers: fantasy worlds or places remote in time or place. Unconventional behavior is less threatening when it occurs far away from ordinary life; nice girls in the next generation after Cherry Ames and Nancy Drew broadened their vision by reading about Karana far away on her nineteenth-century island, or Meg Murry whizzing among the planets in Madeleine L'Engle's *A Wrinkle in Time* (1962). That science fiction adventure started at the home of a scientist couple and their children, then expanded to show a struggle of good and evil throughout the galaxies. Thirteen-year-old Meg was stubborn and sometimes obnoxious, and (like Mary Call) this helped her save her family.

Meg was transported along with her friend Calvin and her telepathic brother Charles Wallace to a sick, dark planet in an attempt to rescue their captured father. Camazotz was a *1984*-type of planet where "EVERYTHING IS IN PERFECT ORDER BECAUSE EVERYBODY HAS LEARNED TO SUBMIT," as the children were told by the dictator "It"—a huge, bodiless brain. "THAT'S WHAT WE HAVE ON CAMAZOTZ. COMPLETE EQUALITY. EVERYBODY EXACTLY ALIKE." Defiant Meg wouldn't buy this: "NO!" SHE CRIED TRIUMPHANTLY. "*LIKE* AND *EQUAL* ARE NOT THE SAME AT ALL!" She freed her father and escaped from Camazotz with him, but they seized and brain-washed her little brother. So now the Murrys had to rescue him, which would be an important victory in the continuing war of good guys against evil powers. Meg began to despair: SHE HAD FOUND HER FATHER AND HE HAD NOT MADE EVERYTHING ALL RIGHT. THERE WAS NOTHING TO GUARANTEE IT WOULD ALL COME OUT RIGHT IN THE END. It became clear that the responsibility was hers: no one else was as close to Charles Wallace and no one else had a chance at calling out his own, trapped self.

Finally Meg agreed to return alone to Camazotz. "I'M SORRY, FATHER. I WANTED YOU TO DO IT ALL FOR ME. SO I TRIED TO PRETEND THAT IT WAS ALL YOUR FAULT. BECAUSE I WAS SCARED, AND I DIDN'T WANT TO HAVE TO DO ANYTHING MYSELF." "DO YOU HAVE THE COUR-AGE TO GO ALONE?" MRS WHATSIT ASKED HER. MEG'S VOICE WAS FLAT. "NO. BUT IT DOESN'T MATTER. YOU KNOW IT'S THE ONLY THING TO DO." Meg set forth; she found that her tenacity and anger, her hatred, got her a long way but not far enough. To release her brother and weaken Camazotz she needed to use the power of her love for Charles Wallace. Her strength and her love, together, defeated the horrible It. This outcome may *seem* to resemble earlier stories where a tomboy girl learned she must tame her fierce ways and become a softer member of her society. The difference here, how-ever, is much greater than the likeness: Meg did not give up her fierceness, her rage; rather, she added and activated and focused the positive love that she always possessed. She became herself; she did not—like those earlier sad Katys and Caddies and Jo's—abandon her central self and become somebody else's idea of what a nice girl should be.

As girl characters became bolder and more active in the 1960s, some interesting ones appeared in realistic settings. Two popular books presented restless girls from privileged families seeking ad-venture in New York City. Harriet, in *Harriet the Spy* (1964) by Louise Fitzhugh, and Claudia, in *From the Mixed-up Files of Mrs. Basil E. Frankweiler* (1967) by E.L. Konigsberg, showed initiative and met challenges in contemporary, urban ways. Harriet and Claudia were too sharp and curious to remain nice complacent private-school girls. They were true descendents of Alice—that wandering girl created a century before, who frightened softer girl readers like myself with her cool toughness in a weird world.

Eleven-year-old Harriet Welsch announced "I WANT TO KNOW EVERYTHING IN THE WORLD. I WILL BE A SPY AND KNOW EVERYTHING." Clearly she was destined to become a writer: she invented a game called Town, with detailed stories for each citizen, and wrote copiously in the notebooks that were her most important possession. Each day after school in Manhattan she followed her spying route and wrote down what she saw and what she thought: studying the owners of an Italian grocery, staking out a bachelor with cats, even sneaking into the kitchen dumbwaiter of a townhouse to spy on the woman who lived there. Harriet's nanny, Ole Golly, encouraged her, saying "LIFE IS A STRUGGLE AND A GOOD SPY GETS IN THERE AND FIGHTS." Harriet flung herself into things wildly, like rolling and bumping around the floor of her room to figure out how to play an onion in a school pageant.

Energy and imagination could be dangerous. After Harriet's school friends found her notebook, full of the caustic things she had written about them, they banded together to ostracize her. This was already a lonely time, as Ole Golly had married and moved away. Would the traumatic incident tame Harriet's independence and curiosity, and make her realize that conventional behavior is kindest and most comfortable for everyone? She did not sell out, though she finally agreed to a compromise. At first, she was outraged at her classmates; her notebook had only told the truth. But a teacher lured her back from despair by selecting Harriet to write the class newspaper. Ole Golly sent bracing advice, telling Harriet she would have to apologize to her friends and even lie, because she hurt them. REMEMBER THAT WRITING IS TO PUT LOVE IN THE WORLD, NOT TO USE AGAINST YOUR FRIENDS. BUT TO YOURSELF YOU MUST ALWAYS TELL THE TRUTH. Without sacrificing ambition, Harriet was learning empathy. Her perspective opened up in ways that would benefit both her writing and her relationships: I HAVE THOUGHT A LOT ABOUT *BEING* THINGS SINCE TRYING TO BE AN ONION. I HAVE TRIED TO BE A BENCH IN THE PARK, A CAT, AND MY MUG IN THE BATHROOM. I THINK I DID THE MUG BEST BECAUSE WHEN I WAS LOOKING AT IT I FELT IT LOOKING BACK AT ME AND I FELT

LIKE WE WERE TWO MUGS LOOKING AT EACH OTHER. I WONDER IF GRASS TALKS.

The end is gratifying because of its priorities. Harriet issued a retraction and was forgiven by her friends; then she wrote in her notebook, NOW THAT THINGS ARE BACK TO NORMAL I CAN GET SOME REAL WORK DONE. She knew Ole Golly had been right to say, I HAVE DECIDED THAT IF YOU ARE EVER GOING TO BE A WRITER IT IS TIME YOU GOT CRACKING. YOU ARE ELEVEN YEARS OLD AND HAVEN'T WRITTEN A THING BUT NOTES. Talent and ambition caused her trouble and always would, but she didn't give up on them and she refused to see them as shameful.

From the Mixed-up Files of Mrs. Basil E. Frankweiler is another recent story that showed a girl hero who could return to her home base and accept it, while strengthening rather than sacrificing the core of her developing self. Twelve-year-old Claudia Kincaid grew tired of her suburban, straight-A life and determined to run away. As she liked comfort and elegance she chose for her destination the Metropolitan Museum of Art; as her finances were meager she invited her younger brother to join her and contribute his savings. For a week the children hid in the museum, sleeping in a sixteenth-century bed, bathing at night in the museum fountain, buying food with coins from the fountain.

Claudia craved excitement and the crude danger of hiding out began to pale, so she began a more sophisticated quest: to solve the mystery of a statue's origin which was stumping the art world and the media. Studying the beautiful little angel statue at night did not bring the answer, nor did research in the Public Library. The next step was to take a train to the Connecticut mansion of the statue's eccentric donor, Mrs. Basil E. Frankweiler, and confront her: Did she know the secret? Was the angel really made by Michelangelo?

Mrs. Frankweiler, a modern good fairy, put Claudia through some tests to see if she was worthy and then bestowed on her the secret of the statue. She helped the girl see what she was really seeking: not just the excitement of running away from home and being different, but the deeper excitement of having important secrets, your own knowledge that you keep inside. The adventure is in the knowledge. Mrs. Frankweiler told Claudia, "SOME DAYS YOU MUST LEARN A GREAT DEAL. BUT YOU SHOULD ALSO HAVE DAYS WHEN YOU ALLOW WHAT IS ALREADY IN YOU TO SWELL UP INSIDE OF YOU UNTIL IT TOUCHES EVERYTHING. IF YOU NEVER TAKE TIME OUT TO LET THAT HAPPEN, THEN YOU JUST ACCUMULATE FACTS, AND THEY BE-GIN TO RATTLE AROUND INSIDE OF YOU. YOU CAN MAKE NOISE WITH THEM, BUT NEVER REALLY FEEL ANYTHING WITH THEM. IT'S HOLLOW." While riding home in Mrs. Frankweiler's chauffeured Rolls Royce was good, knowing important secrets about the statue and about herself was even better, the best outcome of Claudia's adventure.

Claudia's and Harriet's stories were closer to real life than fantasy tales were, but they did not describe typical lives of ordinary girls. In the second half of the century the founding mother of that genre was Beverly Cleary, who sent four-year-old Ramona hurtling into the literary world in 1955. Ramona had dozens of descendents in the next forty years—Lowry's Anastasia, Naylor's Alice, Cameron's Julia, Greene's Isabelle and Al—and some of those series were captivating, but it was hard to beat the energy and conviction of the original little kid girl hero.

Ramona Quimby was not just an interesting small girl, she was an interesting small *child*. Her thoughts and actions were hers because she was a unique self, not because she belonged to the category "Girl." Her odd, naughty behavior—taking one bite out of each apple in a basket, crashing her tricycle into the coffee table, squeezing out a whole toothpaste tube, playing an interminable game of smashing bricks into dust—was judged for itself, not held against a ruler measuring girlish deportment. Her best friend Howie never got excited but that was the way he was; he wasn't different just because he was a boy. If you compare this series to, say, the Peppers books with their stereotypes, you can see how enormous a change has taken place.

By the time Ramona moved from nursery school to kindergarten (in her second book, *Ramona the Pest*) certain things about her were clear. Her mind was logical so she did weird things for good reasons, such as refusing to leave her seat at school because the teacher had told her "sit there for the present" and she wanted to wait for her present. Her chief goal was to know who she really was and be known to others. Learning to write her name was not enough—she had to make it unique by drawing cat ears and whiskers on the Q in Quimby. A Halloween party frightened her because many children were wearing the exact same mask; she realized people couldn't see her individual self any more.

So identity not gender was Ramona's theme and problem. When she noticed TWO KINDS OF CHILDREN WENT TO KINDERGARTEN she was not thinking boys and girls, but good and bad: THOSE WHO LINED UP BESIDE THE DOOR, AS THEY WERE SUPPOSED TO, AND THOSE WHO RAN AROUND THE PLAYGROUND AND SCRAMBLED TO GET INTO LINE WHEN THEY SAW MISS BINNEY APPROACHING. RAMONA RAN AROUND THE PLAYGROUND. Was she a bad person? And why was life sometimes unfair? It took her seven books to get such questions sorted out. Some of the incidents did involve boy vs. girl behavior—could girls wear brown galoshes?—but these were no more crucial and defining than gender-neutral incidents where Ramona wore pajamas to school under her clothes or scrunched up Susan's paper owl in a rage.

Leftover Messages in Recent Classics

Even as girls were breathing fresh air with Pippi and Ramona in the 1950s, they were still exposed to the familiar polluted, sexist air in books by some of the masters of children's fiction. "Masters" is the right word, because E. B. White, C. S. Lewis, and Susan Cooper used their broad and deep talents in support of hierarchical, gender-stereotyped societies. The female spider in *Charlotte's Web* (1952) is such a great character that it is painful to point out the dreariness of the girl character. Eight-year-old Fern's behavior was enterprising at the start; she shouted at her father until he agreed not to kill the runty pig. "IT'S UNFAIR," CRIED FERN. "IF *I* HAD BEEN VERY SMALL AT BIRTH, WOULD YOU HAVE KILLED *ME*?" She raised her piglet, Wilbur, carefully, and became joyously involved in the conversations and adventures of the barn animals.

Later, when Wilbur's life was threatened again by slaughtering season, the spider saved him with her brilliant public relations scheme of weaving captions into her web, such as SOME PIG! and RADIANT. Fern admired Charlotte's genius as much as the animals did but gradually she lost interest. In the last scenes, when her Wilbur was awarded a special prize at the state fair for being radiant and terrific, Fern was nagging her parents for money so she could go on the ferris wheel with Henry Fussy. When Charlotte was dying at the fair far from home, having used up her strength weaving messages for Wilbur, Fern was not around. Charlotte's nobility was memorable; so was Fern's callousness. White was writing about the cycles of nature—Fern was simply growing up, just as Charlotte was growing old (for a spider)—but the effect was nasty. The story showed that a human girl would be self-centered, frivolous, unreliable. You can forgive the author only because of his portrayal of Charlotte: witty; blood-thirsty but kind; good at her work and good at making babies. IT IS NOT OFTEN THAT SOMEONE COMES ALONG WHO IS A TRUE FRIEND AND A GOOD WRITER. CHARLOTTE WAS BOTH.

C. S. Lewis's Narnia tales from the 1950s have also been well loved. They are stuffed full of magic and wars and journeys; fauns, beasts; and a variety of human children some of whom became kings and queens of Narnia. Aslan, the Christlike lion, lovingly watched over his land and people while other characters fumbled, doing their best. The problem is that the Narnia books measured the children not just against Lewis's Christian ideals but also, blatantly, against old standards of gender-appropriate behavior. The girl characters tended to be more sensitive and nurturing; Lucy in particular was the healer and was the first to understand Aslan's true nature and power. The boys were efficient in planning and bold in battle. Sometimes the girls did brave deeds but mostly they floated in a bath of clichés. In a battle scene, ROUND AND ROUND THE COMBATANTS CIRCLED, AND SUSAN (WHO NEVER COULD LEARN TO LIKE THIS SORT OF THING) SHOUTED OUT, "OH, *DO* BE CAREFUL." Lucy was praised as being "AS GOOD AS A MAN, OR AT ANY RATE AS GOOD AS A BOY. SUSAN IS MORE LIKE AN ORDINARY GROWN-UP LADY." When Peter kissed the furry head of a helpful badger, IT WASN'T A GIRLISH THING FOR HIM TO DO, BECAUSE HE WAS THE HIGH KING.

The author thought he was distinguishing children who were good examples and children who were bad examples of their gender; even so he condescended to the girls. It wasn't just frivolous

Lasaraleen who yearned for fancy stuff—"DARLING, ONLY THINK! THREE PALACES, ONE ON THE LAKE. ROPES OF PEARLS. BATHS OF ASSES' MILK." Even Lucy behaved as a real girl was supposed to: Back in the palace she went off with a friend TO TALK ABOUT ARAVIS'S BEDROOM AND BOUDOIR AND ABOUT GETTING CLOTHES FOR HER, AND ALL THE SORT OF THINGS GIRLS DO TALK ABOUT. With this regressive garbage still in their heads in the 1950s, girls needed books like *Island of the Blue Dolphins* and *Julie of the Wolves*.

Narnia in the 1950s was followed by Susan Cooper's Dark Is Rising series in the 1970s. Here, things had not improved for female characters, who were even more thoroughly relegated to supporting roles. Of the five children involved only one was a girl, an uninteresting one at that. Dozens of characters appeared in Cooper's five-volume series about the the Old Ones' struggle to defend the Light against the rising of evil forces of the Dark. Only three of the good guys and bad guys were women, and the neutral nature deity was female, the Greenwitch. Everyone else was male; they were the players. An ancient manuscript that turned up to guide the Old Ones referred to "HEATHEN *MEN* OF EVIL" and "THE *MAN* WHO FINDS THE GRAIL. . . ."

Will Stanton, an ordinary eleven-year-old who was the last of the circle of Old Ones, developed heroic qualities throughout the series, pursuing a terrifying magic quest with Bran, the Welsh heir to King Arthur. Jane, the one girl, was an important character only in one book of the series, where she won the Greenwitch over to the side of the Light by showing a spontaneous sympathy for the Greenwitch's loneliness. So readers learned that a girl could help the cause through feminine instinct, not by brains and courage. The only time Jane took decisive action, her action was disastrous: she revealed secrets to one of the enemy in disguise. A girl should have known better than to take the initiative. All the children were frightened when things went wrong, but Jane surpassed the boys in whining and snivelling. She remarked about little Barney, "I'M GLAD HE'S SO BRIGHT ABOUT IT ALL. I WISH I WERE. IT'S AS IF THERE'S SOMEONE WAITING BEHIND EVERY CORNER TO POUNCE ON US. I ONLY FEEL SAFE WHEN I'M IN BED." Once again, the girl felt safest when she was horizontal.

Recent Series

Even in the third quarter of this century, then, strong girl heroes did not dominate girls' fiction; they still competed with stereotyped characters and plots in books by some of the best writers. If E. B. White and C. S. Lewis were so obtuse, could we expect anything better from feeble formula series? Some sleazy sexist books did continue to appear. One popular series from the 1980s, Sweet Valley High, trained children to become the kind of women who read Harlequin romances. (One Sweet Valley girl noticed THERE WAS A MANLIKE HARDNESS TO HIS BRONZED BUILD SHE FOUND DANGEROUS AND EXCITING . . . IN HER NEW RED STRING BIKINI SHE WAS A MATCH EVEN FOR "MS. 10," IF SHE DID SAY SO HERSELF.) The heroines of Sweet Valley High were twin sisters, lovably bad Jessica and impossibly good Elizabeth. Their adventures couldn't be more shallow, predictable, and boy-crazy—somebody got in trouble for staying out all night; somebody was jealous of her boyfriend's attention to a rival; somebody wasn't chosen queen of the prom.

The author made a few gestures suggesting new attitudes towards girls: Elizabeth wrote for the school newspaper, took an interest in schoolwork, avoided heavy makeup and sexy clothes. But Elizabeth was really the old good-girl stereotype and nobody read the Sweet Valley books to hear about Elizabeth's ambitions as a journalist—it was those bronzed manlike bodies and cute cheerleading outfits that appealed to the ditzier kind of preteen girl. Many girls read Sweet Valley books in a brief silly phase, aware of their limitations, then moved on to more solid books. By the 1980s, even in the saccharine world of Sweet Valley, there was at least a pretense of respect for sensible, interesting girls.

The same tokenism appeared in an awful book called *Just Another Gorgeous Guy* by Irene Bennett Brown (1984). Forced to spend her seventeenth summer in an old-fashioned Oregon village, spoiled Hillary learned to discard materialistic values, love children and old folks, and date nerdy boys. Since the book's energy (such as it is) lay in Hillary's frivolous "Before" character, the would-be-feminist message is singularly unconvincing. ALL SUMMER LONG SHE HAD BEEN AWARE OF THIS FEVERISH DESIRE TO KNOW HERSELF. TO MAKE GOOD, TO FEEL SOLID AGAIN, A REAL PERSON; yeah, sure. Who could believe in such sentiments after a hundred pages of this other stuff?—A ROCK TUNE POUNDED THROUGH THE WINDOW OF A CAR CRUISING BY. HILLARY TURNED FROM SCOPING THE DRIVER TO CATCH SIGHT OF ANOTHER DREAM, ALL TAN MUSCLES AND SUN-BLEACHED HAIR, LICKING A STACKED ICE CREAM CONE. SHE ALMOST DROOLED, AND NOT BECAUSE OF THE ICE CREAM. SHE WASN'T GOING TO GET INTO TROUBLE. BUT SHE DID PLAN TO MAKE GOOD USE OF HER TIME, A LA MEETING GORGEOUS GUYS. It's rather sweet, though ludicrous, that the same Hillary suddenly developed plans to work for historic preservation and low-income housing; at least the author means well.

The most jarring set of girls' books with a mixed sensibility is the Deathbed books of Lurlene McDaniel, written in the 1990s. Building on the popularity of realistic stories about serious problems, McDaniel created a world of teenagers who were dying and/or disabled or deformed. (This isn't a *series*—you can't sustain a cast of characters when people die all the time.) But she avoided real realism and undercut the seriousness of her subjects by writing superficially, in the clichés of romance fiction. A character might have cystic fibrosis or her boyfriend might have terminal leukemia, but she still would think about AN AWESOME TAFFETA DRESS, A MUSCULAR PHYSIQUE TO DIE FOR. (The latter being an unfortunate turn of phrase under the circumstances.)

In the more upbeat McDaniel stories, pleasant things happened, like a girl with a facial deformity getting together with a blind boy; but most of the books had witless morbid touches that make the 1960s' *Love Story* look cheerful. Julie in *Don't Die, My Love* (1995) went into a terrible depression after her football-player boyfriend died of leukemia in the fall. Then in the spring a friend of Luke's took Julie to the top of the stadium and made her look down. Lo! a bright message from the heavens was spelled out in the grass on the football field: I LOVE YOU, JULIE. Luke had planted tulip bulbs in the fall, presumably staggering out of his hospital bed with a trowel to do so. Julie was then able to accept her loss and, as they say in such circles, get on with her life.

It's hard to know what to make of these books and the girls who read them. Certainly teenagers want to explore all emotions, morbid along with scary, violent, and sexual. McDaniel's books are unusually horrible because they stir up a prurient delight in the weakness and sickly wretchedness of young girls: they encourage the kinds of emotion that the Victorians so enjoyed in the deaths of Dickens's Little Nell and Stowe's Little Eva. Poe's conviction is still abroad in our culture: that the most beautiful and virtuous girl is, like Carol in *The Birds' Christmas Carol*, immobilized. Lurlene McDaniel's characters are not young women responding actively to terrible medical problems, they are old-time heroines steeped in a romantic world of death.

The good news is that these sickly stories are distinctly a minor note in the reading girls are exposed to today. And I have been told by teachers and librarians in several states that the Sweet Valley High books have peaked. When you look at other mass-market series popular in recent years, the picture is surprisingly bright. Apparently American society has changed enough that gross female stereotypes are not acceptable to most parents and daughters. They won't buy rankly sexist books, so publishers are not producing them. As always, to make money, run-of-the-mill series spew forth improbable plots and undeveloped characters. But now at least girl characters do not shrink from danger and exertion; they do not let others tell them how to think and act; and they do not constantly sacrifice their own plans and wishes. The old barrage of weak-maiden messages has virtually stopped in girls' books, and while this change alone will not produce a nation of brave new girls, it will surely help young readers to think of themselves as competent, active people.

Something healthy started happening in the 1960s and 70s. Despite resistance to clumsy terms such as "Ms." and "his/her," changes were taking place in the language of reasonable people and publications. The nagging of determined souls gradually created an awareness that "he" does not properly describe half the world's population; and that gender stereotypes are harmful, not humorous. Just as it became clear to most (even those who didn't care) that ethnic slurs were not going to be tolerated, it also became clear that remarks about dumb blondes, bullying wives, and eager rape victims were made only by idiots. Even the most ordinary, formulaic children's series benefited from this changing perspective. Reading around in these series I found that even superficial, uninspiring stories avoided the gross kind of "girlish" behavior that was taken for granted before 1950.

Judy Blume was the star of this mass-market realm in the 1970s. Her characters had messy problems similar to those her young readers were living through: One was involved in the bullying of a fat girl; one was confused by her mixed religious background; another worried that friends would find out about her phobias. One had a depressed grandmother; another had white parents who didn't like a black family moving next door. The stories are pleasant but thin, the characters created from a menu, not understood from within.

These were typical problem-cases rather than unique characterizations—but at least they were not based on old conventions of proper girlhood. With Judy Blume, even those books that described sex-linked problems like first menstruation or wet dreams were reasonably matter-of-fact: these were just another kind of problem that young people had to handle. That was comforting. An eleven-year-old girl character (and reader) could worry equally about buying a bra and choosing a religion, while a boy could worry about family quarrels and erections in math class. Life included all this, and it could all be coped with or survived. Judy Blume's books were not great contributions to literature but they did avoid the old girls'-book miasma of guilt and sacrifice and anxious virtue.

Judy Blume problem books, and dozens of other recent series like the American Girl history stories, have brought pleasure to little girls and income to publishers. Even more lucrative and titillating are the horror books that swept the publishing world in the 1980s. While booksellers and librarians say that the fad is cooling, children still pore over dozens of books in the various scary series—for instance, R. L. Stine's Goosebumps for younger readers and his Fear Street for middle-level children, and the more recent weird series called Animorphs in which child characters turned into animals and then back again. You might expect that these plot-dominated horror books would play mostly to boys and that they would contain stereotyped images of frightened, feeble girls being saved by stronger boys, yet even in these trashy stories of recent years a fairer picture of girls does prevail.

I haven't read many books by R. L. Stine—my devotion to children's literature has *some* limits—but the four I read show girls to be at least as brave and resourceful as boys. They are definitely more than victims and sidekicks. In *Stay out of the Basement* (1992), one of the silly, supernatural Goosebumps books, the girl and boy children were equally frightened to learn that their scientist father's plant experiments were turning him into a murderous vegetable who ate plant food and slept on a bed full of dirt and worms. Margaret and her brother worked together to break into the basement full of mutant plant-people, and Margaret was the one who identified the real father by cutting his arm to see the red blood flow (the evil clone bled green sap). She didn't faint at the blood, either.

In Fear Street stories *The Wrong Number* and *The Sleepwalker* (both 1990) girl heroes refused to be paralyzed by events; they found clever, risky ways to solve mysteries that were baffling everyone else. *The Sleepwalker* nicely reversed the familiar Gothic-romance plot where a girl would drift helplessly, while terrible things were done to her. In this story a teenager found herself sleepwalking night after night, wandering even to the deep lake's edge. The story started like this: AS PALE AS MOONLIGHT, MAYRA SEEMED TO FLOAT ACROSS THE LAWN. HER LONG COPPERY HAIR BILLOWED IN THE NIGHT BREEZE. HER SILKY WHITE NIGHTGOWN SHIMMERED. Yes, typical. But instead of giving in like a Gothic maiden, Mayra investigated until she figured out what was happening. Then she set a trap for her boyfriend, who had been hypnotizing her into forgetting a car accident in which he had killed somebody. "WHEN YOU OPEN YOUR EYES YOU WILL FEEL COMPLETELY CALM," WALKER SAID SOFTLY. MAYRA, HER EYELIDS CLOSED, NODDED SLOWLY. "AND YOU WILL CONTINUE TO FORGET ABOUT THAT NIGHT ON RIVER RIDGE. YOU WILL HAVE NO MEMORY OF THE ACCIDENT." MAYRA OPENED HER EYES. SHE LEAPT TO HER FEET AND GRABBED WALKER'S SWEATSHIRT WITH BOTH HANDS. "YOU FILTHY CREEP!" SHE SCREAMED. "I *KNEW* THAT'S WHAT YOU DID TO ME THAT HORRIBLE NIGHT! MY SLEEPWALKING—IT WAS ALL YOUR FAULT!" Not graceful behavior (or writing), but satisfying.

Ann Martin in the 1980s had a good idea for an updated kind of girls'-group series. Her Baby-sitters Club books followed an old pattern: a gang of likable characters had mild adventures and solved not-too-threatening problems. Nonetheless, the girls' club was impressive. Creating and running a babysitting service challenged the responsibilty and imagination of five junior high school girls. If you compare the members of the Baby-sitters Club to the "Big Six" children in the Maida books, you can see how far formula writers have advanced. Maida and her friends could not plan a backyard stroll without the help of servants and mentors; the Baby-sitters deftly managed finances, schedules, public relations; they cared for children and reassured parents; they expanded into playgroups and au pair vacations.

These books did include dull descriptions of clothes and giggling gossip about boys, and Judy Blume–like problems were added in predictable amounts: a spoonful of dyslexia, a touch of diabetes; a sprinkling of divorced parents, jealous siblings, dying pets. You can't fault a series for following its formula, though, and these little girls created for themselves a useful, enterprising kind of fun. It would be even more enterprising if they were involved in a business less traditionally girlish than babysitting— bicycle repair, perhaps—but nobody's perfect.

Some people believe that being alert to sexist (or racist or homophobic or xenophobic) images is faddish and unnecessary, a knee-jerk response. But we are constantly hit with so many millions of verbal messages that it seems obtuse or malicious to deny their potency. Little girls who read a lot are now being soaked in the Baby-sitters' cheerful work ethic and the gushing enthusiasms of other series such as The Gymnasts and Girl Talk. Certainly no normal adult could enjoy shallow stories and cute language of the "incredibly cool," "major hunk!" sort of writing. Yet if a child is going to have a phase of reading flimsy stories, it's better she should read healthy flimsy stories than the old sacrificial, guilt-laden kind.

After 1975

Now that the underbrush of girly stereotypes has been pretty much cleared away, there is space for new kinds of books to grow, and they have indeed been growing. In the 1980s and 90s, girl characters in good children's stories have become wonderfully original, thick with reality and ambiguity. I can't begin to list all the interesting new girls' books and authors. Stories set in our own world have girls who are not distorted by old assumptions about fragile females. Stories set in other times and places have complex girls who fight against powerful social forces; they lose particular battles but not their strong selves; they believe in their own value and their own values.

Shabanu, Daughter of the Wind (1989) tells of a desert family in Pakistan and a girl who tried to develop an independent self within the family. Eleven-year-old Shabanu, who tended camels and taught her favorite one to dance, loved her nomadic life but worried about the future: a girl had to be married at puberty to an arranged suitor. Her family was traditional but kind, never making her feel unwanted even though their culture defined girls as inferior. When a deadly feud threatened the family, however, the father brought them safety and wealth by marrying his older daughter to Shabanu's intended, beloved suitor, and selling Shabanu as fourth wife to a fifty-year-old rich man who fancied her.

This man sent her presents. "HOW CAN I ACCEPT A GIFT FROM HIM?" I ASK QUIETLY, "IS HE BUYING ME?" "SHABANU," SAYS DADI, HIS VOICE STERN. "HE ALREADY *HAS* BOUGHT YOU. HE HAS PAID MORE THAN A FAIR PRICE FOR A TROUBLESOME GIRL LIKE YOU. CAN'T YOU SEE HE WANTS YOU TO BE HAPPY?" I AM SMALL AND STRONG WITH TOO MUCH SPIRIT, AND I THINK TOO MUCH. I AM LONELY AND FEARFUL, AND I LONG FOR THE DAYS WHEN I WAS FREE IN THE DESERT. I DO RESENT HIS TRYING TO BUY MY HEART. BRIDE PRICE IS COMMON HERE IN THE DESERT. I DON'T BEGRUDGE MAMA AND DADI THAT. THEY WON'T HAVE TO WORRY ABOUT DROUGHT OR ANYTHING ELSE EVER AGAIN. BUT MY HEART. . . .

The author, Suzanne Fisher Staples, did not oversimplify or demonize. Family customs were warm, desert life was difficult but beautiful. Even so doubts grew in Shabanu about her life and she thought of a cousin who was beaten by her husband, then built up her own herd of goats and left home with her child. Shabanu tried to run away to live with the cousin, Sharma, but was caught by her enraged father. HE CAN BEAT ME TO DEATH IF HE LIKES. THE PAIN GROWS WORSE AS THE BLOWS STRIKE ALREADY-BRUISED FLESH. BUT I TAKE SHARMA'S ADVICE. I RECALL THE BEAUTIFUL THINGS IN MY WORLD AND, LIKE A BRIDE ADMIRING HER DOWRY, I TAKE THEM OUT, ONE BY ONE, THEN FOLD THEM AWAY AGAIN DEEP INTO MY HEART. In the future her only hope would be to keep her strong self hidden but alive, locked away from her husband and master.

Lyddie (1991, by Katherine Paterson) followed a nineteenth-century Vermont farm girl who met challenges boldly. Her family split up and she went to work in a Lowell factory noted for tuberculosis and injuries. Thirteen-year-old Lyddie, PLAIN AS PLOWED SOD and ORNERY AS AN OLD SOW, was tough. She stared down a bear in the family cabin. When a coach stuck in mud she pushed aside the floundering men, FOUND A FLAT STONE AND PUT IT UNDER THE MIRED WHEEL. THEN SHE WADED IN, SET HER OWN STRONG RIGHT SHOULDER AGAINST THE REAR WHEEL, AND CALLED OUT "ONE, TWO, THREE, HEAVE!"

Tending her looms thirteen hours a day in terrible conditions, she became the best factory worker; studying *Oliver Twist*, she became a good reader. Moral challenges were harder. Saving to pay farm debts and reassemble her family, she was tempted to turn in an escaped slave for a hundred dollars but instead lent the man all her money. Later, saving money seemed meaningless after Lyddie's mother went to an asylum, her brother was adopted, and the farm was sold. So Lyddie did not despair at being fired from the factory. She had dumped a water bucket on her overseer to prevent him from raping a friend of hers. Before she left Lowell she confronted the overseer: if he punished the other girl, Lyddie would tell his wife what happened. Then she set off for the West with her savings, determined to become one of the female students at Oberlin College. After a few years she might—or might not—return to Vermont and marry the kind farmer who had been courting her. "I'M OFF..." TO STARE DOWN THE BEAR! SHE WOULD STARE DOWN ALL THE BEARS!

* * *

Many recent books about twentieth-century American children go deeper than the Judy Blume-type stories. *Roll of Thunder, Hear My Cry* and *Let the Circle Be Unbroken* (by Mildred D. Taylor, 1976 and 1981) present the Logans, a black family in Depression Mississippi. Eleven-year-old Cassie was a no-nonsense girl who wanted to take part in whatever was going on, even when the goings-on were terrifying. As she grew up into a dangerous world of lynchings and white-only water fountains, she learned how to survive without losing pride and independence. Her family helped her, and so did her own boldness. When the white schoolbus driver once too often splashed mud on the black children who had no bus, to amuse his little riders, Cassie and her brother dug a ditch in the dirt road so the bus broke down and its children got drenched in the mud. When a rich white girl's teasing went too far, Cassie planned a long campaign of pretending to be her respectful little helper; she eventually discovered Lillian Jean's secrets, then beat her up and threatened to tell the embarrassing secrets if Lillian Jean complained.

Cassie's story did not follow the old plot pattern where a feisty girl gets tamed and weakened. She stayed her own self but from experience gained self-control and perspective. From her family she learned love and loyalty. Her father told about when she was born—"I SAID TO MYSELF: 'WHAT I GOTTA WORRY 'BOUT THESE WHITE FOLKS FOR? OR MONEY I AIN'T GOT? THIS LITTLE GIRL RIGHT HERE, SHE'S WHAT'S IMPORTANT. AIN'T NEVER GONNA BE NOTHING MORE IMPORTANT THAN THIS LITTLE GIRL.' "

Katherine Paterson specializes in children coming to terms with ambivalent feelings, love mixed with bitterness; she creates fine, strong girl characters. In her *Bridge to Terabithia* (1977) Jess, a ten-year-old farm boy who liked to draw, made friends with a girl from the city who opened new worlds of courage and culture. Leslie and Jess found a secret spot in the forest, where she told him stories from books like Narnia and pronounced him a King of Terabithia. THERE IN THE SHADOWY LIGHT OF THE STRONGHOLD EVERYTHING SEEMED POSSIBLE. Jess was jealous because Leslie could run faster and wasn't afraid of things, like swinging across the creek on a rope. But when the rope broke and Leslie was killed,

Jess was able to use the strength he had gained from her. He decided TERABITHIA WAS LIKE A CASTLE WHERE YOU CAME TO BE KNIGHTED. AFTER YOU STAYED FOR A WHILE AND GREW STRONG YOU HAD TO MOVE ON. FOR HADN'T LESLIE TRIED TO PUSH BACK THE WALLS OF HIS MIND AND MAKE HIM SEE BEYOND TO THE SHINING WORLD— HUGE AND TERRIBLE AND BEAUTIFUL AND VERY FRAGILE? SHE WASN'T THERE, SO HE MUST GO FOR BOTH OF THEM.

Elizabeth in *Autumn Street* (by Lois Lowry, 1980) experienced an even more shocking loss, which did not destroy her and helped her to grow. She was only six when her father went off to World War II and she went to live with rich Pennsylvania grandparents. There she found new kinds of understanding—about the labels people put on each other of rich and poor, black and white, master and servant; about the masks people wear to hide their real feelings. She found that cruelty could be anywhere, even in herself— once she lost her temper at her dearest friend Charles, the housekeeper's grandson, and shouted "Nigger."

Frightening spaces lurked inside and outside of people, Elizabeth discovered; she was terrified of the woods beyond the house and the caves that were rumored to lie within them. I WAS FRIGHTENED OF CAVES, OF DARK PASSAGES WITH CONVOLUTED TURNINGS. YOU COULD CALL OUT AND YOUR VOICE WOULD RETURN TO YOU. YOUR *VOICES*, COMING AT YOU, MURMURING; AND YOU WOULD HAVE TO STAND THERE ALL ALONE AND LISTEN TO THE ANSWERS THAT CAME AT YOU FROM INSIDE YOURSELF. This was not the self-satisfied world of earlier girls' stories, and when Elizabeth made a smug Pollyanna-like remark she sounded unconvincing, false: Talking about the dirty, crazy man who wandered through the town muttering and taking handouts, Elizabeth announced, "I WOULDN'T BE SCARED OF HIM. I WOULD PROBABLY SMILE AT HIM SO HE WOULD FEEL BETTER." I PRACTICED A SMALL, SAD, PITEOUS SMILE. In fact, it *was* sad and piteous—and more realistic—that in *Autumn Street* the girl character could not dissolve hostility with a sweet smile. After an incident where white boys hit and taunted little Charles, the child ran off into that dark, convoluted wood and got killed, his throat cut by the crazy man. When Elizabeth's father came home from the war with part of his leg missing, he reassured her that "BAD THINGS WON'T HAPPEN ANY MORE." She knew that was not true; she had family love and other comforts but she would always have a hollow place in her, a cave, after that year in Autumn Street with Charles.

Whereas newer children's books like these take on the same old themes—family and friends, individual identity, loss, coping and growing—they allow girl characters freer choices. Newer fictional worlds are often more terrible than the old ones but they are bigger. Female characters are less confined by convention, and also authors are less confined to a tiny segment of society: much of the excitement of today's children's books is that they represent a larger range of social and ethnic groups. Readers are no longer stuck with stories about little white girls in big houses. Publishers have discovered it is good business to allow good books about different types of people (although formula series still have mostly white, suburban settings).

So readers meet wonderful characters like those in Virginia Hamilton's *Arilla Sun Down* (1976). Arilla, a confused twelve-year-old, learned to handle ambivalence, complexity. She was comfortable in her black community but troubled about the Native-American part of her heritage. Arilla's handsome brother flaunted his Indianness aggressively; their hardworking father broke out of his city life every so often and ran away to his Indian hometown. Arilla had to work out her feelings about all this, and how to like her family and herself. She had to reconcile her town self with her past self, the little girl who listened to the Indian tales of old James. James had named Arilla "Wordkeeper" and "Talking Story." When he died, she asked his spirit, "IS IT FAR-GOING?" IT IS ONLY GOING IN A CIRCLE. "YOU COMING BACK AGAIN?" I AM HERE AND NOW, THEN AND THERE, IN ALL THINGS. AND WORD-KEEPER? "I HEAR YOU." REMEMBER WHO YOU ARE.

Two of the most striking creations of the 1980s are Cynthia Voigt's Dicey and Brock Cole's Celine, girls who struggled to grow up—and succeeded. In *Celine* (1989) the sixteen-year-old heroine spoke in a unique, funny and serious voice as she dealt with divorced parents, obtuse teachers, her own artistic talent, and an annoying boyfriend. When Celine's friends told her that DER-MOT IS A "HUNK," VISIONS OF CHEESE, RAW MEAT, BLUBBER STRIPPED FROM LIVING WHALES, DANCE BEFORE MY EYES. HUNKS. DERMOT IS ONE

OF THOSE PEOPLE WHOM LOVE TURNS INTO A BULLY. BECAUSE HE HAS THIS GREAT PASSION FOR ME, I AM UNREASONABLE AND SELFISH IF I DON'T ACT AS IF I LOVE HIM. IT LOOKS AS IF I WILL HAVE TO SPEND THE REST OF MY LIFE BEING SENSITIVE TO DERMOT'S GREAT NEEDS AND HAVING THESE REALLY TEDIOUS CONVERSATIONS ABOUT HOW DIFFICULT LIFE IS.

Then there was the stepmother Celine lived with. "I LIKE MY DAD AND ALL, BUT HE'S MARRIED THIS LITTLE JERK WHO'S ONLY SIX YEARS OLDER THAN I AM, AND I KNOW FOR A FACT THAT SHE COMES FROM PATERSON, NEW JERSEY, EVEN THOUGH SHE HAS THIS PHONY ENGLISH ACCENT AND KEEPS TALKING ABOUT DERRIDA ALL THE TIME." Interesting and complex things happened in Celine's head as she worked things out. Taking a young neighbor to a shrink appointment, she wandered into a psychologist's office and emerged, after a free session, with a medical excuse to get out of a semester of hated gym classes. It was clear that Celine would keep moving toward that "maturity" her father was always talking about, without sacrificing her own ideas of what maturity is. She would figure out how to deal with the pressure and weirdness around her. She came to tolerate her humorless stepmother; she survived a party from hell (where she helped the hostess make "seafood dip" by mixing catfood and mayonnaise); and she even got rid of the bullying Dermot.

Dicey's challenges were more frightening and primitive than Celine's. The core of her story appears in *Homecoming* (1981) and *Dicey's Song* (1982). Driving the four children from Cape Cod to a relative in Connecticut, Dicey's mother stopped in a parking lot, told the kids to be good, and went into the mall. She never came back. Dicey suspected her mother had just given up; she had been silent and hopeless since losing her meager supermarket job. Thirteen-year-old Dicey, the eldest, feared that the family would be split up if she told the police. She decided to follow the map and walk them all to the great-aunt's address in Bridgeport, though they had never met the woman. The journey was epic, pitiful—four children trudging down commercial Route 1 for weeks, sleeping in parks and behind empty houses—but it was brave and sometimes fun and they were together. With seven dollars and earnings from toting grocery bags, they bought milk and bananas and stale bread. Dicey let the children keep a stolen picnic bag, but when her brother stole money from a boy who had helped them, she lectured him fiercely and explained the difference.

The family was threatened in less obvious ways when they reached Bridgeport and found only a stiff distant relative who took them in out of duty and turned their education over to rigid nuns. Slow Maybeth was diagnosed as retarded and Sammy labeled a troublemaker, so Dicey knew they had to move on. She worked at a job long enough to save train fare to Maryland; then left a note and all four set off to see the grandmother who was estranged from their mother. Dicey's wanderings were not passive and random like Oliver Twist's, or even Alice's. She knew what she wanted to do and figured out how to do it and she knew about dangers and limitations. When she found the reclusive grandmother living on a derelict but beautiful riverside farm, Dicey didn't expect to melt her stony nature with childish sweetness. Instead, like a hero of legend, she earned the woman's respect by performing difficult tasks around the farm and proving her value. She used strength, not girl's weakness, to batter her way into the bitter old woman's life. Dicey is a many-dimensional character who had to learn, in later books, trust as well as independence, flexibility as well as stubbornness. She is a Jo March of the late twentieth-century, a tough, resourceful Jo without Jo's guilt and self-flagellation.

Some parents and teachers think children today face so many problems that their reading should lead them for a while into a gentler world. Others believe that reading about children with difficult lives can bring a child insight and perspective and give her a greater sense of control and freedom. Stories that describe the lives of girls like Shabanu and Lyddie, Cassie and Dicey and Celine, can do much for a child, when they are told with honesty and imagination.

Many of the good new books about girls would be classed as fantasies. In a fantasy the author can work out any theme in any way that works, creating a world with its own rules and possibilities. Some of these are about girls dealing with a harshly patriarchal society. They may triumph over the system, like Menolly in Anne McCaffrey's Dragonsong stories, who became a leader in the powerful Harpers' Guild even though it was taboo for women to be musicians; and like Alanna in Tamora Pearce's Song of the Lioness series, who wanted so to become a knight that she disguised herself as a boy for the grueling three-year period of training and testing at court.

The hero of *The True Confessions of Charlotte Doyle*, a ripping tale by Avi (1990), was different from girls like Menolly and Alanna: she did not start out challenging the male system she lived in. A docile thirteen-year-old in 1832, Charlotte Doyle had to sail from England home to America under the charge of some worthy travelers. The guardians were unable to join the ship and Charlotte was forced to sail anyway, the only female on board. WHAT COULD I DO? ALL MY LIFE I HAD BEEN TRAINED TO OBEY. "PLEASE LEAD ME," I MUMBLED, AS NEAR TO FAINTING AS ONE COULD BE WITHOUT ACTU- ALLY SUCCUMBING. Charlotte scorned the sailors as beneath her, and ignored their warnings about the cruel captain. Through her snobbish blindness, she betrayed plans for a just rebellion and caused the death of a crew member.

Remorseful about the harm she'd done, Charlotte offered to become one of the overworked crew; she discarded her petticoats for the trousers of a ship's boy. Despite terror and aching muscles, she was soon climbing around in rigging and doing all the tasks of a young sailor. Enraged that he could not control her and afraid that she would expose him on land, the captain framed Charlotte for the murder of another sailor and sentenced her to hang. The formerly dainty maiden pushed the captain overboard; the crew named her temporary captain until they landed. They then told the world sadly that the captain had been swept overboard in the hurricane.

Charlotte was reunited with her family but found she could no longer tolerate their repressive ways. She ran off into the night in her sailor-boy clothes and happily rejoined the crew of the *Seahawk*, to live the life she had come to love. I FOUND MYSELF ATOP THE FOREMAST, MY BARE BROWN FEET NIMBLY BALANCING ON THE FOOT ROPES. MY HAIR, UNCOMBED FOR DAYS, BLEW FREE IN THE SALTY AIR. I WAS SQUINTING INTO THE SWOLLEN FACE OF A BLOOD-RED SUN.

AND THERE I WAS, JOYOUS, NEW-MADE, LIBERATED FROM A PRISON I'D THOUGHT WAS MY PROPER PLACE! This must be the first real girl's *Treasure Island*.

Perhaps the most touching tale of a girl fighting a hostile world is Karen Cushman's *The Midwife's Apprentice* (1995). Gradually, painfully, the scrawny beggar girl called Brat or Dung Beetle created herself out of nothing. She forced a grudging midwife to teach her her profession. She gave herself a real name—Alyce—and she created a family out of a stray cat and a little beggar boy. She took revenge on cruel neighbors by frightening them with devil footprints she made with carved wooden hooves. She learned to sing, laugh, and read. When asked by a friendly scholar, "What do *you* want?"—a question she had never considered before—she finally answered, "I KNOW WHAT I WANT. A FULL BELLY, A CONTENTED HEART, AND A PLACE IN THIS WORLD."

The most swashbuckling adventure is Cynthia Voigt's *Jackaroo* (1985). If *Charlotte Doyle* is the girls' *Treasure Island*, *Jackaroo* is a terrific girls' *Robin Hood*. An imaginary feudal kingdom was in chaos. The peasants were wracked by famine, preyed on by thieves, neglected by warring nobles. Gwyn, sixteen-year-old daughter of an innkeeper, chafed under the rules of her society: her life would consist of conformity and obedience. But Gwyn was good at grabbing opportunities. Fascinated by legends of Jackaroo—a masked hero who returned in bad times to punish thieves, help poor people, and rob nobles—she saw possibilities when she found an old costume in an abandoned cottage.

Wearing the red cape, black boots, and mask of Jackaroo, and riding a borrowed horse, Gwyn became Jackaroo. She delivered gold coins to a desperate father, goats to a poor old woman, an orphan baby to a childless woman. She forced corrupt officials to execute thieves and murderers. Gwyn's story used old conventions of heroic male exploits. At the same time it challenged those conventions in a new way: During one of her Jackaroo rides, Gwyn was astonished to see *another* masked, caped rider swoop onto the scene, confusing her pursuers and allowing her to escape. That turned out to be her friend and future husband Burl, but a third Jackaroo appeared on another occasion to do more good deeds.

Is this supposed to be farce? No, it is a new type of heroic tale, and it is a kind that accepts female heroes more easily than the old heroism did. This kind of heroism knows that individual action is important but also admits that truly useful action must be multiple, communal. Goals are never accomplished all at once, by one person. Gwyn loved the thrill of acting alone, winning and helping; she also came to love the pattern of a whole harmonious society, which she was helping to create: "THE LAND SERVES THE PEOPLE, THE PEOPLE SERVE THE EARLS, THE EARLS SERVE THE KING, AND THE KING SERVES THE LAND." EVEN JACKAROO, GWYN THOUGHT TO HERSELF, FIT INTO THAT CIRCLE. HE SERVED THE PEOPLE. HE SERVED THEM OUTSIDE OF THE LAW, BUT WITHIN THE TURNING OF THE WHEEL. ... IT WAS ODD THAT DRESSED UP AS JACKAROO SHE FELT MORE LIKE HERSELF. SHE LIKED HERSELF, AND IN DISGUISE SHE WAS FREE TO DO WHAT SHE REALLY WANTED TO DO, MUCH FREER THAN WAS GWYN, THE INNKEEPER'S DAUGHTER. A friend of mine once said apologetically that as a child she had a ridiculous fantasy of being a girl Robin Hood. Imagine how many girls today are being confirmed and expanded, not truncated, by reading books like *Jackaroo*. They don't think it's ridiculous.

Perhaps the best sign of progress away from sexist stories is that today many books show strong girl characters doing important things as a matter of course, with no fuss about their being girls. Philip Pullman has written two books in an ambitious fantasy series for young people—*The Golden Compass* (1995) and *The Subtle Knife* (1997). They are about parallel worlds, innocence and knowledge, religion and science. They are set in nineteenth-century and also twentieth-century Oxford, the North Pole, and other intertwined universes. The fate of all these universes depended on the actions of the main characters. The most central of those main characters was a little girl named Lyra, a daring but sensible child who simply did what she had to do. Adult characters knew she was a crucial figure in the wars of the worlds and tried either to protect her or to harm her—but they didn't much notice that Lyra was a girl rather than a boy. She was merely a young person of importance.

Natalie Babbitt's *Tuck Everlasting* (1975) seems equally unconcerned about the gender of its hero. After ten-year-old Winnie ran away from her dry, fenced yard and fussy parents, she was seized by the Tuck family, who grabbed her away from a woodland stream so they could explain their secret. Eighty-seven years earlier the parents and two sons had happened to drink from that stream. Over the next years they found they were no longer changing; they did not age. They realized the world would collapse into chaos if people learned about the magic water that stopped death, so they desperately hid this knowledge, moving to a new place when their unchanging appearance started to cause talk.

The Tucks were kind, earnest people, and Winnie came around to their viewpoint. She willingly got herself in trouble helping them escape a situation that would expose the secret. Jesse Tuck invited her to drink from the stream when she turned seventeen and then join the Tucks in their wanderings. But, as Pa Tuck said, "EVERYTHING'S A WHEEL, TURNING AND TURNING, NEVER STOPPING. THE FROGS IS PART OF IT, AND THE BUGS, AND THE WOOD THRUSH, TOO. AND PEOPLE. BUT NEVER THE SAME ONES. ALWAYS COMING IN NEW, ALWAYS GROWING AND CHANGING. DYING'S PART OF THE WHEEL. YOU CAN'T PICK OUT THE PIECES YOU LIKE AND LEAVE THE REST." Winnie chose to stay on the wheel, pouring into the dirt her bottle of magic water. Winnie is presented as a person who happened to be a girl just as she just happened to be a person who had brown hair and a person who liked toads.

So children's stories may at last have moved beyond their traditional, dreary preoccupation with the compulsory girlishness of girls. A girl character now can do whatever things a boy can do, taking part even in the most dangerous adventures. Jane Yolen managed something remarkable in *The Devil's Arithmetic* (1988) and *Briar Rose* (1992): she tried to present the truth and horror of the Holocaust in a form that young people could grasp without total despair. In both books Yolen distances the horrible events but does not avoid describing them. In *The Devil's Arithmetic* present-day Hannah in New York resented her grandfather's constant talk of his time in the camps. Then she found herself transported in time and space to a Polish village just before Jews were rounded up and imprisoned. Even with her knowledge of what was to come she was helpless, but she was able to make a choice that made a difference in her family's history. In *Briar Rose* a young American woman tracked down the history of her melancholy grandmother, uncovering Holocaust stories of good and evil so extreme as to be almost unbelievable. Becca, like Hannah in the other book, happened to be female, but femaleness is certainly not the point of the story—except that women are shown to be as courageous as men.

I started this project knowing a lot about children's books before 1950 but not much about later books, and I made a guess about the later ones that proved to be too pessimistic. I am happy to find that I underestimated the recent changes in girl characters, their minds and their actions. By and large, recent stories show girls as active not passive; loud not silent. Even in books about both boys and girls, girls are central, not peripheral. They are competent not limited, assertive not submissive. They act for themselves, not just for and with their community. They have goals other than romance and marriage, though these are important to many of them. Instead of "Sit Still," their motto is "Don't Just Sit There, Do Something."

If the old images have disappeared, then why should we examine the old stories at all? Because the old images are still strong in many parts of our culture, openly or covertly; because children's books are only one of the forces helping to form young girls, and many of the others have gotten not better but more harmful in recent years. As Mary Pipher, Carol Gilligan, Emily Hancock, and others have argued, girls today face great emotional and physical danger, especially at puberty. The girl culture is full of depression, eating disorders, self-mutilation, drugs, pregnancy, family disruption, sexual and other violence. Pressures tend to silence girls—pressure to conform, to be perfect, to be popular, to be beautiful. Even if *fictional* girls have become stronger and more confident, today's real-life girls are often like yesterday's girls; and they know they are objectified and judged by their appearance, which they feel is never good enough. The ghosts of old sacrificial storybook heroines are still floating in the air (and on the airwaves), whispering sit-still, look-good messages.

Many groups of people are trying in many ways to encourage girls to develop into strong individuals; but *boys* are mostly not happy about this. Research like the Sadkers' in *Failing at Fairness* (1994) shows that boys in classrooms still demand most of the attention, squashing the participation and ideas and confidence of girls. Barrie Thorne's *Gender Play* (1993) tells of the fear little boys have that girls are "polluting": "Girls as a group are treated as an ultimate source of contamination." She says boys consider girls' objects polluting—if you touch them; you get cooties or some other kind of pollution, such as "girl stain." Girls do not fear boys' objects the same way.

The saddest expression of boys' feelings about girls appears in *Failing at Fairness*. Schoolchildren in different states, in the 1980s and 90s, were asked to write down how they would feel if one morning they woke up and found they had switched to the other sex. Girls responded with a realistic sense of their place in the world: If I wake up to find I am a boy, "People will listen to what I have to say and will take me seriously"; and "When I grow up I will be able to be almost anything I want." But the boys responded with panic: When I woke up and found I was a *girl*, "No cat liked me. No animal in the world. I did not like myself." "My friends would treat me like dirt." Some boys said they would kill themselves. "I would stab myself in the heart." Their reactions showed deep contempt and loathing for girls. As adolescent girls look to boys for approval and popularity, it is not surprising if they have problems of self-esteem.

Girls' confidence and autonomy are also damaged when behavior that departs from gender norms is still, in some circles, punished severely. *Gender Shock*, a shocking book by Phyllis Burke (1996), tells of a disorder listed in the 1980 and 1994 editions of the *Diagnostic and Statistical Manual* of the American Psychiatric Association—"GID," Gender Identity Disorder. This includes among its disease symptoms "intense desire to participate in stereotypical games and pastimes of the other sex." A girl who reacts intensely against wearing dresses may be diagnosed as having GID, and so may one who prefers "rough-and-tumble play and traditional boyhood games." Since the 1970s hospitals and clinics in California, Florida, Chicago, and other places have engaged in behavior modification, sometimes including drug therapy, on children with unconventional behavior. In 1978 in

Florida an eight-year-old girl was sent to a treatment program by her parents, who worried about her "masculine" behavior. With headphones giving instructions in her ears in the lab and at home, Becky learned over seven months to shun boys' toys and clothes and act more like a girl. (The checklist marked it *feminine* to stand with feet together, *masculine* with feet apart, for instance.) Becky was eventually pronounced cured; she was now asking for jewelry and perfume. Boys in parallel cases were deemed disturbed when they were "interested in arts and crafts" or when they "liked neat hair and color-coordinated clothing." Becky's program was funded by the federal government. It can hardly be claimed that today all girls are comfortably free to be themselves, and need no encouragement.

People are coming to recognize the destructive forces pushing at girls in their developing years, and various movements are springing up to support them. There are books suggesting rituals to make girls realize their importance and celebrate themselves; techniques to help them counter gender stereotypes; programs to provide mentoring support and career exploration. There are groups in the educational world seeking ways to encourage girls so they will take part more actively in class and so they will study math, science, and technology, traditionally male fields that foster success and independence. There are more and better sports and outdoors opportunities for girls, because sitting still doesn't create strong people—only motion can do that. Fathers are taking a larger part in childraising.

Books are less influential now than they were in my childhood; mine was the last generation to live all or most of childhood without television. But girls can still be profoundly affected by books. At least three reference books appeared in 1997 alone suggesting book lists for girls and book clubs for girls and their mothers. Kathleen Odean presents a sensible viewpoint in *Great Books for Girls*: In children's stories "the problems the girls solve may seem commonplace, but the very act of a girl having an adventure, or puzzling out her own solution, sets her apart from more traditional fictional girls. Girls don't need any more lessons in being nice; they need lessons in making decisions for themselves." Books soak into the mind; they don't flicker past in a dazzling confusion like TV images. A girl can brood her way into the soul of Cassie Logan or Jackaroo-Gwyn. She can see herself as Harriet the Spy or Julie of the Wolves. Books can be one influence helping a girl get up from the chair where she is sitting still (perhaps staring at her imperfect appearance in a mirror) and take a step or two. Through stories, she can explore good ways to develop a self and examine bad ways that hinder the self. She needs all the help stories can give her, so she will not be damaged by boys who grow up still thinking "I'd rather be dead than be a girl"; so she will not be damaged by her own suspicion that she is worthless.

I did much of my childhood reading in an old scratchy green armchair in a little hot room called "the maid's room"—as we had no maid, the room was mostly a storeroom. Once my visiting cousin Peter came in while I was reading, noticed the flat roof outside covering a back porch, and hopped out the window to stroll around on it. Such alien behavior!—I would no more have climbed out on the roof than I would have tried to fly.

But my niece's six-year-old daughter plans to be Pippi Long-stocking next Halloween, "because she is so strong she could pick up your house." *Pippi* is her favorite book. Emily also likes *Alice*, but thinks she wasn't very smart about one thing. Why didn't she just go back up the rabbit hole if she wanted to go home?—she could eat a piece from the side of the mushroom that makes you big and climb out of the hole, and then once she's out, eat a piece from the side that makes you little, which she would be carrying with her, and then she would be back to normal again.

Clearly, no one has been telling Emily that girls don't develop problem-solving skills. I ask her: Do you ever read stories about girls who get scared of everything, and think boys are stronger and smarter? She smiles and shakes her head. "*Jeb* gets scared of a lot of things," she says thoughtfully, "but I don't."

In a 1976 essay P.L. Travers, creator of Mary Poppins, suggests that "the hero is one who is willing to set out, take the first step. Perhaps the hero is one who puts his foot upon a path not know-ing what he may expect from life but in some way feeling in his bones that life expects something from him." Recent children's stories turn this stepping-out hero into a "she." In "The Moon Ribbon" (1976), a modern fairy tale, Jane Yolen describes three stages of Sylva, A PLAIN BUT GOODHEARTED GIRL. Orphaned Sylva suffered at the hands of a cruel stepmother until one night a magic river carried her to the shining house of her real mother's spirit. A SILVER RIVER RIPPLED IN THE MOONLIGHT. SHE FLOATED LIKE A SWAN AND THE RIVER BORE HER ON. AT LAST SHE WAS CARRIED AROUND A GREAT BEND IN THE RIVER AND DEPOSITED GENTLY ON A GRASSY SLOPE. This first journey moved her partway toward her goal but it was not enough: she was only passive, floating, like the girl heroines we have read about for centuries.

Another night a silver highway appeared before her as she sat on the ground. SYLVA GOT UP AND STEPPED OUT ONTO THE ROAD AND WAITED FOR IT TO BRING HER TO THE MAGICAL HOUSE. BUT THE ROAD DID NOT MOVE. "STRANGE," SHE SAID TO HERSELF. "WHY DOES IT NOT CARRY ME AS THE RIVER DID?" SYLVA WAITED A MOMENT MORE, THEN TENTATIVELY SET ONE FOOT IN FRONT OF THE OTHER. AS SOON AS SHE HAD SET OFF ON HER OWN, THE ROAD SET OFF, TOO, AND THEY MOVED TOGETHER PAST FIELDS AND FORESTS, FASTER AND FASTER. From such stories, perhaps, our own daughters are learning to set one foot in front of the other, and set off on their own down their own silver highways. If they do this they will not be lying abed all their lives like crippled Carol Bird in her pretty bower in 1886, growing stiller and stiller and dying at last of her own excessive virtue.

Index